D. James Kennedy, Ph.D.

Dear Friend,

Thank you for your support of Coral Ridge Ministries. It is my pleasure to present you with this special edition of *The Marketing of Evil.*

This is a remarkable book. Here, between two covers, author David Kupelian dissects and exposes the brilliant and malign techniques employed by merchants of evil who "sell us corruption disguised as freedom."

The effort to change America's mind on issues like abortion, homosexuality, church-state separation, and more is not a happenstance undertaking. Instead, as Kupelian shows, it is a well-thought-out strategic campaign that uses the methods of Madison Avenue to market rank lies.

But the good news is that by God's grace, the truth will eventually win out, and Kupelian's important and groundbreaking book makes enormous progress toward that end. It brings into the light these works of darkness for all to see.

This is vital information to immunize you, your loved ones, and your friends to the carnival mirror distortions employed by those who market evil to America—and to equip you to counteract the lies with the truth.

I am grateful for your friendship and support for our outreach to reclaim America for Christ. Thank you for standing with me as we "market" the grace of God and the healing balm of biblical truth to this generation!

Sincerely in Christ,

D. James Kennedy, Ph.D.

PRAISE FOR DAVID KUPELIAN'S
THE MARKETING OF EVIL

"David Kupelian dares to tell the truth about the overwhelming forces in our society which take us far away from our original American concept of freedom with responsibility, happiness with commitments, and traditional values. *The Marketing of Evil* is a serious wake-up call for all who cherish traditional values, the innocence of children, and the very existence of our great country."

> —Dr. LAURA SCHLESSINGER, internationally syndicated radio talk-show host and best-selling author of *The Proper Care and Feeding of Husbands*

"It's often said that marketing is warfare, and in *The Marketing of Evil*, David Kupelian clearly reveals the stunning strategies and tactics of persuasion employed by those engaged in an all-out war against America's Judeo-Christian culture. If you really want to understand the adversary's thinking and help turn the tide of battle, read this book!"

> —DAVID LIMBAUGH, nationally syndicated columnist and best-selling author of *Persecution* and *Absolute Power*

"*The Marketing of Evil* takes no prisoners. David Kupelian brilliantly explains how a clever, radical elite is persuading Americans to accept evil as good, and good as evil. With precise clarity, the book blows the lid off the most successful—and dangerous—cultural scams. In addition, Kupelian's personal vignettes and vigorous writing hold the reader's interest throughout."

> —ROBERT KNIGHT, director of the Culture and Family Institute, an affiliate of Concerned Women for America, and author of *The Age of Consent: The Rise of Relativism and the Corruption of Popular Culture*

"Excellent! Simply excellent. If you want to solidify your Christian world view—or just understand what the culture war is all about—you owe it to yourself to read David Kupelian's *The Marketing of Evil*."

> —DONALD E. WILDMON, chairman and founder of the American Family Association

"Did you ever want to know—I mean *really* know—how and why America is being transformed from a unified, Judeo-Christian society into a divided, false, murky, neopagan culture? Even if you think you know the answers to those questions, in fact, *especially* if you think you know the answers, you must read David Kupelian's *The Marketing of Evil*. So clearly does it expose the incredible con game to which Americans have been subjected that it offers real hope—because when our problems come this sharply into focus, so do the solutions."

—JOSEPH FARAH, founder and CEO of WorldNetDaily.com and WND Books, syndicated columnist, national radio talk-show host, and author of *Taking America Back*

"Every parent in America needs to read this book. David Kupelian skillfully exposes the secular left's rotten-apple peddlers in devastating detail. From pitching promiscuity as 'freedom' to promoting abortion as 'choice,' the marketers of evil are always selling you something destructive—with catastrophic results. Kupelian shines a light on them all. Now watch the cockroaches run for cover."

—MICHELLE MALKIN, Fox News Channel analyst, nationally syndicated columnist, and author of *Invasion*

"David Kupelian's book is like a giant x-ray machine that exposes the atheistic, secular left's brilliant marketing campaigns aimed at seducing America away from its founding Judeo-Christian faith. If you want to know how such a thoroughly decent country as America could go so wrong so fast, you simply have to read *The Marketing of Evil*."

—HAL LINDSEY, columnist and best-selling author of 20 books, including *The Late, Great Planet Earth*

"David Kupelian's new book *The Marketing of Evil* is brilliant! He combines superb common sense (that is so rare in our society) with the important biblical command to expose "the fruitless deeds of darkness" (Ephesians 5:11). By doing so, he breaks the spell of the carefully marketed lies that are destroying our civilization, and sets the stage for revival and reformation. *The Marketing of Evil* must be read by every concerned American."

—Dr. TED BAEHR, chairman of the Christian Film and Television Commission, publisher of MovieGuide, and author of *The Media-Wise Family*

DAVID KUPELIAN

THE MARKETING OF EVIL

How Radicals,

Elitists, and Pseudo-Experts

Sell Us Corruption

Disguised as Freedom

WND BOOKS

AN IMPRINT OF CUMBERLAND HOUSE PUBLISHING, INC.

NASHVILLE, TENNESSEE

To my wife, JEAN,
and
our children, SARAH and JOSHUA

CONTENTS

INTRODUCTION

As AMERICANS, WE'VE COME to tolerate, embrace, and even champion many things that would have horrified our parents' generation. Things like abortion-on-demand virtually up to the moment of birth, judges banning the Ten Commandments from public places, a national explosion of middle-school sex, the slow starvation of the disabled, thousands of homosexuals openly flouting the law and getting "married," and online porn creating late-night sex addicts in millions of middle-class homes.

At the same time, our courts have scrubbed America's schoolrooms surgically clean of every vestige of the religion on which this nation was founded—Christianity.

Indeed, in fifty years we've gone from a nation unified by traditional Judeo-Christian values to one in which those same values are increasingly scorned, rejected, and demonized.

What's going on? Are today's Americans inherently more morally confused and depraved than previous generations?

Of course not. But we have been taken in—big-time—by some of the boldest and most brilliant marketing campaigns in modern history.

A generation ago, in his perceptive best seller *The Hidden Persuaders,* Vance Packard explained how Madison Avenue was greedily using knowledge of mass manipulation gleaned from modern psychology and psychiatry to induce us to buy everything from cigarettes to cars to soap.

But do we really think modern marketing's sophisticated and powerful propaganda techniques are being used just to sell soap? No, there are far more precious commodities being sold to us every day—namely, new beliefs and, especially, new *feelings* about things we formerly rejected. And we've bought some whoppers in recent years.

The plain truth is, within the space of our lifetimes, much of what Americans once almost universally abhorred has been packaged, perfumed, gift-wrapped, and sold to us as though it had great value. By skillfully playing on our deeply felt national values of fairness, generosity, and tolerance, these marketers have persuaded us to embrace as enlightened and noble that which all previous generations since America's founding regarded as grossly self-destructive—in a word, evil.

In his classic book, *People of the Lie*, Dr. M. Scott Peck reflects on what "evil" actually means:

> It is a reflection of the enormous mystery of the subject that we do not have a generally accepted definition of evil. Yet in our hearts I think we all have some understanding of its nature. For the moment I can do no better than to heed my son, who, with the characteristic vision of eight-year-olds, explained simply, "Why, Daddy, evil is 'live' spelled backward." Evil is in opposition to life. It is that which opposes the life force.[1]

Peck also points out that people caught up with evil are liars, "deceiving others as they also build layer upon layer of self-deception."[2] The marketers of evil not only lie to us continually—and to themselves—but the purpose of their lies is to promote behavior and beliefs that oppose life.

For instance, most people believe—in accord with our modern cultural mythology—that the "abortion rights" and "gay rights" movements were spontaneous grassroots uprisings of neglected or persecuted minorities wanting to breathe free. Few people realize America was actually "sold" on abortion thanks to an audacious, calculated, and brazenly deceptive public relations plan that relied heavily on lies and fabrications—as the campaign's cofounder confesses in these pages. Or that giant corporations voraciously competing for America's $150 billion teen market routinely infiltrate young people's social groups with undercover "culture spies" to find out how better to lead children into ever more debauched forms of "authentic self-expression."

Few of us realize that the widely revered father of the "sexual revolution" has been irrefutably exposed as a full-fledged sexual psychopath who encouraged pedophilia and whose vaunted "scientific surveys" included interviewing incarcerated sex offenders and prostitutes while pretending they were typical World War II–era Americans. Or that the "gay rights" movement—which transformed America's former view of homosexuals as self-destructive "deviants" into their current status as victims and cultural heroes—is following an in-depth, published plan laid out by professional Harvard-trained marketers.

But beyond exposing these campaigns by today's not-so-hidden persuaders who have transformed modern America, this book will show you how the marketing juggernaut continues at full-throttle into the present. You'll see—often in the marketers' own words—exactly how corruption, selfishness, and foolishness are expertly positioned and packaged so as to make them appear enlightened, liberated, and even spiritually advanced. In effect, turning reality on its head.

How can this be happening in America? How does child molesting become "man-boy love"? How does crushing a baby's skull and sucking out his brains become a "constitutional right"? How does quoting the Bible become "hate speech"? How exactly is evil made to appear good, and good made to appear evil? How has America—which still boasts an 80 percent Christian population—seen fit to embrace what can only be called a culture of death, rather than a culture of life?

We're about to discover how all this has been accomplished—right before our eyes.

Think of this book as an up-close, modern-day look at what is traditionally known as *temptation*—the "art and science" of making evil look attractive by appealing to the weaknesses in all of us that invite such deception.

Thus, while we're discovering why, when, where, and how phony experts and social revolutionaries have sold us the lies that now threaten the future of the greatest nation in history, we'll also discover something else: we'll see clearly how the moral confusion and relativism that have permeated the West, especially since the 1960s, have made us ripe for all this deception—and more. And that's a critically important part of the story.

After all, if we don't understand what the marketers of evil in this world are doing—and especially if we don't comprehend our own inherent flaws that allow us to be conned—our fate is already sealed. But when we finally come to understand, with crystal clarity, the subtle seductions and bold manipulations that have led our culture into captivity, the spell is broken and we're free.

It's that simple. If we know the marketer is a con man, we just tell him to get lost.

We'll start our exploration of *The Marketing of Evil* with one of today's most successful and intimidating public relations campaigns—the selling of homosexuality to America. The explanations by "gay rights" marketers of their own tactics of mass manipulation are so amazingly clear and brazen that they will enhance your understanding of all that follows throughout the book.

So let us begin our journey . . .

THE
MARKETING
OF EVIL

1

MARKETING BLITZ

Selling "Gay Rights" to America

I DID NOT CHOOSE to be homosexual. I would change my sexual orientation if that were within my power."

So confessed Robert Bauman, a powerful conservative congressman from Maryland. Americans were stunned in 1980 when headlines revealed Bauman had been caught red-handed having a sexual rendezvous with a young male prostitute. In his book *The Gentleman from Maryland: The Conscience of a Gay Conservative,* Bauman revealed the conditions that shaped his own tortured double life as a pro-family Republican congressman and closet homosexual.

At the tender age of five, Bauman had been sexually seduced by a twelve-year-old neighbor. Reflecting on that pivotal experience, as well as subsequent similar episodes, Bauman described the powerful feelings he found welling up within him at a young age:

> This was not a matter of chance attraction to a forbidden object. This was a frightening force from deep within my being, an involuntary reaction to the sight, smell, and feel of other boys. I neither understood nor accepted it. And I came to hate myself because of the presence within me of this horrible weakness, this uncleanness of spirit over which I seemed to have no control. . . .
>
> I was sure my predicament was a unique punishment designed only for me. Unable to understand it myself, I could never even attempt an explanation to someone else. I countered my dilemma with a plan that constituted

the essence of simplicity. I made up my mind that I was not "queer." I heard all those denunciations of homos by my military school peers and firmly resolved I could never be considered one of such a despicable breed.[1]

Bauman was elected in 1973 as representative of the First Congressional District of Maryland, became chairman of the American Conservative Union in 1979, and, many thought, was on his way to becoming Speaker of the House. But he was leading a double life as a married man with four children while at the same time engaging in anonymous homosexual one-night stands. He described the wrenching emotional aftermath he experienced after every episode: "Each time I would feel great guilt and head for Saturday confession at St. Peter's or St. Joseph's on Capitol Hill so I could make amends with God and be in the state of grace for Sunday Communion. I would always vow to myself and God I would never do it again."[2]

Submerging himself "in the excitement of politics where compliments, victories and deference helped reassure me I was a good person," Bauman looked every bit the quintessential conservative, family-values congressman. "If I could save the world," he later mused, "I might avoid having to save myself."[3]

Looking back on his secret double life, Bauman engaged in some painful self-examination:

> How could any normal and moral human being do what I did? How could anyone, however callous, repeatedly be unfaithful to one's spouse (lying, evading responsibility, breaking solemn vows)? I have described how it could be done. *Why* I did it is the serious question. And I have no answer, even to this day. I do not know. In many ways I was driven by a force over which I seemed to have little control.
>
> Of course, my choice was conscious and deliberate. It could have been altered. But some compulsion drove me, blotting out all I had learned, diminishing in importance all that was most dear and important. I seemed willing to risk my marriage, my wife and children, even life itself.[4]

It's hard not to have compassion on a fellow human being desperately struggling to overcome a powerful compulsion he "neither understood nor accepted." What happened to Bauman was a tragedy. He needed help—not rejection and condemnation for being a "queer," nor acceptance and praise for being an "oppressed minority"—but real help in understanding and overcoming his sexual problem.

In today's polarized climate, however, it seems most of us either condemn homosexuals as evil corrupters of society or we fawn over them as noble victims and cultural heroes. We either accuse them of "choosing" to be "wicked sexual deviants," or we claim—utterly without evidence—that "gayness" is an inborn, genetic trait.

Reality, however, lies somewhere else. Deep down, people of conscience know homosexuality is neither an innocent, inborn "minority" characteristic like skin color, nor a conscious choice to become evil and to corrupt others. But without understanding what we're really dealing with, we're not only powerless to help others but easily confused and corrupted ourselves.

Bauman, under the sway of an overwhelming and self-destructive compulsion, even admits in retrospect that perhaps he *wanted* to be caught so he could get help.

> I can see numerous instances when my conduct, which I thought carefully discreet, was really designed to reveal to someone, anyone, what was happening to me. Perhaps my unconscious conclusion was that someone else must deal with the chaos of my life because I was rapidly reaching the point at which I could not do it myself.[5]

Finally, in 1980, at the age of forty-three, Bauman got his wish and was found out. After the dramatic public exposure of his solicitation of a teenage male hustler, the congressman saw his political career crash. He lost not only his reelection bid but also his family, his historic home, and many of his powerful friends as well.

In truth, Robert Bauman's sad story is in some ways not too different from that of many others in America before today's era of "gay pride," out-of-the-closet politicians and celebrities, "lesbian and gay studies" in most colleges, "Gay Day" at Disneyland, and powerful homosexual lobbying and journalistic and legal groups throughout the land.

Back then, most people like Bauman remained "in the closet" with regard to their homosexuality. And in their secret world they suffered conflict, fear of exposure, and sometimes worse.

Today, thanks to America's politically correct "gay-friendly" culture, millions of human beings in the grip of this same unnatural sexual compulsion find it much easier to accept—even to wear as a badge of honor. But they still don't understand it. In fact, they have less desire than ever to understand it—just as the larger society has also lost interest in understanding homosexuality. But sometimes not knowing what you're dealing with can be dangerous. So let's take off the rainbow-colored glasses and objectively explore this phenomenon we call "gay rights." It grew out of the "sexual liberation" movement of the 1960s. To be precise, the June 11, 1969, "Stonewall riot"—when a group of homosexuals at New York City's Stonewall Inn resisted police commands to disperse—is widely regarded as the birth of the "gay liberation" movement.

This emerging political force made considerable strides during the '70s, most notably in persuading—many say intimidating—the American Psychiatric Association in 1973 into removing homosexuality from its official list of mental disorders. But "gay rights" was young, inexperienced, underfunded, and understaffed as political movements go, and the issue received little support from politicians or the nation in general. "Equality for gays" was not yet a phrase that reverberated in the hearts and minds of Americans.

Then came AIDS.

THE PROBLEM OF THE PLAGUE

SURELY, MANY activists thought, this would be their movement's death knell. For while they were trying to convince the mainstream that homosexuals represented a normal, healthy, alternative lifestyle, along comes a modern plague—horrible, incurable, fatal, and spread primarily by promiscuous homosexual men.

AIDS—originally named GRID (gay-related immunodeficiency disease) until activist homosexuals pressured the medical establishment to switch to the generic acronym AIDS (acquired immune deficiency syndrome)—was the ultimate public relations nightmare. It gave society a brand-new reason to fear and shun homosexuals—namely, concern over becoming infected with a nightmarish new disease.

And AIDS did something else. In order for the medical establishment and news media to communicate to the public how the disease was being transmitted, it became necessary to focus publicly on the one thing homosexuals most wanted to downplay—the sometimes-bizarre sexual acts in which they engage and their often astronomically high numbers of sexual partners. (A widely cited 1978 study by Alan P. Bell and Martin S. Wineburg reported that 43 percent of homosexuals had more than five hundred sex partners during their lifetime.)[6]

In addition, the "silver bullet" medical cure Americans had virtually come to expect, having grown up in the age of miracle drugs like the polio vaccine and penicillin, never materialized. Rather, AIDS experts and public health authorities issued dire warnings about a disease reminiscent of the bubonic plague of the Middle Ages:

> By the early years of the next century, we could have lost between 50 and 100 million people worldwide. There's no question about that.—Surgeon General C. Everett Koop

> Ninety percent of the people infected [with HIV] don't even know it.—Dr. Robert Gallo, codiscoverer of the HIV virus

> In many areas, the number of persons affected with the AIDS virus is at least 100 times greater than reported case of AIDS.—Dr. James Curran, director of AIDS and HIV immunology and prevention activities at the Centers for Disease Control[7]

Meanwhile, throughout the '80s and beyond, as AIDS infection and death rates skyrocketed with each passing year, high-profile figures were dying of the disease, including actor Rock Hudson in 1985, ABC News anchor Max Robinson in 1988, and ballet superstar Rudolf Nureyev in 1993.

During this time the public experienced two distinct and widespread reactions to the unfolding AIDS epidemic. One was the natural sympathy evoked by witnessing the terrible suffering and death of AIDS victims. But the other, if less politically correct, was fear and loathing of homosexuals. After all, there was no way back in those early days of the disease to rule out AIDS transmission via "casual contact"—that is, by means other than sex and intravenous drug use. As prominent Harvard AIDS researcher Dr. William Haseltine warned at the time: "Anyone who tells you categorically that AIDS is not contracted by saliva is not telling you the truth. AIDS may, in fact, be transmissible by tears, saliva, bodily fluids and mosquito bites."[8]

Fears that AIDS would "break out" into the general population were further fanned by horror stories such as that of Kimberly Bergalis, a Florida girl who contracted AIDS (along with several other patients) from her homosexual dentist, David Acer.

As a matter of fact, many Americans not part of the two main "at-risk groups" (male homosexuals and IV drug abusers) *were* dying, mostly from HIV-tainted blood transfusions. One of them, Ryan White, an eighteen-year-old Indiana boy with hemophilia who became infected with HIV through a blood transfusion, died of AIDS in 1990 and became the poster boy for rallying Americans to support AIDS research. Two years later tennis great Arthur Ashe, also infected by an HIV-tainted transfusion, succumbed to the disease.

As a public relations matter, AIDS was daunting. This modern plague, if not handled brilliantly in the court of public opinion, could result in homosexuals being widely shunned.

On the other hand, perhaps the sympathy factor could be harnessed and multiplied to advance the activists' cause.

The movement definitely needed help. The defiant, storm-trooper tactics of in-your-face groups like ACT-UP (AIDS Coalition to Unleash Power) may or may not have been successful in pressuring the federal government to increase its commitment to combating AIDS. But such tactics definitely *were* successful in giving activist homosexuals a very bad name.

One infamous incident was the assault on New York's famed St. Patrick's Cathedral on December 10, 1989. While Cardinal John O'Connor presided over the 10:15 Sunday morning Mass, a multitude of "pro-choice" and "gay rights" activists protested angrily outside. Some, wearing gold-colored robes similar to clerical vestments, hoisted a large portrait of a pornographically altered frontal nude portrait of Jesus.

"You bigot, O'Connor, you're killing us!" screamed one protester, while signs called the archbishop "Murderer!"[9]

Then it got *really* ugly. Scores of protesters entered the church, resulting in what many in the packed house of parishioners described as a "nightmare."

"The radical homosexuals turned a celebration of the Holy Eucharist into a screaming babble of sacrilege by standing in the pews, shouting and waving their fists, tossing condoms into the air," recounted the *New York Post*. One of the invaders grabbed a consecrated wafer and threw it to the ground.

Outside, demonstrators, many of them members of ACT-UP, carried placards that summed up their sentiments toward the Catholic Church: "Keep your church out of my crotch." "Keep your rosaries off my ovaries." "Eternal life to Cardinal John O'Connor NOW!" "Curb your dogma."[10]

Clearly, the young movement was flirting with oblivion if it persisted in such ugly, indefensible tactics. It needed a new, more civilized direction if it ever hoped to convince Americans that homosexuality was a perfectly normal alternative lifestyle.

This new direction would somehow have to convert the fearsome AIDS epidemic from a negative into a positive. What was needed was a comprehensive, long-term public relations campaign that had to be brilliantly conceived and skillfully executed.

WAR CONFERENCE

IN FEBRUARY 1988 some 175 leading activists representing homosexual groups from across the nation held a war conference in Warrenton, Virginia, to map out their movement's future.[11] Shortly thereafter, activists Marshall Kirk and Hunter Madsen put into book form the comprehensive public relations plan they had been advocating with their gay-rights peers for several years.

Kirk and Madsen were not the kind of drooling activists that would burst into churches and throw condoms in the air. They were smart guys—very smart. Kirk, a Harvard-educated researcher in neuropsychiatry, worked with the Johns Hopkins Study of Mathematically Precocious Youth and designed aptitude tests for adults with 200+ IQs. Madsen, with a doctorate in politics from Harvard, was an expert on public persuasion tactics and social marketing. Together they wrote *After the Ball: How America Will Conquer Its Fear and Hatred of Gays in the '90s.*

"As cynical as it may seem," they explained at the outset, "AIDS gives us a chance, however brief, to establish ourselves as a victimized minority legitimately deserving of America's special protection and care. At the same time," they warned, "it generates mass hysteria of precisely the sort that has brought about public stonings and leper colonies since the Dark Ages and before. . . . How can we maximize the sympathy and minimize the fear? How, given the horrid hand that AIDS has dealt us, can we best play it?"[12]

The bottom line of Kirk and Madsen's master plan? "The campaign we outline in this book, though complex, depends centrally upon a program of unabashed propaganda, firmly grounded in long-established principles of psychology and advertising."[13]

Arguing that, skillfully handled, the AIDS epidemic could conquer American resistance to homosexuality and form the basis of a comprehensive, long-term marketing campaign to sell "gay rights" to straight America, *After the Ball* became the public-relations "Bible" of the movement.

Kirk and Madsen's "war goal," explains marketing expert Paul E. Rondeau of Regent University, was to "force acceptance of homosexual culture into the mainstream, to silence opposition, and ultimately to convert American society." In his comprehensive study, "Selling Homosexuality to America," Rondeau writes:

> The extensive three-stage strategy to Desensitize, Jam and Convert the American public is reminiscent of George Orwell's premise of goodthink and badthink in "1984." As Kirk and Madsen put it, "To one extent or another, the separability—and manipulability—of the verbal label is the basis for all the abstract principles underlying our proposed campaign."[14]

Separability? Manipulability? Allow me to translate this psychological marketing jargon: We can change what people actually think and feel by breaking their current negative associations with our cause and replacing them with positive associations.

Simple case in point: homosexual activists call their movement "gay rights." This accomplishes two major objectives: (1) Use of the word *gay* rather than *homosexual* masks the controversial sexual behavior involved and accentuates instead a vague but positive-sounding cultural identity— gay, which, after all, once meant "happy"; and (2) describing their battle from the get-go as one over "rights" implies homosexuals are being denied the basic freedoms of citizenship that others enjoy.

So merely by using the term *gay rights,* and persuading politicians and the media to adopt this terminology, activists seeking to transform America have framed the terms of the debate in their favor almost before the contest begins. (And in public relations warfare, he who frames the *terms* of the debate almost always wins. The abortion rights movement has prevailed in that war precisely because it succeeded, early on, in framing the debate as a question, not of *abortion,* but of *choice.* The abortion vanguard correctly anticipated that it would be far easier to defend an abstract, positive-sounding idea like *choice* than the unrestricted slaughter of unborn babies.)

Okay, you might be wondering, even granting the movement's cutting-edge marketing savvy, how do you sell middle America on those five hundred sex partners and weird sexual practices? Answer, according to Kirk and Madsen, you don't. Just don't talk about it. Rather, look and act as normal as possible for the camera.

"When you're very different, and people hate you for it," they explain, "this is what you do: *first* you get your foot in the door, by being as *similar* as possible; then, and only then—when your one little difference is finally accepted—can you start dragging in your other peculiarities, one by one. *You hammer in the wedge narrow end first.* As the saying goes, allow the camel's nose beneath your tent, and his whole body will soon follow."[15]

In other words, sadomasochists, leather fetishists, cross-dressers, transgenders, and other "peculiar" members of the homosexual community need to keep away from the tent and out of sight while the sales job is under way. Later, once the camel is safely inside, there will be room for all.

Rondeau explains Kirk and Madsen's techniques of "desensitization," "jamming," and "conversion" this way:

> Desensitization is described as inundating the public in a "continuous flood of gay-related advertising, presented in the least offensive fashion possible. If straights can't shut off the shower, they may at least eventually get used to being wet." But, the activists did not mean advertising in the usual marketing context but, rather, quite a different approach: "The main thing is to talk about gayness until the issue becomes thoroughly tiresome." They add, "[S]eek desensitization and nothing more. . . . If you can get [straights] to think [homosexuality] is just another thing—

meriting no more than a shrug of the shoulders—then your battle for legal and social rights is virtually won."

This planned hegemony is a variant of the type that Michael Warren describes in "Seeing Through the Media" where it "is not raw overt coercion; it is one group's covert orchestration of compliance by another group through structuring the consciousness of the second group."[16]

"Structuring the consciousness" of others? If that phraseology is uncomfortably reminiscent of various mind control and brainwashing tales you might have heard over the years, don't be surprised. Manipulating the emotions and thereby restructuring the thoughts and beliefs of large numbers of people is what modern marketing is all about.

THE ROAD TO CONVERSION

"JAMMING," EXPLAINS Rondeau, "is psychological terrorism meant to silence expression of or even support for dissenting opinion."[17] Radio counselor and psychologist Dr. Laura Schlessinger experienced big-time jamming during the run-up to her planned television show. Outraged over a single comment critical of homosexuals she had made on her radio program, activists launched a massive intimidation campaign against the television program's advertisers. As a result, the new show was stillborn.

But perhaps the highest-profile example of jamming occurred after the 1998 murder of University of Wyoming freshman Matthew Shepard. Lured from a bar, robbed and savagely beaten by two men, Shepard died five days later of head injuries. In the frenzied, saturation media coverage that followed, the press and homosexual activists singled out conservative Christians as having created a "climate of anti-gay hate" in which such a brutal act could happen.

NBC's *Today* show took the lead, focusing on a Christian ad campaign running at the time that offered to help homosexuals change their orientation. Reporter David Gregory narrated: "The ads were controversial for portraying gays and lesbians as sinners who had made poor choices, despite the growing belief that homosexuality may be genetic. . . . Have the ads fostered a climate of anti-gay hate that leads to incidents like the killing of Matthew Shepard? Gay rights activists say the ads convey a message that gay people are defective."[18]

And in a now-infamous interview, *Today*'s Katie Couric asked Wyoming Governor Jim Geringer: "Some gay rights activists have said that some conservative political organizations like the Christian Coalition, the Family Research Council and Focus on the Family are contributing to this anti-homosexual atmosphere by having an ad campaign saying if you are a homosexual you can change your orientation. That prompts people to say, 'If I meet someone who's homosexual, I'm going to take action to try to convince them or try to harm them.' Do you believe that such groups are contributing to this climate?"[19]

Consciously or not, the media were following Kirk and Madsen's playbook to the letter, discrediting anyone who disagreed with the homosexual agenda by associating them with lowlife murderers. In reality, none of the Christian groups smeared by NBC had ever condoned mistreatment of homosexuals—in fact, they had explicitly condemned it.

As if to add even more shame to the whole-hog jamming of Christians after the Shepard murder, in 2004 a comprehensive new investigation by ABC News *20/20* concluded that homosexuality very likely *wasn't a factor* in Shepard's murder, but rather Shepard had been targeted for his money.

So much for desensitization and jamming. But what about "conversion"? Here, Kirk and Madsen announce defiantly:

We mean conversion of the average American's emotions, mind, and will, through a planned psychological attack, in the form of propaganda fed to the nation via the media. We mean "subverting" the mechanism of prejudice to our own ends—using the very processes that made America hate us to turn their hatred into warm regard—whether they like it or not.[20]

Transforming another person's hatred into love ("warm regard") is the object of classic brainwashing. As Kirk and Madsen explain:

In Conversion, we mimic the natural process of stereotype-learning, with the following effect: we take the bigot's good feelings about all-right guys, and attach them to the label "gay," either weakening or, eventually, replacing his bad feelings toward the label and the prior stereotype. . . .

Whereas in Jamming the target is shown a bigot being rejected by his crowd for his prejudice against gays, in Conversion the target is shown his crowd actually associating with gays in good fellowship. Once again, it's very difficult for the average person, who, by nature and training, almost invariably feels what he sees his fellows feeling, not to respond in this knee-jerk fashion to a sufficiently calculated advertisement.[21]

We're talking about some serious messing around with Americans' minds here. Do the homosexual activists thus engaged really know they're deceiving the public, or are they convinced they're just telling the truth?

"It makes no difference that the ads are lies," write Kirk and Madsen, "not to us, because we're using them to ethically good effect, to counter negative stereotypes that are every bit as much lies, and far more wicked ones."[22]

HOMOSEXUALIZING HISTORY

ANOTHER IMPORTANT technique promoted by *After the Ball,* and employed repeatedly to great effect in recent years, is to claim that famous historical figures—"from Socrates to Eleanor Roosevelt, Tchaikovsky to Bessie Smith, Alexander the Great to Alexander Hamilton, and Leonardo da Vinci to Walt Whitman"—were homosexual or bisexual. Although the authors know these claims are unproven at best and often baseless (they refer to them as "suspected 'inverts'"), that doesn't stop them from advocating the tactic.

A recent example of this was the highly publicized, though utterly unsubstantiated, speculation that Abraham Lincoln was a homosexual. Even more outrageous was the suggestion by openly "gay" New Hampshire Episcopal Bishop Gene Robinson—a comment he quickly retracted after a firestorm of protest—that Jesus Christ was a homosexual!

As Kirk and Madsen explain:

Famous historical figures are considered especially useful to us for two reasons: first, they are invariably dead as a doornail, hence in no position to deny the truth and sue for libel. Second, and more serious, the virtues and accomplishments that make these historic gay figures admirable cannot be gainsaid or dismissed by the public, since high school history textbooks have already set them in incontrovertible cement.[23]

The flip side of this "celebrity endorsement" tactic consists of associating all detractors of the radical homosexual agenda with negative images of universally despised tyrants and lowlifes. *After the Ball* lists some of the negative images with which opponents should be associated—including "Klansmen demanding that gays be slaughtered or castrated," "hysterical backwoods preachers, drooling with hate," "menacing punks, thugs and convicts who speak coolly about the 'fags' they have bashed," and a "tour of Nazi concentration camps where homosexuals were tortured and gassed."[24]

Indeed, says Rondeau, "perhaps the most menacing focus of the campaign is the special treatment reserved for the religious dissenters. The strategy is to 'jam homohatred by linking it to Nazi horror.'"[25]

Kirk and Madsen explain the leverage gained by this nasty technique:

> Most contemporary hate groups on the Religious Right will bitterly resent the implied connection between homohatred and Nazi fascism. But since they can't defend the latter, they'll end up having to distance themselves by insisting that they would never go to such extremes. Such declarations of civility toward gays, of course, set our worst detractors on the slippery slope toward recognition of fundamental gay rights.[26]

Homosexual activists love to compare their opponents with Adolf Hitler and Nazis, apparently undaunted by the fact that, according to William L. Shirer's twelve-hundred-page *The Rise and Fall of the Third Reich,* widely regarded as *the* definitive book on Nazi Germany, "many of the early Nazis" *were* homosexuals.[27]

But this is not about truth. It's about manipulation. In a sense, modern psychology–based marketers understand people better than people understand themselves. They use emotional threads to tie their "product" (in this case, homosexuality) to preexisting positive attributes in the consumers' mind. And in a cultural-political campaign like this, they also successfully tie all who oppose their agenda to preexisting negatives, such as Nazis. The net effect of this conditioning can be so powerful over time that ultimately one's prior beliefs—based on experience, religious training, conscience, and common sense—are overwhelmed and replaced as a result of successive waves of emotion-driven reprogramming.

Still, one wonders how the press could allow itself to be used in such a blatantly propagandistic way and in pursuit of such a subversive agenda. And make no mistake, the "gay rights" agenda, which includes indoctrinating kindergartners with pro-homosexual propaganda and legalizing same-sex marriage, is extraordinarily subversive to America's foundational values and institutions. For the answer to that question you have to realize what's happened to the news media in recent years.

As you no doubt already know, the establishment press is oriented far to the left of the American mainstream, as study after study for the past three decades has documented beyond rational dispute. But did you know that, in addition, a major *homosexual* presence has emerged in the "mainstream" media, especially since the dawn of the 1990s?

Indeed, part of the mobilization that occurred in the wake of the 1988 War Conference was the recognition that the news media represented *the* prime tool for changing the hearts and minds of Americans. And if getting your message before the media was the name of the game, how much better would it be to actually *be* the media? Thus 1990 saw the launch of the National Lesbian and Gay Journalists Association (NLGJA), which has since grown into a formidable organization.

To celebrate its tenth anniversary, homosexual journalists from many major news organizations gathered in San Francisco for NLGJA's gala conference held September 7–10, 2000. The discussion on center stage was surreal. It focused on the question of whether or not, when reporting on stories related to homosexuality, mainstream journalists have a responsibility to include any viewpoints that contradict those of homosexuals. (You heard me right.)

MSNBC producer Ramon Escobar framed the issue this way: "This whole issue of 'balance' that we as journalists are supposed to achieve. . . . When we cover the black community, I've never seen a newsroom where you're covering one side and then you have to go run out and get the Klan's point of view: 'Well, I've got to go do my Klan interview.' How do you be fair?"[28]

NLGJA member Jeffrey Kofman, at the time a CBS correspondent who later migrated to NBC, restated the question: "The argument [is]: Why do we constantly see in coverage of gay and lesbian, bisexual and transgender issues the homophobes and the fag-haters quoted in stories when, of course, we don't do that with Jews, blacks, etcetera?"

Paula Madison, vice president of diversity at NBC and news director of WNBC in New York, added: "I agree with him. I don't see why we would seek out . . . the absurd, inane point of view just to get another point of view."

"All of us," Kofman rejoined, "have seen and continue to see a lot of coverage that includes perspectives on gay issues that include people who just simply are intolerant and perhaps not qualified as well."

Are you getting the picture? Whereas fifty years ago a news story portraying homosexuality as normal and respectable was unheard of, now we're facing exactly the opposite spectacle. Up on that glitzy convention stage were representatives of top broadcast news networks debating whether or not professional journalists should give voice to the Christian or traditional viewpoint on homosexuality. Or, they suggested, wouldn't it be better just to censor such "hateful" and "bigoted" viewpoints as being the moral equivalent of a "pro-racism" or "pro-bigotry" viewpoint, and thus beyond the margins of civilized debate?

By the way, lest you think this was just an unrepresentative group of radical journalists blowing off steam in their off-hours, here's who sponsored this particular homosexual journalists conference: Hearst Newspapers; Knight-Ridder, Inc.; CBS News; Gannett Foundation; CNN; Bloomberg News; NBC News; the *Dallas Morning News;* Fox News Channel; the *Los Angeles Times;* the *New York Daily News;* the *San Francisco Chronicle;* Time, Inc.; the *Wall Street Journal;* the *Washington Post;* and the *San Jose Mercury News.*[29]

No wonder the "mainstream press," overwhelmingly sympathetic toward the "gay rights" agenda, seems to be on the same page as homosexual activists engaged in desensitizing, jamming, and converting Americans to their world view. As a matter of fact, as we saw in the Matthew Shepard case, it's hard to tell them apart.

Thus a lot of the credit for the "gay-ing of America" can be laid at the door of the news media who, intentionally or not, have worked in tandem with the movement's public relations machinery for years now.

WE FORGOT ONE THING

TODAY THE homosexual activist movement is a juggernaut, racking up success after success. Even the occasional losses, such as voter rejection of same-sex marriage in the 2004 election, are simply the expected "one step back" in the time-honored "two steps forward one step back" mode of most long-term political wars. (After all, by audaciously conducting thousands of illegal same-sex marriage ceremonies, homosexuals all but guaranteed legal and social acceptance of their fall-back position—homosexual civil unions with the full legal force of marriage, something most Americans regarded as radical and unacceptable just a few years ago.)

As just one of a multitude of success indicators, consider that the popular teen magazine *Seventeen* conducted a reader poll in 1991, shortly after activist homosexuals abandoned the streets in favor of the television studio. At the time, only 17 percent of the magazine's adolescent readers accepted homosexuality as appropriate. In 1999, after eight years of intense "gay rights" marketing, a whopping 54 percent, more than three times as many teens, accepted homosexuality as appropriate.[30]

This stunning turnaround is reflected in virtually every area of society. Whether in culture, politics, law, business, the news media, entertainment, education, or even the church, homosexual strides have been nothing short of astonishing. Once condemned as "immoral deviants," homosexuals and lesbians today are honored, idealized, defended as victims, and celebrated as role models. Thanks to "hate-crimes" legislation, they are now afforded extra protections as a special class of people— protections not granted to all members of society. (If you were assaulted, the perpetrator would get one sentence, but if you were assaulted because of your homosexuality, the perpetrator would receive a more severe sentence under hate-crimes sentencing guidelines.)

Meanwhile, in what was once a vibrant Judeo-Christian culture, Christians and other proponents of traditional biblical principles are routinely cast as bigots and "homophobes," thanks to constant jamming. Direct quotes from the Bible regarding homosexuality are routinely condemned as "hate speech," and—as we have seen—pro-homosexual journalists piously agonize over whether or not they should dignify the traditional, biblical viewpoint by even acknowledging it.

Multitudes of activists—with almost limitless time and energy to devote to advancing their agenda, largely unencumbered by any need to change diapers, pay for dental braces, or attend their children's soccer games, as do most heterosexual married people—have succeeded in their goal of transforming society. As public relations campaigns go, it's been an unqualified success.

However, in the "gay rights" movement's relentless struggle to legitimize homosexuality, and in the greater society's veneration of them as heroes of the great civil rights crusade of the new millennium, we've forgotten one thing. In the endlessly clever media campaign that's bamboozled everyone, "restructured their consciousness," turned their hate into love and their rejection into acceptance, something crucial has been lost.

We've forgotten about reality. We've been living in a Madison Avenue fantasy world of marketing images and carefully crafted rhetoric in the foreground, with court battles, fascistlike intimidation, and relentless waves of persuasion in the background.

But what about the truth we've left behind? What about the reality of homosexuality, of what causes it, and of what it means physically and spiritually for those so oriented? Do we even care any more?

Let's rewind and go back to former Congressman Robert Bauman, who in poignantly describing his internal struggles against his homosexual compulsions confided that he had been sexually seduced when he was five years old by an older boy.

Did that experience have anything to do with Bauman's future homosexuality?

There was a time when psychiatry, psychology, religion, and common sense all said "yes." In fact, sexually abused young males are "up to 7 times more likely to self-identify as gay or bisexual than peers who had not been abused," concludes the peer-reviewed 1998 study, "Sexual Abuse of Boys," by William C. Holmes, M.D. and Gail B. Slap, M.D.[31]

On that topic, a reader recently wrote to me: "We are a family of eight siblings and the oldest is gay, and has lived with the same partner for 41 years. At various times, my siblings and I have tried to discover why he is gay and none of the rest of us are. We finally found out through an older cousin that my brother was repeatedly sexually molested when he was six years old by a 19-year-old man."[32]

Even Kirk and Madsen, who advise activists to claim they were born homosexual, know better. "We argue that, for all practical purposes, gays should be considered to have been born gay," they write, "even though sexual orientation, for most humans, seems to be the product of a complex interaction between innate predispositions and environmental factors during childhood and early adolescence."

If "environmental factors" are involved—and everyone knows they are, whether or not they publicly admit it—why then advise homosexuals to claim they were "born gay"?

"To suggest in public that homosexuality might be chosen," Kirk and Madsen explain, "is to open the can of worms labeled 'moral choices and sin' and give the religious intransigents a stick to beat us with. Straights must be taught that it is as natural for some persons to be homosexual as it is for others to be heterosexual: wickedness and seduction have nothing to do with it."[33]

Unfortunately, with all the brainy marketing behind the campaign to mainstream homosexuality, what's been swept under the rug is the recognition—once commonplace in America—that flawed early relationships or sexual victimization can put a child on the road to homosexuality.

Children are exquisitely impressionable, so much so that sexual seduction or assault is a major trauma that can, and often does, reprogram the victim's identity—his view of who and what he is. While the Holmes and Slap study confirms this, the point is self-evident: our prisons are full of child molesters who were molested as children and batterers who were battered as children.

What about the twelve-year-old who molested Bauman? What caused him to sexually seduce a five-year-old boy? No doubt he felt a strong compulsion to do to a new kid what had been done to him. But why?

An innocent young child has a "bright light" quality that feels mysteriously threatening to those in the grip of corruption. In fact, many see this dynamic at the core of a great deal of child abuse.

To the person who's already been "converted" and is acting out the homosexual "lifestyle," it's deeply satisfying—*far* beyond mere sexual pleasure—to "initiate" an innocent person. Doing so serves to anesthetize his own conscience and assuage his inner conflict by destroying the innocence of another person, since that innocence tends to make him aware of his own corruption.

There was a time when most Americans knew that homosexuals were not "born that way" but rather had their normal gender-identity development disturbed and redirected through early childhood experiences. There was a time when we recognized on some level that unhealthy relationships with mothers and fathers could cause girls and boys to grow up with gender confusion—just like emotionally devastating traumatic experiences of molestation—if not dealt with properly.

But that was a time before much of America itself was seduced into believing there was no God, or if there was a God, He is inconsequential to the affairs of the world. It was a time when Judeo-Christian morality inspired the culture and laws of the land.

Today we've basically abandoned "old-fashioned" notions of right and wrong in favor of "consensuality," which means two people can do whatever they want, no matter how abominable, as long as they "don't hurt anybody else." The problem with that—aside from the fact that it denies the existence of God and His laws—is that in such a deluded state you have no basis for determining if you're hurting another person or not. A pedophile justifies sex with children precisely because he doesn't believe he's hurting the child; rather he believes he's loving him!

You might wonder: Where and when will this "gay rights" public relations steamroller stop? The end game is not only to bring about the complete acceptance of homosexuality, including same-sex marriage, but also to prohibit and even criminalize public criticism of homosexuality, including the quotation of biblical passages disapproving of homosexuality. In other words, total jamming of criticism with the force of law. This is already essentially the case in Canada and parts of Scandinavia.

"Why?" you might ask. "I thought gays just wanted equal rights and to be free to do what they want in their own bedrooms." No, they've had that for years.

Their campaign will not end until Christians and other traditionalists opposing homosexuality are shut up, discredited, and utterly silenced—and all because of a little factor we've forgotten about in our cleverness, namely this: In truth, there *is* something wrong with homosexuality. Simply put, it *is* unnatural and self-destructive—just as Western civilization has long understood it.

Homosexual activists fancy their cause as identical to that of blacks and the '60s civil rights movement. But being black is not unnatural and self-destructive. Being of African origin obviously doesn't involve fleeing one's own conscience and the author of that conscience—God.

But it is precisely because of this difference that the "gay civil rights" movement is not about changing the laws so homosexuals can have equal opportunity for advancement or access as it was for blacks during the '60s. Homosexuals already live in freedom and can reside, work, or play virtually anywhere they want. In fact, as a group, homosexuals enjoy a *higher income level* than the general American population.

It's not about rights. It's about redefining truth and censoring all criticism so that militant homosexuals can be comfortable in their "lifestyle" without having to be disturbed by reality.

Remember, all of us—homosexuals included—have a conscience (that other-dimensional standard that God has tucked away inside each of us) that causes us inner conflict when we're doing the wrong thing. But if we tumble into the grip of dark forces we don't understand and then start to *defend* our obsessions and compulsions, we inevitably come to regard our conscience as an enemy. And although we may be somewhat successful in drowning out that inner warning bell, what happens when this same rejected conscience factor appears in another person and gets too close to us for comfort? We feel threatened.

Therefore, we feel compelled to silence the "voice of conscience"—not just the one inside of us, but the one in other people, which tends to revive our own conscience with which we're at war. This means we can't tolerate dissent. We simply can't stand it. It makes us want to scream.

To the homosexual living in denial, then, even a loving offer of help from, say, a Christian ex-gay ministry or "reparative therapy" counselor (to help overcome homosexual addiction) feels like the most vile, abusive hatred. In fact, it's real love—which we misinterpret as hatred and "bigotry" simply because it causes us to confront a truth that is not welcome in us.

LOVE AND REDEMPTION

WHEN ALL is said and done, the "mainstreaming" of homosexuality over the last few decades has been a great tragedy. But of all the societal confusion, chaos, and corruption it has ushered in, the most tragic dimension of all is what it has done to people struggling with homosexual and "transgender" attractions and compulsions.

Remember, our conflicts contain the seeds of redemption—that is, as long as we know we have a problem, there's hope for a change. But if we deny there's a problem, we are literally robbed of the chance to find healing. That's exactly what America has done in buying into the "gay rights movement." We have betrayed our homosexual brothers and sisters.

Glorifying dysfunctionality and corruption, we have relieved homosexuals of the inner conflict they once felt over their condition—something they desperately need, indeed all of us need, if we're ever going to overcome our problems and find wholeness.

A generation ago, we understood there is such a thing as sin, and that sin is a serious matter and to be avoided. Now there is no societal consciousness of sin—only limitless "freedom," "choice," and "consensual relationships." Beguiled by our scientific and technological advances into believing we are enlightened, in reality as we move further and further away from our Judeo-Christian spiritual roots, we actually understand less and less about ourselves. Most of all, we've forgotten as a society what love is, because supporting and justifying homosexuality is *not* real love any more than glorifying drinking helps the alcoholic or celebrating smoking helps wipe out lung cancer.

We defend our own corruption at great peril. And if defending that corruption becomes a national movement, as it has with our cultural and legal adoption of the "gay rights agenda," we're all in serious trouble.

In truth, most homosexuals experience guilt and conflict when they first discover homosexual urges. Thus there is a strong temptation—especially in today's pro-"gay" culture—for them to "resolve" the conflict by giving in to the compulsion and affirming, "It's okay to be gay." But if they do, there is just no way out for them. For this reason, the most loving stance for others to take is not to serve as enablers of self-destructive and immoral compulsions, but to stand in patient but firm opposition. In other words, we need to side with the afflicted person's conscience.

In America, we've done the opposite.

"Hating the sin but not the sinner," the classic Christian expression for loving your struggling neighbor by nonjudgmentally disagreeing with his errant behavior, actually has great power—more than we realize. By resisting the temptation to hate, yet still standing firm against what's wrong, God's love is able to come through that obedient "neutral zone."

We started this journey into the world of "gay rights" with the poignant words of former congressman Robert Bauman, who said: "I did not choose to be homosexual. I would change my sexual orientation if that were within my power." Sadly, we've failed Bauman and millions suffering with similar sexual problems by glorifying and pandering to their dysfunction and pretending it's normal.

In the end, we have to ask ourselves which is worse—the previous era in America, when homosexuals were reviled and driven underground? Or today's America, when the pendulum has swung so far in the other direction that those in the grip of powerful self-destructive compulsions are fawned over and lionized as heroes?

Either way, because the rest of us have failed to find real love, they remain victims.

2

BUYING THE BIG LIE

The Myth of Church-State Separation

GET YOUR HANDS OFF our God!" shouted one indignant protester.

Others, urging him to stay calm, knelt on the ground and prayed. Still other demonstrators took to chanting, *"Put it back! Put it back! Put it back! . . ."*

Prominent national voices wailed in indignation. Dismayed and angered Americans unleashed a fusillade of letters, faxes, and e-mails to politicians and newspapers and each other. Evangelical leader Dr. James Dobson, who had urged his three million radio listeners to head to Montgomery, Alabama, in a show of support, fervently warned that America was witnessing a campaign "to remove every vestige of faith or reverence for God from the public square."

But all the agonized protests were to no avail.

The spectacular fifty-three-hundred-pound monument of the Ten Commandments, installed in the courthouse's rotunda by then-Alabama Supreme Court Chief Justice Roy O. Moore, was being kicked out.

It took little more than an hour for three workers and a security guard to hoist the washing machine–sized granite cube onto a dolly and scoot it out of sight of television cameras to an undisclosed location—and out of public view.

To top off the spectacle, Moore was then suspended from his position as the state's top jurist for defying the mandate of U.S. District Judge Myron Thompson, who had ordered the monument's removal.

Exactly why, you ask, did the Ten Commandments—the spiritual basis for America's laws, which are also carved into the U.S. Supreme Court building in Washington DC—have to be banished from the Alabama Judicial Building?

You see, Judge Thompson had determined that the monument violated the First Amendment's establishment clause, which says, "Congress shall make no law respecting an establishment of religion."

"Congress shall make no law." Thompson never explained how a granite display of the Ten Commandments in a courthouse constituted Congress "making a law."

But that didn't matter. Somehow, though the vast majority of Americans are repulsed by it, a virulent and increasingly pervasive legal theory of the First Amendment holds that Christmas manger scenes must be eliminated from public places, commencement exercises conducted without a prayer, and kids must refrain from saying "Merry Christmas" at school.

How far, millions wonder aloud, can this judicial assault on the nation's religious and traditional values—a jihad waged most prominently and notoriously by the American Civil Liberties Union (ACLU)—possibly go before *someone* stops it?

The truth is, the notion of "the constitutional separation of church and state" that underlies all of these cases, indeed, that underlies the legal transformation of America into a de facto atheistic, secular state, is a lie.

It is one of the truly outrageous, malignant—and provably false—"Big Lies" of our generation.

Secularist Fantasy

THINK BACK. If you attended public school in the last few decades, you probably remember being taught that America was founded by a lively assortment of slaveholding Christians, deists, and freethinkers who insisted on instituting a "constitutional separation of church and state." Thomas Jefferson, you were reminded, had famously affirmed this "wall of separation" in his 1802 letter to the Danbury Baptists.

You could be forgiven for inferring from all this "education" that, back in the good old days at least, government scrupulously kept religion at arm's length.

But that would be a truly deluded secularist fantasy. In reality, throughout the late 1700s—the era of the Revolutionary War and the subsequent adoption of the U.S. Constitution and Bill of Rights, including the First Amendment—Christianity permeated America from top to bottom.

- In 1777, with the Revolutionary War threatening the flow of Bibles from England, Congress approved the purchase of twenty thousand Bibles from Holland to give to the states.

- No fewer than six of the thirteen original states had official, state-supported churches—"establishments of religion"! I'll bet you didn't know that. In fact, these states—Connecticut, Georgia, Maryland, Massachusetts, New Hampshire, and South Carolina—refused to ratify the new national Constitution unless it included a prohibition of federal meddling with their existing state "establishments of religion."

- Other states *required* those seeking elected office to be Christians.

- The Continental Congress routinely designated days of fasting and prayer and other religious observances, appointed government-funded chaplains, and appropriated money to pay for Christian missionaries to convert the Indians.

In other words, the original American government under the Constitution would have driven the ACLU stark, raving mad.

What a difference two hundred years can make. Today, for every big case that makes the evening news—like the banishment of the Ten Commandments from the Alabama courthouse or the judicial ban on the "Under God" phrase from the Pledge of Allegiance—there are countless other smaller cases, every bit as mind-boggling:

- A federal court ruled that a schoolteacher couldn't be seen in school with his own personal Bible and later ruled that a classroom library containing 237 books must remove the 2 titles dealing with Christianity.[1]

- A criminal, convicted and sentenced by a jury for brutally clubbing to death a seventy-one-year-old woman with an axe handle so he could steal her Social Security check, had his sentence overturned. Why? The prosecuting attorney, in a statement lasting less than five seconds, mentioned a Bible verse in the courtroom.[2]

- A public cemetery, ruled a federal court, couldn't have a planter in the shape of a cross, since, as the court explained, the mere sight of it could cause "emotional distress" to a passerby and thus constitute "injury-in-fact."[3]

"Injury-in-fact"? From looking at a planter?

Isn't it about time we face the painful truth—that we Americans have had our Constitution, and therefore the very reins of power, stolen from us while we were busy going to work, raising our kids, paying the bills, and watching *Jeopardy?*

WHAT "WALL OF SEPARATION"?

FIRST A quick civics lesson. The section of the Constitution that deals with religion is the First Amendment of the Bill of Rights—the first sixteen words of it, anyway.

There's the establishment clause ("Congress shall make no law respecting an establishment of religion") and the free exercise clause ("or prohibiting the free exercise thereof").

The establishment clause—that's the one today's courts almost always focus on—simply prohibits the federal government from "establishing" a national church or from interfering with the established churches in the states! (Remember, several states already had state-supported "establishments of religion.")

Possibly you wonder whether the issue is really this cut-and-dried. After all, for the last half-century, judicial activists on the Supreme Court and lower courts, ACLU lawyers, the press, and the secular culture in general have embraced "the constitutional separation of church and state" as though it actually existed somewhere in the Constitution. Of course, none of these words—"separation," "church," or "state"—are in the First Amendment.

Let's go back in time and witness the conversation among those who debated and approved the wording of the Bill of Rights and find out what they really meant.

The date is June 8, 1789. James Madison—key architect of the Constitution and a leading member of the First Congress—is proposing the following wording for what ultimately will become the religion clauses of the First Amendment: "The civil rights of none shall be abridged on account of religious belief or worship, nor shall any national religion be established, nor shall the full and equal rights of conscience be in any manner, or on any pretext, infringed."

The representatives debate this for a bit and then turn it over to a committee consisting of Madison and ten other House members, which comes up with a new version: "No religion shall be established by law, nor shall the equal rights of conscience be infringed."

More debate. Madison explains that "he apprehended the meaning of the words to be, that Congress should not establish a religion, and enforce the legal observation of it by law, nor compel men to worship God in any manner contrary to their conscience."

Rep. Benjamin Huntington complains the proposed wording might "be taken in such latitude as to be extremely hurtful to the cause of religion." So Madison suggests inserting the word *national* before the word *religion* to assuage the fears of those concerned over the establishment of a national religion—and of being compelled to conform to it. (After all, wasn't that precisely the reason the Puritans had come to America in the first place—to escape the tyranny of England's compulsory state religion?)

But Representative Eldridge Gerry balks at the word "national," because, he argues, the Constitution created a federal government, not a national one. So Madison withdraws his latest proposal but assures Congress his reference to a "national religion" had to do with a national religious establishment, not a national government.

A week later, the House again alters the wording this way: "Congress shall make no law establishing religion, or to prevent the free exercise thereof, or to infringe the rights of conscience."

Meanwhile, the Senate debates other versions of the same amendment and on September 3, 1789, comes up with this wording: "Congress shall make no law establishing articles of faith or a mode of worship, or prohibiting the free exercise of religion."

The House doesn't like the Senate's changes and calls for a conference, from which emerges—finally—the wording ultimately included in the Bill of Rights: "Congress shall make no law respecting an establishment of religion, or prohibiting the free exercise thereof."

Okay, now that we've "witnessed" the debate over the First Amendment, do you really believe the Founding Fathers wanted to make kids into criminals for saying "Merry Christmas" at school? Did they intend for the Supreme Court to outlaw prayer in the nation's learning institutions when all of their own congressional sessions to this very day open with a prayer?

Of course not. In fact, Joseph Story, appointed by President James Madison to the Supreme Court in 1811, where he served for the next thirty-three years until his death, explained exactly how the high court regarded the First Amendment in his celebrated *Commentary on the Constitution of the United States.*

> Probably at the time of the adoption of the Constitution, and of the amendment to it now under consideration [First Amendment], the general if not the universal sentiment in America was, that Christianity ought to receive encouragement from the State so far as was not incompatible with the private rights of conscience and the freedom of religious worship. An attempt to level all religions, and to make it a matter of state policy to hold all in utter indifference, would have created universal disapprobation, if not universal indignation.
>
> The real object of the [First Amendment] was, not to countenance, much less to advance Mahometanism [Islam], or Judaism, or infidelity, by prostrating Christianity; but to exclude all rivalry among Christian sects, and to prevent any national ecclesiastical establishment, which should give to an hierarchy the exclusive patronage of the national government.[4]

Even today Supreme Court Chief Justice William Rehnquist, in reviewing the same 1789 First Amendment deliberations you just "witnessed," comes to the same conclusion as Story:

> On the basis of the record of these proceedings in the House of Representatives, James Madison was undoubtedly the most important architect among the Members of the House of the Amendments which became the

Bill of Rights. . . . His original language, "nor shall any national religion be established," obviously does not conform to the "wall of separation" between church and State idea which latter-day commentators have ascribed to him. His explanation on the floor of the meaning of his language—"that Congress should not establish a religion, and enforce the legal observation of it by law" is of the same ilk. . . .

It seems indisputable from these glimpses of Madison's thinking, as reflected by actions on the floor of the House in 1789, that he saw the Amendment as designed to prohibit the establishment of a national religion, and perhaps to prevent discrimination among sects. He did not see it as requiring neutrality on the part of government between religion and irreligion.

Rehnquist adds tellingly, "None of the other Members of Congress who spoke during the August 15th debate expressed the slightest indication that they thought the language before them . . . would require that the Government be absolutely neutral as between religion and irreligion. The evil to be aimed at, so far as those who spoke were concerned, appears to have been the establishment of a national church, and perhaps the preference of one religious sect over another; but it was definitely not concerned about whether the Government might aid all religions evenhandedly."[5]

Oh, by the way, as if to thumb its nose through time at the ACLU two centuries later, the very day after the House of Representatives adopted the First Amendment's religion clauses, Rep. Elias Boudinot proposed a resolution asking President George Washington to issue a national Thanksgiving Day Proclamation.

Boudinot said he "could not think of letting the session pass over without offering an opportunity to all the citizens of the United States of joining with one voice, in returning to Almighty God their sincere thanks for the many blessings he had poured down upon them."

On September 25, 1789, Boudinot's resolution was passed, and within two weeks Washington responded with the following proclamation. Read it carefully:

Now, therefore, I do recommend and assign Thursday, the 26th day of November next, to be devoted by the people of these States to the service of that great and glorious Being who is the beneficent author of all the good that was, that is, or that will be; that we may then all unite in rendering unto Him our sincere and humble thanks for His kind care and protection of the people of this country previous to their becoming a nation; for the signal and manifold mercies and the favorable interpositions of His providence in the course and conclusion of the late war; for the great degree of tranquility, union, and plenty which we have since enjoyed; for the peaceable and rational manner in which we have been enabled to establish constitutions of government for our safety and happiness, and particularly the national one now lately instituted; for the civil and religious liberty with which we are blessed, and the means we have of acquiring and diffusing useful knowledge; and, in general, for all the great and various favors which He has been pleased to confer upon us.

And also that we may then unite in most humbly offering our prayers and supplications to the great Lord and Ruler of Nations, and beseech Him to pardon our national and other transgressions; to enable us all, whether in public or private stations, to perform our several and relative duties properly and punctually; to render our National Government a blessing to all the people by constantly being a Government of wise, just, and constitutional laws, discreetly and faithfully executed and obeyed; to protect and guide all sovereigns and nations (especially such as have shown kindness to us), and to bless them with good governments, peace, and concord; to promote the knowledge and practice of true religion and virtue, and the increase of science among them and us; and, generally, to grant unto all mankind such a degree of temporal prosperity as He alone knows to be best.

These inspiring words from the father of our country would no doubt have inspired a lawsuit threat from the ACLU had the group been around then.

WHAT HAPPENED TO GOD?

FOR THE next 150 years or so, America's judiciary interpreted the First Amendment in accord with what you have just read—as prohibiting the establishment of a single national denomination. Court rulings and public policies reflected that common understanding.

But then, halfway through the last century, something happened that changed all that.

This something first showed its face in 1947, in the landmark Supreme Court case *Everson v. Board of Education*. Speaking for the majority, Justice Hugo Black announced a new and previously unknown legal principle: "The First Amendment has erected a wall between church and state. That wall must be kept high and impregnable. We could not approve the slightest breach."

Ever since then, the high court's rulings have progressively and relentlessly aimed at removing every vestige of Christian language, imagery, or symbolism from public property.

From the decisions of the 1960s outlawing prayer and religious instruction in the schools to today's surreal court battles over whether it's okay for school kids to pledge allegiance "Under God," today's judiciary interprets the First Amendment in a radically different way than did its predecessors during America's first one and a half centuries.

Time to ask some disturbing questions.

First, about these judges. When they create legislation through judicial fiat that no legislature in the nation could, or would, dare enact—as the Massachusetts Supreme Judicial Court did in November 2003 when it *mandated* same-sex marriage in that state—do these judges realize what they're doing? Do they understand that they're flouting the U.S. and state constitutions, violating their oaths of office, betraying the trust of current and future generations of Americans, and usurping power that's not legally theirs?

You might think, How could they not know? After all, these judges are all lawyers and supposedly constitutional scholars. They've sworn an oath to uphold the Constitution. Before rendering a decision they presumably have conducted a thorough investigation into what the Constitution says—and means—about the matter at hand.

Keep in mind that, despite what you may have been led to believe, it's a simple task to ascertain the original meaning of any part of the Constitution or its amendments. We've more or less demonstrated that in these pages by briefly examining the debate over the First Amendment's religion clauses. The Constitution is not long, mystical, and transcendent like the Bible, open to all sorts of conflicting interpretations. Rather, it is a short, clear, relatively recent, English-language contract that was written for the average person. Its original intent is an open book and therefore beyond reasonable dispute.

How about some more specific questions:

• How can Supreme Court Justice Ruth Bader Ginsburg, sworn to uphold the U.S. Constitution, proclaim that she and her fellow justices are now looking to international law to guide their decisions, as she did in a 2003 speech to the American Constitution Society? "Our island or lone-ranger mentality is beginning to change," she proclaimed, adding that justices "are becoming more open to comparative and international law perspectives."[6]

• Similarly, how could Justice Stephen Breyer, on ABC News's *This Week,* question whether the Constitution will be sufficient to govern America in the future? Breyer said to host George Stephanopoulos: "We see all the time, Justice [Sandra Day] O'Connor and I, and the others, how the world really—it's trite but it's true—is growing together. Through commerce, through globalization, through the spread of democratic institutions, through immigration to America, it's becoming more and more one world of many different kinds of people. And how they're going to live together across the world will be the challenge, and whether our Constitution and how it fits into the governing documents of other nations, I think will be a challenge for the next generations."[7]

Say what? "*Whether* our Constitution"? "*How* it fits"? What happened to the Constitution being the "supreme law of the land"?

• How does the Supreme Court justify mountains of federal gun control laws when justices know very well the original intent of the Second Amendment was to guarantee to the individual an unfettered ("shall not be infringed") right to use firearms to defend himself and his family—whether from criminals or, as was the Founders' greater concern, from tyrannical government?

• How did Justice Harry Blackmun, who wrote the majority opinion in the most controversial Supreme Court decision in history, *Roe v. Wade,* divine the right to abortion from the Fourteenth Amendment's supposed "right to privacy," when there simply is no right to privacy in the Fourteenth Amendment or anywhere else in the Constitution?

Let's pause for a moment on *Roe v. Wade*—a decision that opened the door to more than forty million abortions. If we're exploring how and why judges feel perfectly justified in ignoring the Constitution's original intent, let's consider one illuminating little story involving Blackmun and his pregnant daughter.

In March 2004, when Blackmun's private papers were finally released to the public decades after the momentous 1973 *Roe* decision, his daughter, Sally Blackmun, revealed something remarkable. Talking to Women's eNews, she disclosed for the first time that her father consulted with members of his family after being assigned responsibility for writing the majority opinion on *Roe v. Wade*.

"Roe was a case that Dad struggled with," Blackmun told the feminist news service. "It was a case that he asked his daughters' and wife's opinion about."

Most pertinent among those opinions would have been Sally's. Seven years before *Roe v. Wade*, while she was a nineteen-year-old sophomore at Skidmore College in Saratoga Springs, New York, Sally Blackmun discovered she was pregnant.

"It was one of those things I was not at all proud of, that I was not at all pleased with myself about. It was a big disappointment to my parents," she said. "I did what so many young women of my era did. I quit college and married my 20-year-old college boyfriend. It was a decision that I might have made differently had *Roe v. Wade* been around."

Shortly after the wedding, Sally Blackmun lost her child to a miscarriage. Although it took six years to complete her graduation requirements, she questions whether she would have graduated at all had her child been born. Getting pregnant had caused a major dent in the life she had planned. In those same six years, her hastily formed marriage collapsed. By then it was 1972—the same year her father sought her input on *Roe*.

At the time of the Roe decision, Sally Blackmun lived and worked in Washington DC. Although Supreme Court decisions are generally made without advance announcement, Justice Blackmun notified his daughter so she could be present when the decision was read.

"I remember that it was very tense in the courtroom, very crowded. The decorum is such that people aren't yelling and screaming and carrying on. We didn't know how he was going to come down on it. And I was very pleased with the decision and the fact that it gave women that right of choice," Blackmun recalled. "Dad always felt that it was the right thing to do and the necessary thing to do toward the full emancipation of women in this country. So we certainly were in favor of what he did."[8]

The obvious question: Did Justice Blackmun's passion for championing abortion rights have anything at all to do with his daughter's out-of-wedlock pregnancy experience and the pain, embarrassment, and trauma it caused the Blackmun family? Do we need to guess what sort of advice Sally—who later became an attorney and chairwoman of Planned Parenthood of Greater Orlando—might have given her father? And is this how a Supreme Court decision, especially one responsible for more than a million abortions every year for three decades, is supposed to be made?

Is this what we've come to? Judges make rulings based on their personal whims, emotions, and family traumas, oblivious to the fact that they're changing the course of history in profound and destructive ways?

How did we get from having justices like Joseph Story, who reverenced the Constitution and honored the intent and wisdom of the founders, to today's justices? While a minority of modern judges are principled, many are simply unfettered by the Constitution.

Do you really want to know what happened in the mid-twentieth century that caused the Supreme Court to lose its prior allegiance to higher principles? The answer is as obvious as it is unsettling: America as a whole was drifting away from its prior allegiance to higher principles.

Want to know how the Supreme Court could crank out its revolutionary 1962 ruling that outlawed school prayer and its 1963 decision banning Bible reading, religious classes, and religious instruction in the nation's schools? Just look at what was going on in America at the same time.

"Is God Dead?"

THE COVER of the April 8, 1966, issue of *Time* magazine—perhaps its most controversial edition ever—said it all. On a black background, giant red letters trumpeted the scandalous question: "Is God Dead?"

"There is an acute feeling that the churches on Sunday are preaching the existence of a God who is nowhere visible in their daily lives," wrote *Time* reporter John T. Elson, surveying the religious malaise and uncertainty of mainstream Christianity during the 1960s. Leader after religious leader expressed doubt and confusion about the faith of their fathers. Even Francis B. Sayre, then Episcopal dean of Washington's famed National Cathedral, admitted, "I'm confused as to what God is—but so is the rest of America."

In light of the nation's identity crisis during the 1960s, is it so shocking that the Supreme Court would lose its moorings and drift into uncharted legal waters?

Read a little more of what *Time* had to say:

Lutheran Church historian Martin Marty argues that all too many pews are filled on Sunday with practical atheists—disguised nonbelievers who behave during the rest of the week as if God did not exist. . . .

"I love God," cries one anguished teen-ager, "but I hate the church." Theologian Langdon Gilkey says that "belief is the area in the modern Protestant church where one finds blankness, silence, people not knowing what to say or merely repeating what their preachers say." . . .

Says Marty's colleague at the Chicago Divinity School, the Rev. Nathan Scott, who is also rector of St. Paul's Episcopal Church in Hyde Park: "I look out at the faces of my people and I'm not sure what meaning these words, gestures and rituals have for them." . . .

In search of meaning, some believers have desperately turned to psychiatry, Zen or drugs. Thousands of others have quietly abandoned all but token allegiance to the churches, surrendering themselves to a life of "anonymous Christianity" dedicated to civil rights or the Peace Corps. Speaking for a generation of young Roman Catholics for whom the dogmas of the church have lost much of their power, philosopher Michael Novak of Stanford writes: "I do not understand God, nor the way in which he works. If, occasionally, I raise my heart in prayer, it is to no God I can see, or hear, or feel. It is to a God in as cold and obscure a polar night as any non-believer has known."[9]

Whoa, talk about a fiery faith! With shepherds like this, no wonder the 1960s flock was scattered and befuddled. No wonder Eastern and cultic religious movements, from Transcendental Meditation to Hare Krishna, flourished and proliferated. And no wonder government, especially the judiciary, became intoxicated with the idea that it could create a more perfect world by enlarging its scope and power.

There was a spiritual vacuum in America—and government, as it usually does, came whooshing in to fill it.

Time's analysis went on to explain that faith in America was being replaced by a new source of wisdom and truth—namely, science. "The rebellion against this God of faith is best summed up by the word secularization," wrote Elson, who noted that the prestige of science had become so great that it had come to dominate other areas of life.

> In effect, knowledge has become that which can be known by scientific study—and what cannot be known that way somehow seems uninteresting, unreal. In previous ages, the man of ideas, the priest or the philosopher was regarded as the font of wisdom. Now, says [Anglican theologian David] Jenkins, the sage is more likely to be an authority "trained in scientific methods of observing phenomena, who bases what he says on a corpus of knowledge built up by observation and experiment and constantly verified by further processes of practice and observation."[10]

In other words, faith was out as a basis for governing our lives or country. In light of this zeitgeist among America's elite—and believe me, Supreme Court justices live among the elite—is it any wonder that genuine respect for a Constitution and Bill of Rights that were largely the result of a Christian world view would drastically diminish?

Wouldn't this seismic shift in world views, with its worship of scientific progress and dismissive attitude toward traditional faith, fit perfectly with the notion at the heart of all judicial activism that the Constitution is a "living, breathing"—and therefore changing—document?

WHAT'S WRONG WITH LIVING AND BREATHING?

TIMES DO change. The world has been radically transformed by technology. We don't keep slaves any more. So what's *wrong* with regarding the Constitution as a "living, breathing" document as, indeed, a great many people do today?

Of course, the Constitution can be changed through the amendment process—as it has seventeen times since the adoption of the first ten amendments, known as the Bill of Rights. But the idea of a "living" Constitution is very different; it means the contract between America and its government is to be "interpreted" anew by each generation.

Here's the problem. Though our technology, knowledge base, and culture have all changed dramatically over the centuries, human nature and human character weaknesses haven't changed a bit. Objective reality—"the Laws of Nature and of Nature's God" as the Declaration of Independence puts it—hasn't changed. The Bible and the Ten Commandments haven't changed. The universal appeals to personal pride—ambition, greed, lust, envy, power—haven't changed. Specifically, the tendency for too much power to corrupt those entrusted with it has most definitely not changed.

Thus the need for strictly constitutional government with clearly defined and limited powers is still necessary, because, despite our advances, absolute power still corrupts absolutely. Unfortunately, in today's America, the judiciary has assumed something approaching absolute power.

Without question, there are some fine judges in America today, including several on the Supreme Court. Yet far too many see themselves, not as humble servants and guardians of a sacred, two-hundred-plus-year-old contract between Americans and the government they created, but rather as high priests of a new order, chosen to chart the path of civilization in the new, globalist, more enlightened world. It's their job—their destiny, or so they think—to help us lesser folk make the transition from the old days of wooden ships, muskets, and Indians to today's world of microchips, speed-of-light communications, and the long march of man.

Of course, the illogic in all this is that if the Constitution—meant to be the standard by which we measure all other laws—can be changed on the whim of the current court, then we really have no Constitution.

HOW A SLOGAN CAN CHANGE THE WORLD

NOW WE understand who sold us big, secular government and why they did it. But how did they pull it off? Through what sleight of hand did the establishment clause—"Congress shall make no law respecting an establishment of religion"—become transformed into a total ban on religious expression in the public square? It's a fascinating bit of linguistic legerdemain.

First, to better convey the technique, let's recall the Stephen Stills mega-hit song "Love the One You're With." Remember that one? A whole chorus of soulful singers, against a lively, up-tempo disco accompaniment, urged millions of lonesome souls, "If you can't be with the one you love, honey, love the one you're with."

How many adulterous affairs and spontaneous teen hookups resulted from this devious message encouraging sexual anarchy, no one will ever know. But notice how the seduction worked, the way the first phrase ("If you can't be with the one you love") is mirrored in the second phrase ("love the one you're with") by using the same words. The whole equation sounds logical in a rhythmic sort of way—which is to say, if you don't think about it. After all, love is good, right? So if you can't love one person, then love someone else!

"One" in the first phrase refers to your sweetheart, but in the second phrase the same word means someone else. "Love" in the first phrase implies commitment and fidelity—key elements of real love. The same word in the second phrase implies an impulsive, self-indulgent, and very likely immoral and unfaithful act and a betrayal of what love is all about.

This is verbal seduction.

Now look at the First Amendment:

"*Congress*"—We know what that is.

"*shall make no law*"—Well now, I'll bet you thought you knew what that means. You thought it meant Congress shall make no law. But what you didn't know was that in 1940, in the Supreme Court case of *Cantwell v. Connecticut*, the justices decided—citing a mysterious legal principle called "incorporation"—that the First Amendment applied not just to Congress, but to state governments too. So now the federal government could force the states to follow its dictates in regards to prohibiting the "establishment" or prohibiting the "free exercise" of religion. This is obviously something the original thirteen states would have rejected outright, given that half of them had state establishments of religion.

"*respecting an establishment of religion*"—For 150 years an "establishment of religion" in the context of the First Amendment meant that a national church, a particular denomination, wouldn't be supported and imposed on the states by the federal government. But with the decline of Christianity in the United States and, indeed, increasing hostility toward it, the meaning of "establishment of religion" has been radically changed—just like the words in the Stephen Stills song. Today, "establishment of religion" means the mere public mention of God, Christ, the Bible, the Ten Commandments, prayer, and so on. The "God Bless America" banner erected on a California public school to honor those killed in the 9-11 terror attacks was attacked by the ACLU as an unconstitutional establishment of religion.

But to make this seduction even more powerful, the First Amendment religion clauses have been morphed into the phrase "a wall of separation between Church and State"—eight words taken out of context from an incidental letter written by Thomas Jefferson in 1802.

You rarely hear the actual wording of the First Amendment anymore. But "separation of church and state" is one of those phrases that roll off the tongues of judges and journalists so easily and so often that most of us assume it's in the Constitution. In fact, one of the justices on the New York Supreme Court, back in a 1958 First Amendment case called *Baer v. Kolmorgen,* made this very point when he commented: "Much has been written in recent years concerning Thomas Jefferson's reference in 1802 to 'a wall of separation between church and State.' . . . Jefferson's figure of speech has received so much attention that one would almost think at times that it is to be found somewhere in our Constitution."

But there's a method to this constant repetition, as marketers well know: repeat something enough times, and people come to believe it. The celebrated eighteenth-century American philosopher William James put it more pungently: "There is nothing so absurd but if you repeat it often enough people will believe it."

Indeed, there are very few phrases more familiar to Americans than the separation of church and state. Marketers pay millions to brand their product or make their political candidate a household name. But just as with commercial or political marketing, widespread familiarity with a slogan doesn't necessarily mean the message is true.

If Jefferson's wall of separation has come to mean that any reference to God must be eliminated from government, schools, and anything else the government funds, then what did the phrase originally mean, as Jefferson used it?

Ironically, Jefferson intended for his letter to the Danbury Baptists to reassure them that the new federal government would not endanger the free expression of their religion. This is widely known. But what is not well known is that Jefferson did *not* actually coin the phrase "separation of church and state."

Rather, he borrowed the metaphor from the sermon, "The Garden and the Wilderness," which was very familiar to Baptists of the time. As Jim Henderson, senior counsel for the American Center for Law and Justice, explains it:

> That sermon, rendered by Roger Williams (the founder of the Rhode Island Plantation colony, and a Baptist), depicted the church as a garden, the world as a wilderness, and the wall as a device of the Creator's invention that protected the garden from being overrun by the wilderness. Williams explained that, from time to time, for the purpose of disciplining sin in the church, "it hath pleased" the Almighty to break down the wall.
>
> Thomas Jefferson, ever the politician, knew when he communicated with the Baptists that "The Garden and The Wilderness" was well known and widely read nearly two generations later. He appealed to them in the terms of their own great man's idiom.[11]

There you have it. The wall of separation was meant to protect "the garden" of the church from being overrun by "the wilderness" of government. No wonder Chief Justice Rehnquist has said, "The metaphor of a 'wall of separation' is bad history and worse law. It has made a positive chaos out of court rulings. It should be frankly and explicitly abandoned."[12] In other words, it's a lie.

Such lies collapse and self-destruct when examined closely, such as the slogan that asserts "the Constitution is a living document." The opposite of a "living document" is a "dead document," and who wants that? "Living" and "breathing" are positive-sounding attributes. But if you told your spouse that your marriage contract is a living document and therefore you should be able to have intimate relationships with other partners, would your spouse approve? After all, "if you can't be with the one you love," why not "love the one you're with"?

Why not? Because it's a lie. The "living" quality of any contract, including the Constitution, is its integrity, its unchanging nature. What kills a contract are attempts to change, twist, or reinterpret it. So in reality, the secularist's "living" Constitution is dead, while the document, interpreted according to its original intent, is full of life and value.

A QUIET AMERICAN REVOLUTION

COMMON SENSE provides ample proof to a rational person that the First Amendment's religion clauses couldn't possibly mean what the ACLU and many of today's judges say they mean, since there is simply no evidence of it in history. Think about it. It's the first and most important right enshrined in the Bill of Rights, and yet there are no examples of this modern, radical, anti-Christian interpretation being applied during our nation's first 150 years?

I think we all understand the problem. Now the question is, what do we do about it?

In America, unlike virtually all other countries, the power really does reside in the people. We have the legal means of making this the most enlightened nation in history, administered by a limited, constitutional government. After all, it's regular people like you and me who elect the president, who in turn nominates judges for the Supreme Court and other federal courts. It's we who elect the senators who confirm the president's judicial nominees.

Moreover, we elect the congressmen who actually have the constitutional power to control the federal judiciary! As Texas congressman and Constitution champion Ron Paul has explained: "Congress [can] exercise its existing constitutional power to limit the jurisdiction of federal courts. Congress could statutorily remove whole issues like gay marriage from the federal judiciary, striking a blow against judicial tyranny and restoring some degree of states' rights. We seem to have forgotten that the Supreme Court is supreme only over lower federal courts; it is not supreme over the other branches of government."

By becoming part of the Constitution itself, amendments such as the federal marriage amendment or the human life amendment can and will trump any errant Supreme Court decisions. Remember, Supreme Court justices can also be impeached, just like presidents.

And did you know presidents aren't compelled to obey unlawful Supreme Court decisions? Andrew Jackson and Abraham Lincoln actually defied Supreme Court orders.

But, many would warn, a president defying the Supreme Court would lead to a "constitutional crisis." I would call it a "constitutional conflict"—a conflict that can be resolved only by reference back to the nation's founding principles as established in the Constitution.

Whatever we do to rectify this terrible wrong must start with brutal honesty—an unflinching realization of what we have allowed to transpire in our nation. Only by facing these hard truths can we make any real progress.

So let me ask: In allowing the First Amendment to be changed from its original meaning to what it has become today—namely, the prohibition of any acknowledgment of God or His laws inside the schools where most American children spend their youth—do you realize what we're doing? Similarly, in making any reference to God or biblical principles off-limits for those we've entrusted with running this nation's government and charting its future course, do you realize what we're doing?

We are deluding ourselves into believing there is some neutral ground between good and evil, and that this is where the government is supposed to be. But such a neutral ground, if such can even be said to exist, is in itself evil. When Jews are being gassed and cremated down the street, "neutrality" is not neutral—it's collaboration.

When we realize that the Creator has stationed us on this earth in a battleground between a good kingdom and an evil one, and that our real choice in life is between obedience to divine love or disobedience, between honesty and dishonesty, nobility and shallowness, selflessness and selfishness, courage and cowardice, we see there really is no neutral ground.

Thus if government is not populated by godly, principled people, we are doomed to live as glorified serfs. Why? Because true religion and its fruits—love of truth and one another—constitute a powerful force working against the natural tendency of power to corrupt. To put it another way, without having a real relationship with the Living God, men *automatically* become their own miserable "gods." That pathetic, false god in turn owes his allegiance to dark forces he doesn't recognize or comprehend—and if he's in a position of power, he is compelled to become a demagogue or a tyrant.

What we're witnessing is the official, ever-so-gradual squeezing out of everything that's really precious to America. It's as though we're throwing away something so valuable that it goes almost beyond the ability of words to convey it. We're taking the finest life has to offer, like the most precious memories of our children, of their birth, of their accomplishments—and we're taking the sacrifices of our soldiers, of our patriots, our nation's martyrs—and we're junking them.

Think of the Puritans who braved the two-month sea voyage to an unknown land and lost one-half of their number during that first, brutal winter. And the loyal patriot soldiers with George Washington at Valley Forge, shivering shoeless and miserable in the snow. Think of the deaths and sufferings of the millions of Americans lost or maimed in war during the last two centuries. Ponder as well the tremendous sacrifices of their families. Now think of the sustaining role God, faith, prayer, and the Bible had in the lives of all of these people.

If we really have been convinced that our Constitution—conceived, written, believed in, fought for, and died for overwhelmingly by Christians and God-fearing people—requires that the Christian faith be taken out of government, then there's really no hope for us as a nation.

But I don't think we've all bought that big lie.

Yes, we have a lot of judges who offer pious lip service to the Constitution while really believing this two-hundred-plus-year-old document drafted by a bunch of flawed slaveholders is in dire need of major updating by bright, gifted jurists such as themselves.

But then there are those like Judge Roy Moore. Standing on the courthouse steps as his beloved Ten Commandments monument was being dragged away, he commented: "It is a sad day in our country when the moral foundation of our laws and the acknowledgment of God has to be hidden from public view to appease a federal judge."

Focus on the Family's James Dobson summed it all up. Decrying the judicial banishment of the Ten Commandments as part of a movement to remove every trace of "faith or reverence for God from the public square," he warned, "We're at a pivotal point in the history of this country." He added, "Be a participant. Don't sit on the sidelines while our basic freedoms are lost."

KILLER CULTURE

*Who's Selling Sex and Rebellion
to Your Children?*

ASCOUT IS TRUSTWORTHY . . . loyal . . . helpful . . . friendly . . . courteous . . . kind . . ."

I'm watching my twelve-year-old son, Joshua, and two dozen other Boy Scouts together recite the Scout Law at their weekly troop meeting. It's a refreshingly hopeful and manly vignette in an era of wall-to-wall teen confusion.

As I stand in rapt attention—my eyes exploring the boys' uniforms, searching out all the badges, patches, insignias, and other colorful signs of their allegiance to Scouting's high ideals—my mind wanders back a few years to a time when my son wanted to wear a different uniform.

Our family had traveled to Cape May, New Jersey, to vacation on a warm Atlantic beach with close relatives we hadn't seen in a long time. Joshua hit it off great with his cousin, a boy several years his senior. A fun-loving and thoroughly decent kid, the cousin didn't have a mean bone in his body. One little thing, though. He wore a choker around his neck. Of course, Joshua had always regarded necklaces, bracelets, earrings, and the like as strictly girls' stuff and wouldn't dream of donning such gear himself and "looking like a girl" (or a "weirdo").

You guessed it. By the end of one week, Joshua told me he really wanted to get a choker, like his cousin's. He just felt like wearing one, that's all. No big deal, Dad.

I took him for a walk on the jetty where we could be alone. Before long I discovered that not only had my son developed this powerful desire to wear a piece of punk jewelry around his neck—something he had formerly despised—but he was also noticeably hostile toward me for some strange reason, even though he admitted I had done nothing to offend him. As we talked, it dawned on me what was going on. Obviously he wanted to be like his older cousin, who he looked up to and had bonded with—hence the desire to wear a dumb-looking neck choker. But me? He now saw me in uncomfortable contrast to coolness, seeing as I represented his state of mind *before* he was captivated by this alien desire. I was a threat to his new allegiance, so he was rejecting me along with his own previous viewpoint.

As it turned out, I didn't need to say too much. "Joshua, why are you mad at me? Is it because I don't think that deep down you really want to wear a necklace? Tell me something. What would you have thought if, two weeks ago, before we came to Cape May, I had asked you if you would like to wear a clunky wooden necklace. Would you have wanted to?'"

"No way," he replied without hesitation. The trance was broken. Realization set in. He cried briefly, gave me a hug, and assured me manfully he did not want to look like a girl and wear a necklace. When we went into the little gift shop on that beach, he even pointed out the choker he had wanted, displayed there in the showcase, and let me know once again that he wasn't interested. So that was the end of it. But it sure illustrated to me just how sensitive children are to peer pressure.

Gangsta Generation

If Joshua felt the invisible pull of peer pressure to conform to his cousin's fashion preferences, what was influencing his cousin? Indeed, what is exerting this irresistible pressure to conform (by "rebelling") on most of today's youth?

Just as the military and private schools and Boy Scouts have uniforms, so does the prevailing youth culture: baggy pants, backward hats, chokers and other jewelry, body piercings, tattoos, and the like. But if uniforms symbolize values and allegiance, a loyalty to a higher (or lower) order, then in this case it's an allegiance to an increasingly defiant musical, social, sexual, and cultural world, a mysterious (to parents) realm that seems magically to be drawing millions of children into it.

For three years, journalist Patricia Hersch journeyed into this exotic subculture. She observed, listened to, questioned, bonded with, and won the trust of eight teens in the posh, suburban American town of Reston, Virginia, ultimately producing her acclaimed portrait, *A Tribe Apart: A Journey into the Heart of American Adolescence*. The landscape she describes, as ubiquitous across America's fruited plain as McDonald's, is troubling indeed:

> It's hip-hop in suburbia, the culture of rap. Everywhere students wear baseball caps turned backwards or pulled down over their eyes, oversize T-shirts, ridiculously baggy jeans or shorts with dropped crotches that hang to mid-shin, and waists that sag to reveal the tops of brightly colored boxers. Expensive name-brand high-tops complete the outfit. Variations on the theme are hooded sweatshirts, with the hood worn during school, and "do rags," bandannas tied on the head, a style copied from street gangs. Just as ubiquitous are the free-flying swear words, sound bursts landing kamikaze-style, just out of reach of hall guards and teacher monitors. . . .
>
> In the latest exasperating challenge to adult society, black rage is in as a cultural style for white middle-class kids. As in the sixties, when the sons and daughters of the middle class tossed out their tweed jackets and lady-like sheath dresses for the generational uniform of Levi's and work shirts and peacoats in their celebration of blue collar workers, "the Real Americans," so today's adolescents have co-opted inner-city black street-style as the authentic way to be. To act black, as the kids define it, is to be strong, confrontational, a little scary. . . .
>
> "We are living in the gangsta generation," one white high school senior wearing his Malcolm X baseball cap turned backwards explains. "It is all about getting it. I look at what these cool dudes do and how it affects other people. These people are doing more than any faggoty white kid who plays basketball and gets accepted at Duke and has been rich his whole life and maybe gets drunk on the weekend. These kids put their ass on the line every day."

Hersch describes how hip-hop—a multimillion-dollar music industry filled with "the powerful political and sexual images of rap"—has captivated a generation with the drama of the ghetto and its daily struggle for survival:

Hip-hop's in-your-face attitude looks strong and free to kids who feel constrained by expectations of the mundane middle-class world they have grown up in. Rappers have become the most popular attractions on MTV. In an interview on his album "Home Invasion," rapper Ice T refers to the "cultural invasion" that is occurring while unknowing adults sit around with their racist attitudes and their kids sit quietly in their bedrooms, his words pouring into their brains through their headphones: "Once I get 'em under my f—kin' spell / They may start giving you f—kin' hell," he raps. "Start changin' the way they walk, they talk, they act / Now whose fault is that?" The rap world of "hos and pimps, bitches, muthaf—kers, homeys and police" is an attractive diversion from the "ordinary" sphere of dental braces, college boards, and dating. The ghetto—experienced second-hand in movies and music and on the evening news, viewed from the comfort of nice suburban family rooms—holds enormous drama and appeal for young people.[1]

So is that it? Is today's bizarre youth subculture just the latest costume for adolescent rebellion, like the long hair of the 1960s and other, if less conspicuous, rebellious phases of previous generations of youngsters? Is adult concern over today's youth culture just the perennial hand-wringing of parents needlessly worried about their growing offspring's experiments with independence? Or is something else, something far more sinister at work?

"MERCHANTS OF COOL"

"THEY WANT to be cool. They are impressionable, and they have the cash. They are corporate America's $150 billion dream."[2]

That's the opening statement in PBS's stunning 2001 *Frontline* documentary "The Merchants of Cool," narrated by author and media critic Douglas Rushkoff. What emerges in the following sixty minutes is a scandalous portrait of how major corporations—Viacom, Disney, AOL/Time Warner, and others—study America's children like laboratory rats in order to sell them billions of dollars in merchandise by tempting, degrading, and corrupting them.

Think that's a bit of an overstatement?

It's an understatement.

"When you've got a few gigantic transnational corporations, each one loaded down with debt, competing madly for as much shelf space and brain space as they can take," says NYU communications professor Mark Crispin-Miller, "they're going to do whatever they think works the fastest and with the most people, which means that they will drag standards down."[3]

Let's see how far down.

"It's a blizzard of brands, all competing for the same kids," explains Rushkoff. "To win teens' loyalty, marketers believe, they have to speak their language the best. So they study them carefully, as an anthropologist would an exotic native culture."

"Today," Rushkoff discloses, "five enormous companies are responsible for selling nearly all of youth culture. These are the true merchants of cool: Rupert Murdoch's Newscorp, Disney, Viacom, Universal Vivendi, and AOL/Time Warner."[4] The documentary demonstrates how big corporations literally send spies to infiltrate young people's social settings to gather intelligence on what they can induce these children to buy next.

"The entertainment companies, which are a handful of massive conglomerates that own four of the five music companies that sell 90 percent of the music in the United States—those same companies also own all the film studios, all the major TV networks, all the TV stations pretty much in the 10 largest markets," University of Illinois communications professor Robert McChesney reveals in the documentary. "They own all or part of every single commercial cable channel.

"They look at the teen market as part of this massive empire that they're colonizing. You should look at it like the British Empire or the French Empire in the 19th century. Teens are like Africa. You know, that's this range that they're going to take over, and their weaponry are films, music, books, CDs, Internet access, clothing, amusement parks, sports teams. That's all this weaponry they have to make money off of this market."[5]

MTV

What about the cable channel that positions itself as champion of today's teens and preteens—champions of their music, their rebellious free spirit, and their genuine, if ever-changing, notions of what is "cool"? Whatever else MTV might be, at least it's interested in kids, right? Sure, just like the lion is interested in the gazelle.

"Everything on MTV is a commercial," explains McChesney. "That's all that MTV is. Sometimes it's an explicit advertisement paid for by a company to sell a product. Sometimes it's going to be a video for a music company there to sell music. Sometimes it's going to be the set that's filled with trendy clothes and stuff there to sell a look that will include products on that set. Sometimes it will be a show about an upcoming movie paid for by the studio, though you don't know it, to hype a movie that's coming out from Hollywood. But everything's an infomercial. There is no non-commercial part of MTV."[6]

Rushkoff illustrates how the machine works by using the example of Sprite. What was once a struggling, second-string soft-drink company pulled off a brilliant marketing coup by underwriting major hip-hop music events and positioning itself as *the* cool soft drink for the vast MTV-generation market. Connecting the dots between Sprite, MTV, rap musicians, and other cross-promotion participants, Rushkoff lays out the behind-the-scenes game plan: "Sprite rents out the Roseland Ballroom and pays kids 50 bucks a pop to fill it up and look cool. The rap artists who perform for this paid audience get a plug on MTV's show, 'Direct Effects,' for which Sprite is a sponsor. MTV gobbles up the cheap programming, promoting the music of the record companies who advertise on their channel. Everybody's happy."[7]

"So what," you say? "What's wrong with that? Aren't MTV and rappers and clothing companies and others just giving kids what they want?"

That's what they say. But it's not what they do.

In reality, the companies are *creating* new and lower and more shocking—that's the key-word, *shocking*—marketing campaigns, disguised as genuine, authentic expressions of youthful searching for identity and belonging, for the sole purpose of profiting financially from America's children.

They hold focus groups. They send out culture spies (which they call "correspondents") to pretend to befriend and care about teens so they can study them—what they like, don't like, what's in, what's out, what's cool, and what's no longer cool. They engage in "buzz marketing" (where undercover agents talk up a new product). They hire shills to interact with young people in Internet chat rooms, and they engage "street snitches" to loudly talk up a band or other product to raise interest. They bring the entire machinery of modern market research and consumer psychology to bear on studying this gold mine of a market—to anticipate the next, and always weirder and more shocking, incarnation of "cool."

This would be bad enough—if corporate America were just following and marketing the basest instincts of confused, unsupervised teenagers. But they are not following, they are leading—downward. Exhibits A and B: the "mook" and the "midriff," two creations of this corporate youth-marketing consortium.

The mook is a marketing caricature of the wild, uninhibited, outrageous, and amoral male sex maniac. "Take Howard Stern," says Rushkoff, "perhaps the original and still king of all mooks. Look how Viacom leverages him across their properties. He is syndicated on 50 of Viacom's Infinity radio stations. His weekly TV show is broadcast on Viacom's CBS. His number one best-selling autobiography was published by Viacom's Simon and Schuster, then released as a major motion picture by Viacom's Paramount Pictures, grossing $40 million domestically and millions more on videos sold at Viacom's Blockbuster video." Rushkoff adds: "There is no mook in nature. He is a creation designed to capitalize on the testosterone-driven madness of adolescence. He grabs them below the belt and then reaches for their wallets."[8]

A great deal of MTV's programming features and markets to the mook in America's boys. For instance, a major venue of the mook is professional wrestling—one of the most-watched types of television among adolescent boys in America today.

Okay, what about the midriff?

Girls, says Rushkoff, "get dragged down there right along with boys. The media machine has spit out a second caricature. . . . The midriff is no more true to life than the mook. If he is arrested in adolescence, she is prematurely adult. If he doesn't care what people think of him, she is consumed by appearances. If his thing is crudeness, hers is sex. The midriff is really just a collection of the same old sexual clichés, but repackaged as a new kind of female empowerment. 'I am midriff, hear me roar. I am a sexual object, but I'm proud of it.'"[9]

And what is the purpose of these debauched role models for America's future, fashioned out of market research compiled by culture spies hired by corporations to predict what the likely next step *down*—the next *shock wave* disguised as authentic "cool"—will be for the MTV generation? Why, to sell kids more stuff, of course.

"When corporate revenues depend on being ahead of the curve, you have to listen, you have to know exactly what they want and exactly what they're thinking so that you can give them what you want them to have," explains NYU's Crispin-Miller. However, he adds, "the MTV machine doesn't listen to the young so it can make the young happier. . . . The MTV machine tunes in so it can figure out how to pitch what Viacom has to sell."[10]

And how do they manage to bond kids—imprint them—with the next round of musical, clothing, and lifestyle choices they should be buying into?

"Kids are invited to participate in sexual contests on stage or are followed by MTV cameras through their week of debauchery," says Rushkoff. "Sure, some kids have always acted wild, but never have these antics been so celebrated on TV. So of course kids take it as a cue, like here on the strip in Panama Beach, Florida, where high schoolers carry on in public as if they were on some MTV sound stage. Who is mirroring whom? Real life and TV life have begun to blur. Is the media really reflecting the world of kids, or is it the other way around? The answer is increasingly hard to make out."

Then the really devilish part of the marketers' modus operandi comes into view, as host Rushkoff relives his own epiphany:

> I'll never forget the moment that 13-year-old Barbara and her friends spotted our crew during a party between their auditions. They appeared to be dancing for us, for our camera, as if to sell back to us, the media, what we had sold to them.
>
> And that's when it hit me: It's a giant feedback loop. The media watches kids and then sells them an image of themselves. Then kids watch those images and aspire to be that mook or midriff in the TV set. And the media is there watching them do that in order to craft new images for them, and so on.[11]

"Is there any way to escape the feedback loop?" Rushkoff asks. Only in the kids' minds, he reveals, noting that "cool"-seeking youths continually reach downward to a new, raunchier, more outrageous expression—something, *anything,* as long as it hasn't been exploited and ripped off by the corporate world.

That said, Rushkoff rolls tape of a large, demonic-looking group of teens, faces painted, chanting and screaming obscenities in downtown Detroit on Halloween night. He explains:

> A few thousand mostly white young men have gathered to hear a concert by their favorite hometown band, Insane Clown Posse. ICP helped found a musical genre called rap metal or rage rock, which has created a stir across the country for its shock lyrics and ridicule of women and gays. . . . Rock music has always channeled rebellion, but where it used to be directed against parents, teachers or the government, today it is directed against slick commercialism itself, against MTV. These fans feel loyalty to this band and this music because they experience it as their own. It hasn't been processed by corporations, digested into popular culture and sold back to them at the mall.[12]

A member of Insane Clown Posse explains the group's attraction: "Everybody that likes our music feels a super connection. That's why all those juggaloes here, they feel so connected to it because it's—it's exclusively theirs. See, when something's on the radio, it's for everybody, you know what I mean? It's everybody's song. 'Oh, this is my song.' That ain't your song. It's on the radio. It's everybody's song. But to listen to ICP, you feel like you're the only one that knows about it."

"These are the extremes," intones Rushkoff, "to which teens are willing to go to ensure the authenticity of their own scene. It's the front line of teen cultural resistance: Become so crude, so intolerable, and break so many rules that you become indigestible." To complete the mood, in the background Insane Clown Posse is rapping "Bitch, you's a ho. And ho, you's a bitch. Come on!" and other uplifting lyrics.[13]

Then comes the betrayal. "The Merchants of Cool" shows how Insane Clown Posse and other "authentic" groups—untouched by commercialism—are ultimately bought off by the marketing machine, packaged, and sold back to the youth market. Of course, when the shock value wears off, and the mantle of cool—untouched and uncorrupted by corporate America—moves downward to the next, even more outrageous level of depravity—MTV, Viacom, and the other corporate giants will be there to package it and sell it, once again, to our children.

Oh, but don't bother trying to tell your kids about this fiendish game. You see, says Crispin-Miller, "It's part of the official rock video world view, it's part of the official advertising world view, that your parents are creeps, teachers are nerds and idiots, authority figures are laughable, nobody can really understand kids except the corporate sponsor."[14]

Okay, so is that it? America's teens are in the grip of a malignant marketing campaign by big, greedy, uncaring corporations? And hopefully the kids will grow out of it and become normal sometime? End of story?

Not quite. To be sure, millions of youths are in the grip of something destructive, but the corporate aspect is just the visible part. *Behind* both the corporate manipulators and the youths caught in their selfish and shameful influence lurks another, much more formidable and all-pervasive marketing campaign—a malevolent dimension that has no one's best interests at heart and which is programmed to devour all in its path, from the highest to the lowest.

That something, which we shall try to identify shortly, is intent on degrading this generation so totally that little hope would be left for the next generations of Americans.

No Limits

IF YOU doubt there's anything more than youthful rebellion and soulless marketing at work in today's youth culture, read on. But fasten your safety belt.

Remember how Sodom and Gomorrah were portrayed in the classic biblical epic films of the 1950s? Drunken men with multiple piercings and bright red robes, one loose woman under each arm, cavorting in orgiastic revelry against a background of annoying, mosquito-like music? Maybe a bone through the nose as well? Hollywood took pains to depict these lost souls in the most debauched and irredeemable manner—to justify their subsequent destruction with fire and brimstone as punishment for their great sinfulness.

Guess what? Those Hollywood depictions don't even *begin* to capture the shocking reality of what is going on in America's culture today—they're not even close.

First of all, there's sex. Very simply, there seem to be neither boundaries nor taboos anymore when it comes to sex. Anything goes—from heterosexual to homosexual to bi-, trans-, poly-, and you-don't-want-to-know sexual experiences. Sex has become a ubiquitous, cheap, meaningless quest for ever-greater thrills. As Dr. Laura Schlessinger quipped, "Men are astonished to discover they don't even need to court a woman, tell little romantic lies about love or the future. All they have to do is show up!"[15]

Moreover, with the evolution of online pornography, every type of sexual experience has literally been shoved under the noses of millions of Americans against their will. They find their e-mail filled with hard-core sexual images. As a result, many pastors are struggling with how to deal with large numbers of churchgoers reportedly caught up with Internet pornography.

What about body piercing? It has progressed from traditional earrings for females, to earrings for males (eager to display their "feminine side" which the '60s "cultural revolution" sold them), to multiple piercings for both males and females in literally every part of the body—the tongue, nose, eyebrow, lip, cheek, navel, breasts, genitals—again, things you don't really want to know.

It's the same progression to extremes with tattooing. But why stop with conventional piercing and tattooing? Ritual scarification and 3D-art implants are big. So are genital beading, stretching and cutting, transdermal implants, scrotal implants, tooth art, and facial sculpture.

How about tongue splitting? How about branding? How about amputations? That's right—amputations. Some people find these activities a real turn on.

There are no bounds—no lower limits. Whatever you can imagine, even for a second in the darkest recesses of your mind, know that someone somewhere is doing it, praising it, and drawing others into it via the Internet.

Strangest of all is the fact that any behavior, any belief—no matter how obviously insane—is rationalized so it sounds reasonable, even spiritual. Satanism, and especially its variant, the worship of Lucifer (literally,

"Angel of Light") can be made to sound almost enlightened—of course, only in a perverse way. But if you were sufficiently confused, rebellious, and full of rage—if you had been set up by cruelty or hypocrisy (or both) to rebel against everything good—the forbidden starts to be mysteriously attractive.

Let's pick just one of these bizarre behaviors. How about hanging by your skin from hooks? It's called suspension. In literally any other context, this would be considered a gruesome torture. But to many people who frequent suspension parties, it's a spiritual experience. Consider carefully what Body Modification Ezine (www.bmezine.com)—the Web's premiere site for body modification—says about suspension:

WHAT IS SUSPENSION?

The act of suspension is hanging the human body from (or partially from) hooks pierced through the flesh in various places around the body.

WHY WOULD SOMEONE WANT TO DO A SUSPENSION?

There are many different reasons to suspend, from pure adrenaline or endorphin rush, to conquering one's fears, to trying to reach a new level of spiritual consciousness and everything in between. In general, people suspend to attain some sort of "experience."

Some people are seeking the opportunity to discover a deeper sense of themselves and to challenge pre-determined belief systems which may not be true. Some are seeking a rite of passage or a spiritual encounter to let go of the fear of not being whole or complete inside their body.

Others are looking for control over their body, or seek to prove to themselves that they are more than their bodies, or are not their bodies at all. Others simply seek to explore the unknown.

Many people believe that learning how one lives inside one's body and seeing how that body adapts to stress—and passes through it—allows one to surrender to life and explore new realms of possibility.

Gosh—"control over their body," "discover a deeper sense of themselves," "conquering ones fears," "trying to reach a new level of spiritual consciousness." What could be wrong with that?

Or, how about tongue splitting—literally making yourself look like a human lizard—how could that be a positive, spiritual experience?

"The tongue," explains the BME website, "is one of the most immense nervous structures in your body. We have incredibly fine control over it and we receive massive feedback from it. When you dramatically alter its structure and free yourself of the physical boundaries your biology imposes, in some people it triggers a larger freeing on a spiritual level."

Here's one more experience I'll bet you didn't realize was so uplifting—getting AIDS.

Oh, you haven't heard about "bug-chasing"? *Rolling Stone* did a controversial exposé on this new underground movement. Very simply, bug-chasers are people for whom getting infected with the AIDS virus is the ultimate sexual experience. You heard it right: the main focus of their lives is to seek out sexual encounters that will infect them with HIV.

Reporter Gregory A. Freeman explained the phenomenon, focusing initially on a bug-chaser named Carlos:

> Carlos is part of an intricate underground world that has sprouted, driven almost completely by the Internet, in which men who want to be infected with HIV get together with those who are willing to infect them. The men who want the virus are called "bug chasers," and the men who freely give the virus to them are called "gift givers." While the rest of the world fights the AIDS epidemic and most people fear HIV infection, this subculture celebrates the virus and eroticizes it.
>
> HIV-infected semen is treated like liquid gold. Carlos has been chasing the bug for more than a year in a topsy-turvy world in which every convention about HIV is turned upside down. The virus isn't horrible and fearsome, it's beautiful and sexy—and delivered in the way that is most likely to result in infection. In this world, the men with HIV are the most desired, and the bug chasers will do anything to get the virus—to "get knocked up," to be "bred" or "initiated into the brotherhood."

And what, exactly, motivates Carlos and his bug-chasing colleagues?

For Carlos, bug chasing is mostly about the excitement of doing something that everyone else sees as crazy and wrong. Keeping this part of his life secret is part of the turn-on for Carlos, which is not his real name. That forbidden aspect makes HIV infection incredibly exciting for him, so much so that he now seeks out sex exclusively with HIV-positive men. "This is something that no one knows about me," Carlos says. "It's mine. It's my dirty little secret."

Deliberately infecting themselves, explains Freeman, "is the ultimate taboo, the most extreme sex act left on the planet, and that has a strong erotic appeal for some men who have tried everything else."[16]

No question about it: the forbidden is very attractive. As pop star Britney Spears admitted to an interviewer: "When someone tells me not to do something, I do it, that's just my rebellious nature." Similarly, Carlos's thrill at having a "dirty little secret" is a very common theme sounded by people explaining why they had some hidden body part pierced.

Why are so many attracted to the forbidden? Why is it so exciting?

In Love with Death

IN THE West we marvel at the death-oriented Islamic jihad subculture, which in some areas, particularly among the Palestinians, has become the dominant culture, a culture of death. We shake our heads sadly as we contemplate children growing up with the desire, above all else, to martyr themselves—which to them means blowing themselves up while killing as many Jews as possible and believing they're going to heaven.

These young people, caught up in the rage-fueled Islamist marketing campaign of global jihad, can look you right in the eye and express with great passion their conviction that committing mass murder is the mystical doorway to eternal life. Yet, in much the same way, bug-chasing men who seek AIDS, people suspending themselves from the ceiling by meat hooks, those who literally slice their own tongues in two—and even, albeit on a much more subtle level, "regular" people obsessed with the thought of getting their next piercing or tattoo—feel as though they, too, are moving, not toward death, but toward life and greater "spirituality," a more unique and authentic sense of self. Somehow the ritual of pain and mutilation or, in extreme cases, death drives out their awareness of inner conflict, replacing it with an illusion of freedom and selfhood.

Here's how psychotherapist Steven Levenkron, best-selling author and one of the nation's foremost experts on anorexia and other emotion-based illnesses, explains it in his landmark book *Cutting: Understanding and Overcoming Self-Mutilation:* "The self-mutilator is someone who has found that physical pain can be a cure for emotional pain."

After years of counseling patients, mostly young women, who purposely cut their bodies with razors and knives to obtain relief from emotional conflict, Levenkron concluded:

> Self-mutilators have many different reasons for their actions and are tormented by a spectrum of different feelings. Yet I consistently encounter two characteristics in all self-mutilators:
>
> 1. A feeling of mental disintegration, of inability to think.
> 2. A rage that can't be expressed, or even consciously perceived, toward a powerful figure (or figures) in their life, usually a parent.

> For the self-mutilator, the experience of one or both of these feelings is unbearable and must therefore be "drowned out," as they report, by some immediate method. Physical pain and the sight of oneself bleeding become solutions because of their ability to overpower the strength of those feelings.

> Usually, the first incident begins with strong feelings of anger, anxiety, or panic. If the feeling is not too intense, throwing an object, or breaking or knocking something over, may settle the person down. It's when the person becomes so overwhelmed that none of these "remedies" help that we may see them plunge a fist into a wall or through a window, bang their head against a wall, or finally take a weapon to use against themselves.

> Someone who stumbles upon self-injury in this manner and discovers that it relieves one of the painful states listed above will be inclined to use this discovery again in the future. The individual who needs this kind of solution is a person who cannot redress the grievances she has with others, who is afraid to argue, to articulate what she is so angry about. The self-mutilator is ashamed of the mental pain that she experiences and has no language with which to describe it to others.

> However they came to it, the self-mutilator is someone who has found that physical pain can be a cure for emotional pain. . . . When a person

attacks his or her own body with an instrument that will wound the skin, and often worse, it means that the person feels helpless to use any other means to manage the mental anguish and chaos that is borne out of unmanageable feelings.[17]

Although Levenkron is describing a psychiatric syndrome afflicting young girls who ritualistically cut themselves to relieve inner pain, much of the same dynamic is at work to some degree in multitudes of people today finding solace and identity in self-destructive sexuality, pain, and disfigurement. For example, here's how one person explained her decision to have her tongue pierced, writing on the BME Web site:

I love piercings and wanted to do it but the guy that I'm interested in disapproved of it. So, I was reluctant to do the piercing seeing as I didn't want to start a relationship and having a piercing in an area that would affect our physical activities. Anyway, it turns out the bastard slept with my best friend the other night and I knew a new piercing had to take place. Weird, but getting a new piercing helps me to focus all my mental pain and then release it with the physical and also it leaves a nice looking piece of jewelry as well!

Her anger is extinguished, at least temporarily, by piercing her own body.

PIERCING THE VEIL

"FOR WE wrestle not against flesh and blood, but against principalities, against powers, against the rulers of the darkness of this world, against spiritual wickedness in high places" (Ephesians 6:12).

Earlier in this exploration of youth culture we "pierced" the corporate veil, discovering the shameful marketing reality behind today's youth culture. Let's go the rest of the way now and pierce the spiritual veil.

History is full of times and places when *something*—call it a spirit if you wish—sweeps over a particular society. This something is drawn, as into a vacuum, into societies that have lost their way and have harkened to the voice of deceitful leaders and philosophies. During the mid-twentieth century a malevolent spirit swept over Germany, leading to unspeakable crimes being perpetrated against millions of Jews and other "undesirables" in the name of progress. In the late '70s the demonic spirit of Marxist "cleansing" swept through Cambodia like a raging wildfire, resulting in the brutal deaths of perhaps two million. And today we see the worldwide spread of a maniacal jihad suicide cult that is attracting literally millions of Muslims.

But this phenomenon is evident not only in genocidal frenzies. The counterculture revolution of the 1960s was, to many, a spiritual phenomenon with profound reverberations to the present. Likewise, the New Age movement, the preoccupation with "channeling" and UFOs, and other similar movements have an uncanny spiritual, religious dimension that can't be ignored.

True, mass conformity even to bizarre beliefs and practices can be explained somewhat by the sheer power of peer pressure, but there is more to it. It's more akin to mass hypnosis, where large numbers of people simultaneously adopt the same bizarre mind-set, beliefs, and practices. Such instances of spiritual "possession" of a society, of a people made ripe for such a downward transformation by their sins and rebellion against God, are evident throughout history.

Well, now, is it just my imagination, or is there something about today's celebratory piercing and tattooing of the body and the free sex that permeates this culture that literally evokes the spirit of Sodom and Gomorrah? It's as though the rebellious spirit of reprobate, pagan civilizations of the past was being tapped into by today's pop culture.

"Oh, come on," you might say, dismissively. "They're just adorning the human body to make it more beautiful and unique. Let them have their fun. Who are they hurting?" Such mellifluous excuses spring up in our minds quite easily, as most certainly they did also in the time of Sodom, Gomorrah, and other perverse societies.

The fact is, what has risen "out of the pit" in today's world bears a striking resemblance to the ageless spirit of defiant paganism, a spirit now inhabiting millions of people "freed" by trauma (drugs, illicit sex, bodily mutilation, and so on) from the pain of their own conscience—which is to say, freed from God and the divine law written deep down in every person's heart. Why? Same reason as always: so they can be their own gods and make up their own rules.

Of course, in a very real sense they are also victims—they've been set up for all of this. For not only has today's popular culture—from its astonishing gender confusion to its perverse and powerful musical expression—become toxic virtually without precedent in modern history, but also most parents have not protected their own kids from it.

In past eras, if parents were very imperfect, even corrupt, children still had a reasonable chance of "growing up straight," since the rest of society more or less reflected Judeo-Christian values. The youngster could bond to a teacher, minister, mentor, or organization that could provide some healthy direction and stability. But today, because of the near-ubiquitous corruption "out there," if parents fail to properly guide and protect their children, the kids get swallowed whole by the culture. And as talk-show host Bob Just puts it so aptly, "Today's culture is a child molester."[18]

Let me make the point this way: Your being any way other than *genuinely virtuous*—not perfect, mind you, but honestly and diligently seeking to do the right thing at all times—will tend to drive your children crazy. Here's how the craziness unfolds. Children deserve and desperately need firmness, patience, fairness, limits, kindness, insight, and a good, nonhypocritical example. In other words, they need genuine parental love and guidance. If they don't get this, they will resent you. Even if you can't see it, even if they can't see it, and deny it, they will resent you for failing to give them real love.

And that resentment—which becomes suppressed rage—is a destructive, unpredictable, radioactive foreign element in their makeup, which then transmutes into every manner of problem, complex, and evil imaginable. It makes children feel compelled to rebel against you and against all authority out of revenge for your having failed them. And it makes everything forbidden—from sex to drugs to tongue studs to things worse—seem attractive, like a road to personal freedom. Rationalizations and philosophies that they would have once laughed at as ridiculous now make sense to them. Practices they would have shunned in more innocent times, they now not only embrace but celebrate. All of this usually occurs below the level of consciousness.

Today's youth rebellion is not only against failing parents but against the entire adult society—against the children of the 1960s cultural revolution who grew up to become their parents. Unfortunately, many of us never shook off the transforming effects of that national trauma, which birthed the "sex, drugs, and rock 'n' roll" youth counterculture, the left-ist hate-America movement, the women's liberation movement, and overriding all, of course, the sexual revolution.

So we grew up to elect one of our own—a traumatized, amoral baby boomer named Bill Clinton. If you don't think Clinton's escapades with Monica Lewinsky—covered by the media like the Super Bowl—had *everything* to do with the explosion of middle-school sexual adventures across America, then open your eyes. We, the parents of this generation, along with the degrading entertainment media, the biased news media, the lying politicians, the brainwashing government school system, and the rest of society's once-great institutions whose degradation we have tolerated, are responsible.

No wonder our children are rebelling. And today's insane Sodom-and-Gomorrah culture, which we have allowed and in many ways created, stands waiting in the wings to welcome them with open arms.

THE WAY OUT

TODAY'S CULTURE is so poisonous that your only hope is to literally create (or plug into) another culture entirely—a subculture. Just as today's homosexual culture, for example, used to be a miserable subculture lurking in public toilets and seedy clubs, but today has become the sophisticated culture of the "beautiful people" and Hollywood, so must your true American culture—if it's ever to come back—begin again as a subculture.

The best solution I know of for accomplishing this is to homeschool your children and network with other like-minded parents in your area. Trust me, it's already being done, you're not reinventing the wheel. Sports, music, drama, Scouts, 4-H, whatever extracurricular activities you want are all available to homeschoolers. You can literally pick and choose the culture in which your children grow up, and you can actively participate in its creation. I believe homeschooling today represents the single most important and promising avenue for the true rebirth of American Judeo-Christian culture. The real America is now being re-born in families where children are raised with real understanding and insight and protected from the insanity of the popular culture until they're big enough and strong enough in their convictions to go out in the world and make their mark. May it only grow.

What if your children are already caught up in the youth subculture? Is it too late?

No, it's not. But it may be a difficult and long road back. It's a lot easier to be corrupted than to become uncorrupted. Just know this: there is something almost magically liberating about confession. For parents to honestly confess their mistakes, regrets, failings, selfishness, and blindness to their errant offspring is a spiritual experience for all involved. Of course, when youngsters have been "converted" to new loyalties and beliefs, maintained by unconscious rage and rebellion (and perhaps the desire for revenge), they may or may not right away want to come back over to your side. But by being truly repentant over your own culpability in their problem, and confessing this openly and genuinely—and from now on being the kind of person you always should have been—you are giving them the best chance possible to forgive you and find redemption themselves.

Even if they don't come around, or if it takes a long time, your honest self-examination and confession as a parent will free you from your own guilts and past sins. Beyond this, we need to have faith that, with God, all things are possible.

FOLLOWING HIGHER LAW

"**A** SCOUT is trustworthy . . . loyal . . . helpful . . . friendly . . . courteous . . . kind . . . obedient . . . cheerful . . . thrifty . . . brave . . . clean . . . and reverent."

As I stand there, listening to these boys recite the Scout law, I know what I'm looking at. These kids—young men, really—their afterburners roaring on a fabulous fuel mixture of youthful energy, playfulness, intelligence, testosterone, and dedication to higher things, are literally the future of America. I am grateful that at least a few institutions in today's world still exert a positive influence on children. I marvel at the powerful pull the Scout ethic has on them. It binds their lower impulses, hems them in, and appeals to the "better angels" of their nature.

Now they're reciting the Scout oath: "On my honor, I will do my best to do my duty to God and my Country, and to obey the Scout Law, to help other people at all times, to keep myself physically strong, mentally awake and morally straight."

Or course—the Scouts, as well as other good institutions like our churches and even marriage itself—are torn at mercilessly from the outside by heartless activists. And they are torn at from within—by the occasional rotten Scout leader whose ultimate aim is to molest children. And yes, even within Scouts, the kids bring a bit of that *killer culture* in with them. Yet the Scout oath and law, the adult leaders, the time-tested-and-proven program, and the *positive* peer pressure—all of these beckon the boys to embrace a higher calling.

May we all do likewise. If we do, we can redeem our wretched culture one child, one family at a time. And those little swatches of the real American culture, the bits of heaven on earth residing in this home and that home and this church and that Scout troop will one day, please God, join together to form the fabric of a reborn American culture of virtue. Each of us must take that lonely high road. Otherwise, the marketers of evil will lead us all down to ever darker and lower levels of hell on earth.

4

MULTICULTURAL MADNESS

How Western Culture Was Turned
Upside Down in One Generation

T HIS IS A TRUE story about America, about how the magnificent Judeo-Christian culture of my youth—which represented the hope of liberty for the world's oppressed—was so easily turned into mush in my lifetime.

Let me begin with a brief story about my father. When he was only three years old, my dad was sentenced to death. That's right. The Turkish government was engaged in a deliberate campaign to force him, his mother, and his infant sister, along with hundreds of thousands of other Armenians, into the Syrian desert where they would die of starvation, disease, or worse—torture and death at the hands of brutal soldiers or roving bandits.

It was 1915, at the peak of Islamic Turkey's gruesome, premeditated genocide of the Christian Armenian population in that country. Those not butchered outright—the men were often killed immediately—were driven into the Derzor, the Syrian desert east of Aleppo, to perish. My father's father, a doctor, had been pressed into the Turkish army against his will to head a medical regiment.

"One of my earliest recollections, I was not quite three years old at the time," my dad, Vahey Kupelian, told me shortly before he died in 1988, was that "the wagon we were in had tipped over, my hand was broken and bloody, and mother was looking for my infant sister who had rolled away. The next thing I remember after that, mother was on a horse, holding my baby sister, and had me sitting behind her, saying, *'Hold on tight, or the Turks will get you!'*"

The three of them rode off on horseback, ending up in Aleppo, one of the gateways to the desert deportation and certain death. Once there, my grandmother Mary, always a daring and resourceful woman, realized what she needed to do.

After asking around to find out who was in charge, she bluffed her way into getting an audience with Aleppo's governor-general. Since her Armenian husband was in the service of the Turkish army—albeit by force—she played her one and only card, brazenly telling the governor-general, "I demand my rights as the wife of a Turkish army officer!"

"What are those rights?"

"I want commissary privileges and two orderlies," she answered.

"Granted."

In this way, by masquerading as a Turkish officer's wife, Mary bluffed her way out of certain death, saving not only her own life and those of her son and daughter, but also the lives of her husband's two brothers, whom she immediately deputized as orderlies. The group then succeeded in sneaking several other family members out of harm's way, and my grandmother kept them all from starving by obtaining food from the commissary. Thus was my family spared, although little Adolphina, my father's infant sister, was unable to survive the harshness of those times and died shortly thereafter.

As for my grandfather, Simeon Kupelian, after an unusually bloody battle between the Turks and the British, he and the other doctors, all Armenians, tended to the Turkish wounded as best they could. Immediately after this, a squadron of Turkish gunmen came and killed them all, including my grandfather.

One and a half million Armenians perished in those years at the hands of the Turkish regime, the twentieth century's first genocide.

On returning to their beautiful home in Marash a couple of years later, Mary and son Vahey, who was then about six years old, found it had been ransacked. Their fine tapestries had been pulled off the walls, ripped, and urinated on. Everything that could be carried out had been stolen, and everything else had been deliberately broken. *Everything.* Every pane of glass in the French doors was broken, even handles on drawers were destroyed.

Eventually, the hardships of their life led my father and grandmother to do what millions of persecuted people have done over the last few hundred years. They made the long voyage to the one country that welcomed them and offered them freedom and an opportunity for a new life—the most blessed nation on earth, their promised land: America.

Life wasn't easy in this new land, but both mother and son managed to overcome many obstacles, learned English eagerly, built a life for themselves, went to college and pursued careers. Dad got married and had a family; I was the middle of three children growing up in the suburbs of Washington DC. He provided for us, protected us, worried about us, loved us. He also rose to the top of his chosen profession—aeronautical engineering—becoming the army's "Chief Scientist for Ballistic Missile Defense." He lived a good and full life in a blessed land.

That's just one story—my dad's story. Now multiply it by millions of similar cases of dispossessed and persecuted people coming to America, and you'll have a vague idea of what America has long represented to the freedom-loving people of this world.

Born Greek-Armenian, my dad became an American, as did thousands of other Armenians fleeing the genocide. As did Jews fleeing the Nazi Holocaust, Chinese seeking freedom from totalitarianism, Vietnamese and Cambodians escaping from their war-ravaged land, and countless others coming to America for a better life—starting with the English Pilgrims that came here to escape religious persecution. In short, the "huddled masses yearning to breathe free" have come to these shores from every land, speaking every language—but all wanting to become Americans.

"MOTHER OF EXILES"

INSCRIBED IN bronze at the base of the Statue of Liberty, Emma Lazarus's transcendent 1883 poem, "The New Colossus," captures the spirit of America's big-heartedness and generosity perhaps better than anything else, except for "Lady Liberty" herself.

> Not like the brazen giant of Greek fame,
> With conquering limbs astride from land to land;
> Here at our sea-washed, sunset gates shall stand
> A mighty woman with a torch, whose flame
> Is the imprisoned lightning, and her name

Mother of Exiles. From her beacon-hand
Glows world-wide welcome; her mild eyes command
The air-bridged harbor that twin cities frame.

"Keep, ancient lands, your storied pomp!" cries she
With silent lips. "Give me your tired, your poor,
Your huddled masses yearning to breathe free,
The wretched refuse of your teeming shore.
Send these, the homeless, tempest-tossed to me.
I lift my lamp beside the golden door."[1]

There has always been something different about America that enabled this magnanimous nation to wrap her arms around the "wretched refuse" of other nations.

This nation of immigrants was bound together by a spirit, you might say. For although one cannot become French or Chinese or Russian, one *can* become an American by embracing that spirit.

Becoming a naturalized American citizen therefore meant more than passing the federal government's screening process and stumbling through a few civics questions. It meant an implicit and heartfelt agreement to abide not only by the nation's laws, but by its hidden, unwritten "laws" as well—the principles that made up the invisible but vital fabric of Western civilization: the individual as citizen-sovereign; a balance of freedom and responsibility; unlimited opportunity—to succeed or fail; independence and self-reliance; tolerance; the work ethic; equality under the law; and other core Judeo-Christian values.

Underlying all of this, in turn, was the common belief—a belief so deep and unquestioned that it underpinned all of our major institutions—that there is a God, that He is the God of the Bible, that the Ten Commandments and the Sermon on the Mount are the foundation of a good life and a great society, and that America had been uniquely blessed by that God. These were the underlying assumptions infusing America's dominant culture.

All that started to change in the 1960s. Actually, the nation's moral and cultural foundation had been under attack for decades, but the '60s is when the attacks spilled out into America's streets, resulting in unprecedented cultural chaos by decade's end.

One of the first times I remember feeling the foundations of America tremble was in 1964 during my ninth-grade civics class. A girl—I don't remember her name, but I think she was from Tennessee, and she had a very thick southern accent—answered a question from the teacher by mentioning something about God.

"How do you know there *is* a God?" the teacher shot back.

It was like an earth tremor—just a faint quiver really, a precursor to the tidal waves to come a few years later—a smiling, casual, offhanded swipe at the world as we knew it.

How did the little southern girl know there was a God? Clearly taken aback, she answered the teacher earnestly, incredulously, her voice breaking: "Because . . . there *is!*" She had, quite naturally, offered up the best answer anyone could possibly give.

The teacher had questioned the unquestionable, injecting doubt into a room of impressionable young boys and girls. It was one of those moments you remember forty years later because it created a spark, a momentary contact with another dimension—that alien dimension of cynicism and disbelief.

Within a few years the gathering tides of rebellion against traditional America came crashing down with great ferocity and on many shores. One key area was the civil rights movement. Despite the fact that America had long-since forsaken slavery and—thanks to the movement led by Martin Luther King Jr., which culminated in the landmark 1964 Civil Rights Act—had outlawed segregation and made great strides in moving beyond racism altogether, a demand for "black studies" nevertheless arose in the nation's colleges. The idea was that past denigration and mistreatment of blacks necessitated special emphasis on their culture and accomplishments. "Black pride" was born and "black studies," "black history," and the like proliferated through the nation's university campuses. That sounds fine, but there was more going on behind the scenes.

Although most people didn't comprehend it at the time, black pride and similar "liberation movements" did *not* arise out of the mainstream of the civil rights movement, which had arrived, in King's famous "I have a dream" speech, at the ultimate solution to racism: the color-blind society where people would "not be judged by the color of their skin, but by the content of their character." This enlightened vision of America—which would have completed the promise of the Declaration of Independence that "all men are created equal"—was hijacked by forces of the '60s radical left. These were people who did not want peace and racial harmony. They condemned racial integration as "Uncle Tomism" and "co-optation." Their aim was to indict America as a racist oppressor as a means to foment division, revolution, and societal transformation. But all this was off the radar of most Americans, who, under the sway perhaps of the nation's collective guilt over slavery and segregation, accepted what amounted to "radical black studies."

It didn't end there, however. Soon there were women's studies and gay and lesbian studies. Before long, the world of academia was awash in "multiculturalism."

"Wait a minute," you might say. "What's wrong with multiculturalism? Doesn't exposing students to other cultures and values serve to enrich their understanding of the world and its peoples?"

Of course. And there would be nothing wrong if that was what was actually going on. In reality, however, as Judge Robert Bork explained in *Slouching Towards Gomorrah,* multiculturalism had been conjured up solely to serve as a battering ram, "a philosophy of antagonism to America and the West," an "attack on America, the European-American culture, and the white race, with special emphasis on white males." The proof, he noted, is evident in the multicultural curriculum choices:

> A curriculum designed to foster understanding of other cultures would study those cultures. Multiculturalism does not. Courses are not offered on the cultures of China or India or Brazil or Nigeria, nor does the curriculum require the study of languages without which foreign cultures cannot be fully understood. Instead the focus is on groups that, allegedly, have been subjected to oppression by American and Western civilization—homosexuals, American Indians, blacks, Hispanics, women, and so on. The message is not that all cultures are to be respected, but that European culture, which created the dominance of white males, is uniquely evil. Multiculturalism follows the agenda of modern liberalism, and it comes straight from the Sixties counterculture. But now, in American education, it is the dominant culture.[2]

To fathom what's been happening to America, you must understand that during the 1960s the moral foundation of America came under a full-blown assault. The radicals of the '60s—including, by the way, Bill and Hillary Clinton—have today either taken over or profoundly altered the key institutions they originally wanted to destroy, from government to the news media, from education to religion.

A generation later, the various "liberation" movements—sexual liberation, women's liberation, gay liberation, and so on—have blossomed into rampant infidelity, divorce and family breakdown, gender confusion, AIDS, abortion, and other mammoth problems. Moreover, the multicultural madness that started in the '60s has infused virtually all of American society with unending confusion.

Today, in the rarified but toxic air of multiculturalism and political correctness, all cultures and all values are of equal value. The most ignorant, oppressive, suffocating, women-hating kind of culture—where young people's hands and feet are amputated as punishment for petty offenses—is now worthy of equal respect to Western culture, which has provided most of the world's knowledge, progress, food, medicine, technology, quality of life, representative government, and liberty.

This virtual brainwashing of a generation has had its intended effect. *New York Times* journalist Richard Bernstein spent two years documenting the effects of multicultural ideology. The result, notes Bork, "is not an impressionistic book or one based on an ideological predisposition; it is a report of empirical findings."

> He points, for example, to the remarkable change in attitude towards Christopher Columbus between 1892 and 1992. Though not a single new fact about Columbus's life and exploits had been uncovered, the country's mood swung from one of uncritical adulation to one of loathing and condemnation, at least among the members of the "intellectual" class. The change was accomplished by the aggressive ideology of multiculturalism. The Columbus turnaround is merely a specific instance of more general alterations in our moral landscape.[3]

This moral inversion caused by multiculturalism, which proclaims that *all cultures are equal,* has extended to virtually every area of society:

• *All religions are equal:* Witches and Satanists are now afforded the same respect as Christians and Jews. As just one example, U.S. District

Court Judge Dennis W. Dohnal ruled in 2003 that officials in Chester-field County, Virginia, discriminated against Cyndi Simpson, a Wiccan, when they barred her from opening the board of supervisors' meetings with prayer.[4]

Britain's Royal Navy went a step further, allowing an officer to conduct satanic rituals on board one of its ships. Chris Cranmer, a twenty-four-year-old naval technician and noncommissioned officer on the frigate *Cumberland,* was given his own satanic altar where he could dress in black robes and perform ceremonies to worship the devil using bells and candles. Cranmer says he's a "Magistrate of the Society of the Onyx Star Black Guard" and believes he is evil.

"From a military perspective, I believe in vengeance. If I were asked if I were evil, I would say yes," he told London's *Daily Mail* newspaper, which notes that permission to worship on board ship was granted the Satan worshiper under equal-opportunities legislation.[5]

As with religion, where good and evil now are afforded equal respect, so in the area of sexuality, what was bizarre and unmentionable a generation ago is today a civil right:

• *All sexuality is equal:* In 2004, thousands of same-sex marriage ceremonies were conducted throughout the United States—in open defiance of the law—under the banner of fundamental fairness and nondiscrimination.

Even adult-child sex—euphemistically called "intergenerational sex"—is making surprising headway into the mainstream based on today's pervasive climate of moral equivalence among all forms of consensual love. Self-righteous child molesters claim their cause is simply the latest in a long line of civil rights movements and eagerly anticipate the day society will shed its ancient taboos and grant full "sexual rights" to young children and the adults who "love" them.

This world view whereby we declare all human cultures and moral codes, from the fairest to the foulest, to be equal in value is made possible only by the total abandonment of any objective standard of right and wrong. The absurdity of this becomes even more evident when we take the next step downward in the game of making everything equal in value to everything else. I'm talking about a major outgrowth of multiculturalism—namely, the radical animal rights movement.

"ALL LIFE IS EQUAL"

"**A** RAT is a pig is a dog is a boy."

Ingrid Newkirk, founder of the world's largest animal rights organization, the six-hundred-thousand-member People for the Ethical Treatment of Animals (PETA), made this amazing statement to *Vogue* magazine in 1989. Although PETA representatives occasionally try to deflect criticism by claiming Newkirk's statement was taken out of context (saying, for instance, that their founder was only comparing various mammals' capacity for pain), here is the actual quote as she gave it to the *Vogue* reporter:

> Animal liberationists do not separate out the human animal, so there is no rational basis for saying that a human has special rights. A rat is a pig is a dog is a boy. They're all mammals.[6]

How, you may be wondering, can anyone equate a boy with a rat? A close look at the radical animal rights movement—I say "radical" so as not to confuse these zealots with the good folks at the Humane Society—is highly instructive in understanding multicultural madness.

PETA puts on a great public face. It has an impressive record of getting business, industry, and government to be kinder to animals. With the central theme of preventing cruelty to animals, the group has waged a long and successful campaign against research as well as scientific and product testing involving animals.

When one looks at PETA's Web site, it's easy to believe the group just wants to put a stop to homeless dogs' being burned alive and similar horror stories. But moving beyond the shiny exterior with its heart-wrenching animal-abuse stories designed to appeal to large numbers of people and attract donations, one finds this: "For kids who want to eat their veggies and not their friends." That's a PETA headline that draws children into campaigns to "Save the Chickens" and "Save the Pigs." But what about "Save the Babies"? I couldn't find that campaign. It's not there. Instead, on its Web site PETA poses and then answers one of the key questions people ask of the organization, and of animal rights activists in general: "Why don't you focus your attention on abortion or child abuse? Why do you care about animals?"

PETA's answer, which it addresses specifically to pro-life readers, goes like this:

> Those who are particularly adamant on the abortion issue should also consider the issue of vegetarianism, as it requires no additional effort and lends the credibility of personal action to their statements about being "pro-life."

> With the issue of abortion, few of us will ever have to make this choice, and no one can make this choice for someone else, however much some people might wish to.

> But there is one area where the solution is simple: the issue of animal abuse on factory farms. Each and every one of us can simply choose not to be animal abusers by becoming a vegetarian.

Okay, let's get this straight. No one has the right to tell another person that it's wrong to kill the living, breathing, pain-feeling human baby living inside its mother. It's her business alone if she wants to kill it, so back off. But it's everyone's duty and moral responsibility to stop the killing of chickens, pigs, and fish everywhere.

There's more: "If we purport to be 'pro-life,' yet we choose to support violence, misery, and death every time we sit down to eat, what does that say about our convictions? For a simple palate preference, we have become 'pro-death,' we are paying for cruelty to animals. The only legitimate Christian or 'pro-life' choice is vegetarianism."

What are we dealing with here? Just some wacky, lovable, slightly-off-base friends of furry little critters?

Let's take a deeper look.

A human baby, from the moment of its conception—and as the delicate and ethereal fabric grows with its tiny, perfectly formed fingers and toes, little heartbeats, little lips, little ears, shrouded peacefully in its mother's womb—is undoubtedly the crowning glory of creation.

"Created in His image," the human baby at whatever stage is simply sacred. So of course good-natured pro-lifers are always scratching their heads and asking the hard-core animal rights crowd, "Why don't you folks care about the aborted babies?"

Take a good look at PETA's response. Look at the tortured reasoning. Notice the unfriendly tone, the disdainful use of quotes around the word *pro-life*. Do these seem like the words of an organization that really cares about aborting humans? No. But they're hoping you won't notice. They're hoping you'll think, "Oh well, PETA just carved out this little niche of saving dogs and cats and chickens and pigs, but they really care about human babies too."

Wrong.

The most PETA can grudgingly offer up in support of human life is, "Those who are particularly adamant on the abortion issue should also consider the issue of vegetarianism, as it . . . lends the credibility of personal action to their statements about being 'pro-life.'"

Pathetic. By the way, PETA's core argument—which it boldly proclaims as justification for all of its edgy public relations campaigns, some of which border on lawlessness—is the prevention of needless suffering. Do they think unborn babies don't suffer? It is indisputable that even in utero human children have a nervous system and feel real pain. Their nerves and pain receptor cells don't suddenly switch on the moment they exit their mother's womb. They feel the abortionist's scalpel, forceps, suction devices, skull crushers, and other torture implements used in the various abortion methods.

If PETA really cared about human life, it would have answered the question something like this: "Although abortion is the most egregious cause of needless suffering on the planet today, we at PETA have chosen to come to the defense of animals, since not many people have the will or the means to do so. But we know our mission pales into insignificance next to the horrendous ongoing tragedy of millions of innocent human babies slaughtered every year while in their mother's wombs. We salute our brothers and sisters in the pro-life movement for their commitment to end this needless suffering and death."

Sorry, that's just a nice dream. In reality, the radical animal rights folks are in the opposite camp from those opposing abortion. Why? Because pro-lifers, by standing up for the little divine spark in God's most perfect and prized creation, are championing the very reality—namely, the existence of the soul in human beings—that the boy-equals-rat crowd wants to forget! The real message of the radical animal rights movement is that people are only animals—and not very good ones at that.

Elevating animals to the level of human beings—as actor Steven Segal, one of PETA's celebrity advocates, puts it, "We have to view all life as equal"—is a roundabout way of saying that human beings are no more than animals and therefore have no souls.

Now why, you might ask, would anyone deny that a human being has a soul? Why would the notion that we have a divine spark within us be repugnant? After all, whatever goodness we humans can muster, whatever kindness and consideration we have for each other, is based on the fact that we know we are dealing with another soul. If we are faithful to our spouse, honorable in business, truthful to each other, willing to sacrifice for our children—whatever we consider to be virtuous and noble is tied up in this conviction that we are more than animals, spiritual beings esteemed by God.

However, for some people there is great satisfaction and "liberation" in believing there is no soul. Because if there is no soul, there is no God. And if there is no God, there's no divine judgment, no accountability for our actions—you get the picture. We're animals, so we can act like animals. But animals mate in the street and run around naked—kind of like the '60s again, with its "sex, drugs, and rock 'n' roll" counterculture of "freedom."

The radical animal rights folks are just cross-species multiculturalists. Do you think the multiculturalists really care about Eskimo music or about why the Ubangis make their lips as big as pancakes? Do they really care about cultures that worship rats, cows, and sex organs? No, their interest is not truly in elevating other cultures, nor in "celebrating diversity." They simply want to reject moral constraints.

In the same way, people who equate boys with rats don't really care for rats. No, their interest is in *tearing down* Western civilization and denying its foundation—namely, the moral laws of life bequeathed to mankind by God. By equating man with a soulless animal, they've effectively negated—in their minds—the existence of any divine authority or judge over their lives. And thus they feel liberated from the "patriarchal," law-giving Judeo-Christian God they're rebelling against.

Now that we've explored the strange reality underlying what is euphemistically called multiculturalism, but which is actually a hatred of and rebellion against Judeo-Christian values, let's see how this toxic world view has brought America to a very dangerous point.

THE INVISIBLE JIHAD

DESPITE THE fact that multiculturalism has rewritten history, demonized Western culture, and turned civilization on its head for a generation, Americans for the most part floated along with this charade, year after confusing year—until September 11, 2001. The otherworldly shock and horror that we experienced on that particular Tuesday morning was followed by a crash course in radical Islam—a very strange and menacing culture indeed.

We learned that those who wantonly murdered thousands of American civilians and threatened even greater destruction justified their acts as being required of them by Allah. We learned that *shaheeds* (martyrs)—those Muslims who die while killing infidels (unbelievers, primarily Jews but also Christians and Americans generally) in jihad or holy war—are indoctrinated, often from an early age, by radical Islamic clerics.

And what is the jihad message taught in so many mosques and madrassas (religious schools) throughout the Middle East? Just this: As soon as the first drop of your blood is shed in jihad, you will feel no pain, all your sins will be forgiven, and you will be transported instantly to paradise where you will recline comfortably for eternity on plush green cushions, to be lavished with the choicest meats, the finest wines and endless sex with seventy virgins. In addition, all of your family members will be admitted into heaven as part of your reward.

We learned that our nation's borders were scandalously unprotected and our immigration policies full of holes easily exploited by terrorists. We learned that our beloved country was targeted for even more horrific terror attacks—using biological, chemical, or even nuclear weapons—by a maniacal cult of jihadists spread out over sixty nations. We learned that terror cells and sleeper suicide warriors were already in the United States, intending to strike and inflict indiscriminate terror and death. We learned that a well-developed network of Islamic terror supporters was operating freely within the open American system—conducting fundraisers and providing support for known terror groups—in mosques, meeting halls, and even on college campuses.

How exactly did the United States "become the scene of one of the most hideously bedeviled conflicts of all time?" asked New York University literature professor Carol Iannone.

Quite simply, it happened because America lost its grasp of its own historic character, and embraced "diversity" as a national goal. In the name of equality and nondiscrimination we invited mass immigration from every part of the globe, and made no demands on the newcomers to become Americans. In fact, we gave up our American core, adopted multicultural- ism and declared all cultures equal. We invited the new groups to celebrate themselves while we cravenly permitted libelous denigration of our own past. Like fools we prated that diversity is our strength, when common sense and all of history tell us that strength comes from unity.

Absolute nondiscrimination meant we no longer enforced standards, made judgments, distinguished between good and evil, friend and foe. We grew lazy, stupid and careless—about our borders, about national security, even about previous terrorist attacks against us. We worried over our "hate crimes" and our "racial profiling," while men resided in our midst who seethed with murderous fury even against our children and plotted our destruction.[7]

A graphic illustration of the powerful grip multiculturalism and politi- cally correct thinking have on America is the official reluctance to admit that the nation is at war—not with all of Islam, of course—but with a major and growing faction within Islam. Just consider the following:

• Before they paralyzed the Washington DC metropolitan area for three bloody weeks in October 2002, Beltway snipers John Muhammad and seventeen-year-old Lee Boyd "John" Malvo had praised the Septem- ber 11 skyjackers and had threatened to commit major terrorist acts within the United States. But after their capture, most in the media, in their search for a motive, ignored Muhammad and Malvo's known ji- hadist sympathies. In fact, the standard analysis of what made Muham- mad tick seemed to include anything and everything *except* jihad.

Thus the *Los Angeles Times* offered up no less than six possible mo- tives for Muhammad's killing spree, reported Daniel Pipes, an expert on militant Islam. They included "his 'stormy relationship' with his family, his 'stark realization' of loss and regret, his perceived sense of abuse as an American Muslim post-9/11, his desire to 'exert control' over others, his relationship with Malvo, and his trying to make a quick buck," said Pipes, "but did not mention jihad." Similarly, Pipes noted, "a *Boston Globe* article found 'there must have been something in his social interaction—in his marriage or his military career—that pulled the trigger.'"[8]

• On July 4, 2002, a cab driver named Hesham Hadayet walked into the Los Angeles International Airport and shot two people to death before being shot and killed by a security guard. Despite the fact that Hadayet was Egyptian and that he had chosen the Israeli El Al ticket counter as the site for venting his rage, any suggestion that Hadayet was carrying out his own personal jihad was immediately dismissed.

"Investigators . . . believe that Hadayet was simply an overstressed man who snapped," reported the *Los Angeles Times.* "He was known as a quiet, observant Muslim," added the *Times,* which explained away the killer's virulent anti-Semitism by saying: "While Hadayet occasionally mentioned a hatred for Israel, [one former employee] saw it more as a cultural perspective on Mideast politics than an emotion that would fuel violence."[9]

• One of the worst air disasters in recent history, Egypt Air Flight 990 crashed into the Atlantic shortly after takeoff from New York in October 1999, killing 217 passengers and crew. Two and a half years later the National Transportation Safety Board finally reached the same conclusion that virtually everyone else had immediately after the crash—the plane's Egyptian copilot, Gameel El-Batouty, had cut power to the engines and intentionally sent the plane plummeting into the ocean, killing all aboard. But the government panel declined to suggest a motive, except to speculate that El-Batouty might have "committed suicide."

Suicide? To most, mass murder or terrorism would better describe the wanton annihilation of hundreds of innocent people. Yet, despite the fact the copilot had calmly repeated over and over the Arabic phrase *tawkalt*—meaning "I rely on Allah"—for almost a minute and a half during his deed, and that such behavior, according to the report, "is not consistent with the reaction that would be expected from a pilot who is encountering an unexpected or uncommanded flight condition," the federal report steered clear of suggesting jihad as a motive.[10]

In spite of this strange official aversion to investigate seriously the jihad factor in attack after attack that Americans have endured, in truth, virtually all terrorist acts against the United States or its interests in recent years have been perpetrated by militant Islamists. Indeed, a glance at the headlines shows we are in the midst of what can only be described as a global Islamist jihad against "unbelievers." Yet the radical Islamic connection is always downplayed by government. Always.

Likewise, the press—the filter through which Americans receive their information—is also paralyzed by political correctness from plainly defining the enemy. In the aftermath of 9-11, major news organizations decided it wasn't appropriate to describe the Islamic terrorists who blew up the World Trade Center and Pentagon, murdering thousands of innocent Americans, as "Islamic terrorists."

As the *Washington Times* reported, "An organization of religion news reporters yesterday suggested that reporters avoid the term 'Islamic terrorist' or similar labels as Muslims and their beliefs receive greater scrutiny. The Religion Newswriters Association said it was 'troubled' by the frequent use of the term in the days after the terrorist attacks in New York and Washington." At its annual meeting, the group adopted a resolution also rejecting "similar phrases that associate an entire religion with the action of a few."[11]

Okay, so we can't say "Islamic." But at least we can still call them "terrorists," right?

Wrong again.

Stephen Jukes, Reuters's global head of news, decreed that the giant wire service's twenty-five hundred journalists should not use the T word unless in a direct quote. "We all know that one man's terrorist is another man's freedom fighter and that Reuters upholds the principle that we do not use the word terrorist," he wrote in an internal memo. "We're trying to treat everyone on a level playing field, however tragic it's been and however awful and cataclysmic for the American people and people around the world."[12] Incredibly, Jukes concluded by instructing Reuters reporters: "To be frank, it adds little to call the attack on the World Trade Center a terrorist attack."

What are we to conclude when the head of one of the world's premiere news organizations is so paralyzed by multicultural orthodoxy that he is unable to call the worst terrorist attack in American history "a terrorist attack"?

"Americans," warned former Reagan staffer and columnist Paul Craig Roberts about the radical Islamic threat to this nation, "might be so politically correct and racially sensitive as to be unable to deal with the problem at all."

MARKETING MULTICULTURALISM

IT's EASY to blame '60s radicals, university Marxists, cowardly politicians, and an elitist press for today's multicultural madness. But the fact is, millions of Americans have bought into it. Why?

Isn't it obvious? Since the 1960s, America—from her government to her schools and even to her churches—has steadily fallen away from the Judeo-Christian values that previously illuminated and gave life and strength to the nation's institutions. This is equivalent to turning out the country's lights. And when you turn out the lights, everything looks the same in the dark—that's multiculturalism.

Moreover, no longer guided by universal standards of right and wrong, Americans have had nothing more reliable than their own feelings to guide them in the moral realm. And as modern marketing well knows, when people are operating primarily on the basis of feelings and emotions, they're wide open to every sort of imaginable manipulation.

Marketing is the application of the knowledge of human psychology to the task of persuasion. And what psychology has taught the marketing world is that the most powerful persuasion of all takes place not through above-the-board appeals to reason but by directly targeting the emotions.

By way of illustration, cigarettes were once sold on the basis of "great taste" and "fine tobacco." Not all that convincing, but then there aren't a whole lot of features and benefits to sell with cigarettes. Then along came the Marlboro Man. Created in 1955 for Philip Morris Company by advertising giant Leo Burnett, this icon of the quintessential American cowboy is probably the most famous brand image to appear in our lifetimes. The rugged, masculine trademark made Marlboro the world's best-selling cigarette.

What does the Marlboro Man—a rancher on a horse—have to do with cigarettes? Nothing, except that the ubiquitous cowboy evoked within millions of men feelings of masculinity, independence, wide open spaces, and freedom. So successful has been the decades-old campaign that on some ads the image is reduced to little more than a saddle and a splash of red, but—like Pavlov's bell—it still subtly makes people salivate for the mythical place called Marlboro Country.

For the last generation, commercial marketing has aimed not so much at extolling the intrinsic value or usefulness of a product to consumers but rather at conditioning the consumer to associate the product with a particular feeling. Bottom line: if the marketer can elicit in you a feeling—the right feeling—he has won. Game over.

With this principle in mind, let's look at how the public is so easily persuaded to abandon long-held loyalties. How are people so readily convinced that Columbus, a national hero for five hundred years, as well as the Pilgrims, revered and studied by generations of schoolchildren, were actually genocidal racists? How are our former sentiments opposing homosexuality or Wicca so easily transformed into "enlightened tolerance" and open support?

Pick a topic—let's say, same-sex marriage.

Imagine you're participating in a televised one-on-one debate. You're defending traditional marriage. Facing off against you is a lesbian. But not just any lesbian. An attractive, young, eloquent, educated, sensitive, well-dressed lesbian—and to all appearances a fine human being. She looks you in the eye and says, in a disarmingly mainstream and reasonable tone: "I love my country, I obey its laws and I pay my taxes. I'm an American, and have all the same rights you do. In fact, I've served my country in the military and have put my life on the line. I've lived monogamously with my partner for eighteen years. We truly love each other and want nothing more than to be married and to live out our lives in peace and happiness—just like you. What's the matter with that? Why shouldn't we be allowed to be married? How does it hurt you?"

You have thirty seconds to respond before the commercial break.

How can you neutralize the powerful, positive emotions your opponent has skillfully evoked? Will you offer up a statement about the dangers of altering the traditional definition of marriage? Will you point out that children do better with both a mother and father? Will you say the Bible clearly condemns homosexual acts?

The debate will be won by whoever conjures up the strongest emotions of sympathy in the audience.

Therefore, unless you're an extraordinarily gifted and charismatic debater—you lose. And when you lose, millions of people out in TV land are pulled a few inches further away from commonsense values and a few inches closer to embracing, or at least resigning themselves to accepting, same-sex marriage.

The lesbian debater appeals to Americans' basic traits of tolerance, inclusiveness, fair-mindedness, and honor toward veterans. Every statement she makes tends to create in the viewer positive feelings, not toward same-sex marriage per se, but toward her. Yet it's the viewers' attitudes toward same-sex marriage that will change.

Each hidden persuasion is like money accruing in the emotional bank account of the listener—and when there are enough funds (strong feelings of sympathy) in the listener's account, he or she has been "persuaded" of the justness of these two women being married. Or if not persuaded, at least neutralized in terms of offering any effective opposition to same-sex marriage.

Watch how the feelings accumulate in the listener's bank account until they reach critical mass: "I love my country" (patriotism—*cha-ching*). "I obey its laws and I pay my taxes" (responsible citizen—*cha-ching*). "I'm an American, and have all the same rights you do" (appeal to fairness—*cha-ching*). "I've served my country in the military and have put my life on the line" (she's a veteran!—*double cha-ching*). "I've lived monogamously with my partner for eighteen years" (loyalty—*cha-ching*). "We truly love each other and want nothing more than to be married and to live out our lives in peace and happiness—just like you" (true love—*cha-ching*). "Why shouldn't we be allowed to be married? How does it hurt you?" (personal intimidation—*cha-ching*).

Now imagine how the television viewers are reacting to this debate.

Many in the audience find our feelings have been stirred by the lesbian's touching appeal. We like her. We want her to be happy. Our positive feelings toward her start to subtly eat away at our long-held conviction that same-sex marriage is wrong. Those warm emotions give rise to a stream of thought whispers that orbit our minds at light-speed: *Maybe I've judged these people too harshly just because they're different.... Maybe they could make each other happy if they were married.... After all, heterosexual married couples have lots of problems, and half of them get divorced—so what difference does it really make?*

We start to doubt our prior beliefs, wondering if they're as hallowed as we've thought, or rather just some antiquated religious notions about sex and sin that don't really apply in today's world. Then the thought occurs to us, as though from divine revelation: *Don't we all long to love and be loved? . . . Maybe that is the ultimate truth. . . . She's right, it doesn't hurt anyone else for her to be married to her partner. . . . It's mean-spirited to deny other human beings their happiness. . . . I like her. . . . I want her to be happy. Besides, I don't want anyone to call me a bigot.*

Seduction complete.

If we were anchored in the Judeo-Christian moral standards that are responsible for the singular success of the Western world, all this emotional persuasion would be for naught. We'd easily discern the truth of the debate and just be amused at the feeble attempts at manipulating our feelings. But after several decades of public education that reflects not the values of the nation's founders but those of '60s radicals and reformers, millions of Americans are just plain confused.

The farther we stray from the rock of unchanging spiritual principles, the easier it is to get swept away by clever appeals to our feelings—including the need to prove to others that we are tolerant. Increasingly, that means tolerant of corruption or, in some cases, outright evil.

There's no end to the variety of emotional manipulations to which we fall prey, and there are no words to describe the stunning ease with which we have been seduced to throw away that which is most precious to us.

In C. S. Lewis's seven-volume Chronicles of Narnia, the poignant and brilliantly insightful final book, *The Last Battle,* describes how the good-hearted but naïve inhabitants of Narnia throw away their cherished civilization—losing both their lives and their world itself—by falling for a shabby ruse perpetrated by a few cunning and unprincipled characters. When you read it, you can't help thinking, "Oh, my gosh, this isn't even a very clever con game; it's crude, full of contradictions, and easily seen through from a thousand different directions." You just want to shake them and say, "Don't you see what you're falling for?" Nevertheless, as the con men ruthlessly play on the doubts and fears of the Narnia folk, their lies take hold, and the light of civilization goes out.

Haven't we in America done exactly the same thing? Look at the shabby ruse we've fallen for. We've traded Western civilization for vain delusions, cheap thrills, and laughably illogical doctrines. Like the townsfolk in *The Emperor's New Clothes,* we all know the king is wearing no clothes—we can plainly see the truth—but we play along out of fear and intimidation. We're afraid of confrontation, of losing the love and approval of others, of being labeled "judgmental," "racist," "bigoted," or "homophobic." So we quietly allow our minds to be twisted as we surrender our former beliefs and bequeath an unknown country to our children and grandchildren.

How strange. Out of the thousands of years of suffering and oppression that comprise human history, a light burns brightly for just a couple of hundred years. The American experiment: a revolutionary idea that the common man can be free, master of his own government, so long as he himself is ruled by God. For a short time this brilliant young country dazzles all the world and all of history, not just with its power and productivity and progress, but with its goodness.

And then, out of pure hatred—the same rage and rebellion institutionalized in communism, Nazism, and all the other "isms" that have paved the world's roads with corpses throughout the last century—haters of truth scheme to extinguish this shining light. So they concoct an absurd, fantastic ruse—that animals should have the same rights as human beings, that white people are inherently racist and oppressive, that self-destructive sexual compulsions are perfectly normal and noble. Each passing year brings new and more bizarre delusions being held up as truth.

How much stranger still that we've bought it.

Can we get the real America back? Only time will tell. But if we do, it very likely will be due to the efforts of the current generation, which still has some memory of the real America.

The great melting pot—*e pluribus unum*—depended on an ideal. But the melting pot has become corrupted without this guiding spirit. Millions now residing here are not loyal to American values. Rather than unified and color-blind, the nation is divided and segregated. On top of everything else, America literally has been invaded, and we are at war.

Recognizing they must take rapid steps to reverse course, policy makers entertain options for better policing the nation's borders, screening potential immigrants, and reevaluating those already in. But just over the horizon is the more painful work—of revisiting the madness of multiculturalism, political correctness, rebellion against America's founding values, and the spiritual confusion that rebellion has caused. But revisit them we must, since it is they that have led to both the present invasion and the resulting near-paralysis over how to deal with the problem.

If we don't change course, America will end up the loser. Even if the current terror war went away—if it were all only a bad dream from which we awoke with the World Trade Center towers still standing—we would still lose America to the long-term invasion and conversion of our basic identity that has been under way for decades.

GRANDMOTHER'S LOVE

TOWARD THE end of her life, my grandmother, Mary Kupelian, wanted to travel overseas one last time to visit her old-country relatives. I went with her, as her bodyguard, you might say. I will never forget the time I spent with her and those in her village—virtually all of whom, it seemed, were somehow related to me. I will never forget her stories about what she and my father went through during the Armenian genocide, and I'll never forget what a survivor she was, to pick up the few shattered pieces of their lives and to come to America to start over.

And I will never ever forget the night we returned to the United States. Our plane from Athens arrived at New York's Kennedy Airport too late for us to make our connection to Washington DC, so Grandmom and I slept in the airport terminal that night, in the second-floor lounge. We were both tired but very happy to be back in America.

After a while, Grandmom shuffled off to the ladies' room. On her return, she described for me—her old woman's voice brimming with excitement—how everything in the rest room was so clean and shiny and modern, how there was hot and cold running water, how everything worked properly—so totally different from where we had just been. And she said she felt like kneeling down and kissing America—right there on the floor of the rest room of JFK airport—so grateful was she for being back in the USA.

My grandmother, who decades earlier as a "homeless, tempest-tossed" immigrant had found refuge in this generous land, had once more come home through the "golden door."

To this day, whether due to some special blessing from God or just because there's so much contrasting darkness throughout the rest of the world, America remains—despite unrelenting assaults by enemies within and without—the national light of the world. But not everybody loves that light. Mary Kupelian did.

FAMILY MELTDOWN

The Campaign to Destroy Marriage

WHEN THIRTY-TWO-YEAR-OLD Paul and his seventeen-year-old fiancée Anna walked into the Norristown, Pennsylvania, courthouse to apply for a marriage license, the justice turned them down flat when he learned they had known each other for only one day.

Yet after much pleading and persuasion, the judge reluctantly granted them their license, and Anna and Paul were married three days later.

The wedding, held at Paul's brother's house, wasn't much—only four people in attendance, no wedding gown, no flowers, no cake, not even a picture taken. He was poor, and she was poorer.

As marriages go, this one didn't sound like it had too much of a future.

Yet, exactly fifty years later, I was privileged to attend the golden wedding anniversary party of Paul and Anna Paulson, my maternal grandparents. It was memorable. They were as loved by their many friends and relatives as George and Mary Bailey in the final scene of *It's a Wonderful Life*. Although their marriage had been arranged by their Greek families according to old-country custom—hence the absence of any courtship—Grandmom and Grandpop had learned to love each other. Along the way they raised four children (including my mother, Louise), kept them safe and sound through the Great Depression, built a successful business, put all four kids through college, saw them all marry and produce thirteen grandchildren, and lived a long and exemplary life of Christian service to others.

What magic kept their marriage so rock-solid despite the tremendous stresses and hardships they endured?

I didn't know the answer to that as a fourteen-year-old boy at their fiftieth anniversary party, nor did the question even occur to me. Why would it? After all, their marriage didn't represent anything out of the ordinary. When I was a kid, marriage was normal. Almost all grownups were married, and the marriage lasted until one of them died. That's just the way it was—or so it seemed.

I had heard about Elizabeth Taylor and other movie stars who scandalously seemed to marry for a short time, get divorced, remarry, redivorce, and remarry yet again. Some would just sleep around and not bother with the charade of marriage at all.

But that was Hollywood. In the real world, where I lived, people got married and stayed married.

I vividly remember the day I discovered divorce. My mother introduced me to Yvonne, a friend of hers who had been divorced. I still recall my feelings of awkwardness and embarrassment, a gut recognition of some private shame. I knew there was something very wrong, something tragic, about divorce.

Today, decades later, every few weeks I hear about another friend or acquaintance whose marriage has detonated. With stunning rapidity, divorce has been transformed from something relatively rare, stigmatizing, and traumatic to something commonplace, accepted—and traumatic.

Indeed, divorce today is almost *expected*, with one in every two marriages ending this way. It is only the numbing frequency and ubiquity of divorce that make us forget the full-blown calamity it really is—the devastation of a family.

"All it takes is one confused spouse who thinks that divorce will solve their unhappiness," said Michelle Gauthier, founder of Defending Holy Matrimony, a Catholic organization. "When that one spouse visits a lawyer, they place the entire family in the hands of a hostile court system. Children become wards of the state, and all marital assets are controlled by the courts. It is truly a tragedy."[1]

A tragedy, yes, and nowhere more so than in its negative impact on children. "National studies show that children from divorced and remarried families experience more depression, have more learning difficulties, and suffer from more problems with peers than children from intact families," wrote Judith Wallerstein, widely considered the world's foremost authority on the effects of divorce on children. In her landmark book, *The Unexpected Legacy of Divorce,* Wallerstein revealed: "Children from divorced and remarried families are two to three times more likely to be referred for psychological help at school than their peers from intact families. More of them end up in mental health clinics and hospital settings. There is earlier sexual activity, more children born out of wedlock, less marriage, and more divorce. Numerous studies show that adult children of divorce have more psychological problems than those raised in intact marriages."[2]

It gets worse. Besides the more obvious results of rampant divorce—such as the massive growth in single-parent homes—"virtually every major personal and social pathology can be traced to fatherlessness more than to any other single factor," concluded author Stephen Baskerville, a professor of political science at Howard University. Citing violent crime, substance abuse, unwed pregnancy, suicide, and other problems, he observed, "Fatherlessness far surpasses both poverty and race as a predictor of social deviance."[3]

Indeed, the growth of the youth-gang culture—police say Los Angeles County alone is home to an estimated 150,000 gang members—is eloquent testimony to the powerful need boys have for a father. If they don't have a real father in their lives, they'll gravitate to another male role model, even a poisonous one.

Equally alarming, although largely unrecognized by most people, is the expansion of government power to which rampant divorce has given rise. As Baskerville described it:

> The result of three decades of unrestrained divorce is that huge numbers of people—many of them government officials—now have a vested professional and financial interest in encouraging it. Divorce today is not simply a phenomenon; it is a regime—a vast bureaucratic empire that permeates national and local governments, with hangers-on in the private sector. In the United States, divorce and custody comprise over half of civil litigation, constituting the cash cow of the judiciary and bringing employment and earnings to a host of public and private officials, including judges, lawyers, psychotherapists, mediators, counselors, social workers, child support enforcement agents and others.

This growth industry derives from the impact of divorce on children. The divorce revolution has spawned a public-private industrial complex of legal, social service and psychotherapeutic professionals devoted to the problems of children, and especially children in single-parent homes. Many are women with feminist leanings. Whatever pieties they may voice about the plight of fatherless, poor, and violent children, the fact remains that these practitioners have a vested interest in creating as many such children as possible. The way to do it is to remove the fathers.[4]

"Where you have minor children, there's really no such thing as no-fault divorce for fathers," says Detroit attorney Philip Holman, vice president of the National Congress for Fathers and Children. "On the practical level, fathers realize that divorce means they lose their kids."[5]

For an out-of-control, ever-expanding government such as America's, divorce represents a hard-to-resist growth opportunity. "Once the father is eliminated," Baskerville explained, "the state functionally replaces him as protector and provider. By removing the father, the state also creates a host of problems for itself to solve: child poverty, child abuse, juvenile crime, and other problems associated with single-parent homes. In this way, the divorce machinery is self-perpetuating and self-expanding. Involuntary divorce is a marvelous tool that allows for the infinite expansion of government power."[6]

This may appear to be a sinister, almost conspiratorial-sounding assessment of government's role in divorce. But if you look objectively at what has happened to the institution of civil marriage since the 1960s and pay attention not to what people and governments say, but to what they actually *do*, Baskerville's harsh conclusions are hard to dismiss.

Consider just how absurdly easy it is to get divorced today. Writer Dennis E. Powell noted how, upon learning his wife desired a divorce, he quickly found the state more than eager to help break up their marriage:

I have discovered how my state—Connecticut—has done all it can to make ending a marriage easy, while making little or no provision for preserving it. In Connecticut, as in other states, "no-fault" divorce means "divorce because it suits the mood of at least one partner." The state has produced an official publication, the "Do-It-Yourself Divorce Guide" to make getting a divorce as simple as mounting a defense against a speeding ticket—even if your spouse has no interest in divorce.

Especially if your spouse has no interest in divorce. The "Do-It-Yourself Divorce Guide" offers everything one needs to know to obtain a divorce, but no guidance as to how one who opposes a divorce might respond. There is plenty on how to battle for a bigger piece of the marital corpse and on getting court orders of alimony, child support, custody, and exclusive use of the family home. There is no mention of another pre-judgment court order . . . available under the law, in which the court may order two sessions with a marriage counselor or other person trained in the resolution of disputes within families. . . .

Filing for divorce, the guide notes, is a simple matter. Fill out a couple of forms, take them to the court clerk, and have copies delivered to your spouse by a process server.[7]

In Connecticut, divorce is routinely granted about ninety days after one spouse files the necessary papers. Total cost to the divorcing party if one represents oneself pro se (without an attorney): approximately $225–$250.

Ninety days. A couple hundred bucks. No reason required—other than "the marriage has irretrievably broken down." Breaking a marriage contract today is easier than firing an employee hired last week or getting out of a cell-phone contract.

In truth, there is no genuine civil marriage in America anymore. The contract part of the marriage contract is nonexistent. After all, how can two parties enter into a contract, and yet either party has the power to end that contract at any time, for any reason, whether or not the other party agrees? Obviously, there never was a true contract, a binding agreement, in the first place.

Yet the binding, extremely-hard-to-break nature of the marriage contract is essential to marriage itself. Marriage is difficult, and there comes a time in many, if not most, marriages when conflicts and suffering cause one or the other spouse to contemplate ending the marriage. The marriage contract is meant to protect both spouses—and their children—against such a period of weakness. No-fault divorce destroys that protection.

How did this happen? How have we managed to cripple civilization's primary institution, marriage, and to do so with such blinding speed?

"MARRIAGE IS LEGALIZED RAPE"

LET'S BEGIN our exploration by considering that a best-selling pro-marriage book almost never saw the light of day just a few years ago.

Harvard University Press had contracted with University of Chicago sociologist and professor Linda J. Waite, a self-described "liberal Democrat," along with coauthor Maggie Gallagher, to write a book based on Waite's studies about marriage.

Apparently, the Harvard-based publishing house expected the book to do the politically correct thing and disparage marriage, as is so common among today's academic elite. But as the Harvard scholars reviewed the manuscript, they found it revealed married men and women live happier, healthier, more financially secure lives, and even have "more and better sex." So naturally, the university's publication board members decided at the last minute *not* to publish the book—titled *The Case for Marriage: Why Married People Are Happier, Healthier and Better Off Financially*—a book they themselves had commissioned.

One Harvard Press reviewer said she didn't like the book's "tone." That's about as close to an answer as the public ever got.

By way of tonal comparison, check out another Harvard Press author, feminist Catharine MacKinnon, who frequently compares male sexual desire to rape—whether women consent to sex or not. Expressing what one reviewer called "a whole-hog hatred of men," MacKinnon explained: "What in the liberal view looks like love and romance looks a lot like hatred and torture to the feminist."[8] A professor of law at both the University of Michigan Law School and the University of Chicago Law School, MacKinnon has written no fewer than five books for Harvard Press. Her message: "Feminism stresses the indistinguishability of prostitution, marriage, and sexual harassment."[9]

So "marriage equals rape" is okay with Harvard University Press, but "marriage equals happiness" is not okay. Fortunately, although Harvard turned down *The Case for Marriage*, at the eleventh hour the book was ultimately published by Doubleday and enjoyed wide readership and critical acclaim.

Flatly contradicting the cherished "divorce may be good for you" myths of the '60s and '70s, Waite and Gallagher argued—using a broad range of indexes—that "being married is actually better for you physically, materially and spiritually than being single or divorced." But they introduced their findings with a warning:

> For perhaps the first time in human history, marriage as an ideal is under a sustained and surprisingly successful attack. Sometimes the attack is direct and ideological, made by "experts" who believe a lifelong vow of fidelity is unrealistic or oppressive, especially to women.
>
> "Even in the early 1960s," sum up social historians Steven Mintz and Susan Kellogg, "marriage and family ties were regarded by the 'human potential movement' as potential threats to individual fulfillment as a man or a woman. The highest forms of human needs, contended proponents of the new psychologies, were autonomy, independence, growth, and creativity," which marriage often thwarted. The search for autonomy and independence as the highest human good blossomed with the women's movement into a critique of marriage per se, which the more flamboyant feminists denounced as "slavery," "legalized rape," and worst of all, "tied up with a sense of dependency." "From this vantage point," Mintz and Kellogg note, "marriage increasingly came to be described as a trap, circumscribing a woman's social and intellectual horizons and lowering her sense of self-esteem."[10]

"Slavery"? "Legalized rape"? How could anyone think of marriage in such terms? Let's travel back to the 1960s and '70s and listen to the feminist drumbeats. And keep in mind that, like much of what was being preached and written about with religious zeal in those days of cultural revolution, even the most absurd ideas had a way of magically morphing into public policy a few years later.

- "We have to abolish and reform the institution of marriage. . . . By the year 2000 we will, I hope, raise our children to believe in human potential, not God. . . . We must understand what we are

attempting is a revolution, not a public relations movement."
—Gloria Steinem, quoted in the *Saturday Review of Education,*
March 1973

- "Being a housewife is an illegitimate profession . . . the choice to
  serve and be protected and plan towards being a family-maker is a
  choice that shouldn't be. The heart of radical feminism is to
  change that."—Vivian Gornick, feminist author and tenured professor at the University of Arizona, *Daily Illini,* April 25, 1981

- "We can't destroy the inequities between men and women until
  we destroy marriage."—Feminist author Robin Morgan, who
  became an editor at *Ms.* magazine[11]

- "If women are to effect a significant amelioration in their condition it seems obvious that they must refuse to marry. . . . The
  plight of mothers is more desperate than that of other women,
  and the more numerous the children the more hopeless the situation seems to be. . . . Most women . . . would shrink at the notion of leaving husband and children, but this is precisely the
  case in which brutally clear rethinking must be undertaken."
  —Germaine Greer, author, scholar, and lecturer at the University of Warwick, England[12]

- "Like prostitution, marriage is an institution that is extremely
  oppressive and dangerous for women."—Radical feminist author
  Andrea Dworkin in 1983[13]

- "Until all women are lesbians, there will be no true political revolution."—Feminist author and journalist Jill Johnson[14]

- "The legal rights of access that married partners have to each
  other's persons, property, and lives makes it all but impossible for
  a spouse to defend herself (or himself), or to be protected against
  torture, rape, battery, stalking, mayhem, or murder by the other
  spouse. . . . Legal marriage thus enlists state support for condi-

tions conducive to murder and mayhem."—Claudia Card, professor of philosophy at the University of Wisconsin–Madison, 1996[15]

First, let's be very clear about what we're looking at—pure rage, an all-consuming hatred of men, and often a hatred of God also. If you think I'm exaggerating, read the writings of these people for yourself. You will be shocked at the depth and intensity of their anger, the kind one associates with deep personal violation or trauma. Indeed, in some well-known cases, feminist leaders report having been sexually abused as children or beaten by a violent husband. Apparently, they have concluded in their blind anger that *all* men are predatory beasts and molesters, and thus are determined to save their fellow women from the "slavery" and "oppression" of family life.

ALIEN NATION

MOST PEOPLE who lived through the '60s remember the militant feminists and their angry speeches, demonstrations, and bra disposals. But when this spectacle left the front page of mainstream consciousness—along with the Beatles, Jimi Hendrix, long hair, LSD, and the rest of the '60s psychedelic cultural revolution—did America just go back to "normal"? No. We had been transformed. Today, a generation later, we debate issues like cohabitation, divorce, same-sex marriage, civil unions, polygamy, and the redefinition of marriage, seemingly oblivious to the fact that marriage as a fundamental institution of civilization was crippled back in the late '60s and early '70s with the advent of no-fault divorce.

Although radical feminism has always been too strident—and frankly, insane—to be embraced by the American public (though it is to this day a powerful molding influence on America's college campuses), its core agenda has mysteriously become our reality.

The same thing happened with abortion, the number-one cause of feminists today. The public has never accepted the radical pro-abortion agenda; national polls consistently show barely 25 percent of Americans embrace unfettered abortion on demand at any time, for any reason. Yet that radical agenda is the law of the land in the United States today. In the same way, the feminist movement—from the mainstream variety that pushed women into the workplace to the man-hating radical variety that demanded an end to marriage and the mainstreaming of lesbianism—has succeeded in turning its agenda into public policy.

Look at what its purveyors wanted: to persuade women to be ashamed of their roles as homemaker and mother and to set their sights instead on the workplace; to institute no-fault divorce; to make lesbianism an acceptable alternative to heterosexuality; and most of all, to "free" women from marriage. They scored big-time. The question is how?

While feminism was relentlessly driving the family apart from the sidelines, what on earth was the mainstream thinking? After all, it was state legislatures and judges and governors, not militant lesbians, who actually tossed out the powerfully binding civil marriage contract by instituting no-fault divorce.

Judith Wallerstein described the seduction of "mainstream" America:

Up until thirty years ago marriage was a lifetime commitment with only a few narrow legal exits such as proving adultery in the courts or outwaiting years of abandonment. American cultural and legal attitudes bound marriages together, no matter how miserable couples might be. Countless individuals were locked in loveless marriages they desperately wanted to end, but for the most part they had no way out. Then, in an upheaval akin to a cataclysmic earthquake, family law in California changed overnight. A series of statewide task forces recommended that men and women seeking divorce should no longer be required to prove that their spouse was unfaithful, unfit, cruel, or incompatible. It was time, they said, to end the hypocrisy embodied in laws that severely restricted divorce. People should be able to end an unhappy marriage without proving fault or pointing blame.

The prevailing climate of opinion was that divorce would allow adults to make better choices and happier marriages by letting them undo earlier mistakes. They would arrive at an honest, mutual decision to divorce, because if one person wanted out, surely it could not be much of a marriage.

These attitudes were held by men and women of many political persuasions, by lawyers, judges, and mental health professionals alike. The final task force that formulated the new no-fault divorce laws was led by law professor Herma Kay, who was well known as an advocate for women's rights. In 1969, Governor Ronald Reagan signed the new law and people were jubilant. It was a time of hope and faith that greater choice would set men and women free and benefit their children. Within a few years, no-fault divorce laws spread like wildfire to all fifty states. People all across the country were in favor of change.[16]

"But," adds Wallerstein, whose groundbreaking work involved a twenty-five-year study of children of divorce, "what about the children? In our rush to improve the lives of adults, we assumed that their lives would improve as well. We made radical changes in the family without realizing how it would change the experience of growing up. We embarked on a gigantic social experiment without any idea about how the next generation would be affected."[17]

Why did Ronald Reagan, a champion of family values, sign the nation's first no-fault divorce bill into law? Years earlier he had been shattered when his first wife, actress Jane Wyman, filed for divorce. Although it was Reagan's growing anti-communist activities that alienated wife Jane—she complained in her divorce papers that "my husband and I engaged in continual arguments on his political views"[18]—she accused him of "mental cruelty," since divorce laws in the 1940s required a charge against the other spouse of adultery, extreme cruelty, willful desertion, willful neglect, habitual intemperance, felony conviction, or incurable insanity.

As son Michael Reagan later explained in his book *Twice Adopted*, "Even though listing grounds for divorce was largely a formality, those words were probably a bitter pill for him to swallow." In signing California's no-fault divorce law, observed Michael, "He wanted to do something to make the divorce process less acrimonious, less contentious and less expensive." But Reagan later regretted the decision as one of the worst he ever made, as divorce rates skyrocketed and divorce conflicts and legal costs remained "as ruinous as ever," Michael added.[19]

Looking back at America's decades-long divorce "experiment," Glenn Stanton, Focus on the Family's marriage expert, summed up its results. While adults suffered terribly, children "fared even worse," he noted. "Many saw the innocence of childhood evaporate the day their parents announced the divorce. Others described being 'scarred for life.' They told countless stories of being crippled by anxiety, possessed by anger, disoriented by confusion and immobilized by fear of total abandonment. Their behavior, grades and physical and mental health plummeted. They were different children. In fact, they didn't see themselves as children any longer. Divorce forced them to become adults, even before they became teens. We now know these children carry these problems cumulatively into adulthood."[20]

Contemplating the stupendous amount of pain, deprivation, and trauma we so jubilantly and foolishly invited into the national family a generation ago—during which time we overthrew most, if not all, of the rules we had lived by for centuries—we must ask ourselves: What happened to America during the 1960s? What *really* happened?

REVOLUTION

WHAT EXACTLY was this mass seduction we colorfully call "cultural revolution" that overtook America during that tumultuous period? It seems a combination of powerful factors—like planets that rarely align—all came together during that particular period and ushered in a transformation of the American mind.

One factor was the assassination of President John F. Kennedy. It was to the '60s generation what September 11, 2001, was to today's Americans—a national shock beyond all other national shocks. It signaled the end of America's innocence, of the '50s world of *Leave It to Beaver* and *Father Knows Best*. The handsome Camelot president—he and Jacqueline were the closest thing to royalty in modern America—had his brains blown out on national TV.

Like everyone else alive then, I remember where I was—in my eighth-grade science class. It was right after lunch, and the teacher walked into the classroom and said: "I suppose you've all heard Kennedy was shot." My first reaction was: *Kennedy? He must mean the boy in our class named Kennedy.* It didn't occur to me that it could be our president. Presidents weren't assassinated—just as married couples didn't get divorced. Assassinated presidents were people like Abraham Lincoln and James Garfield, but that kind of thing didn't happen in today's America.

Kennedy's assassination was a major psychic shock. And shock has a strange way of opening people up to new ideas—and not necessarily good ideas.

Then there was the Vietnam War. From an ideological point of view it was arguably one of America's most altruistic wars, as we were there to stop the spread of communism and had little to gain ourselves. But the war's actual execution by America's leaders was incompetent and disastrous, as Defense Secretary Robert McNamara later famously admitted. The nation was polarized and intensely emotionalized over the controversial war.

Powerful emotion also has a strange way of opening people up to new ideas.

Then there was the rock music invasion from England. What started with the Beatles, Rolling Stones, and other groups immediately exerted a powerful hold on America's youth and soon introduced and sugarcoated the psychedelic drug subculture—"Turn on, tune in, drop out"—which was, in turn, energized and unified by opposition to the Vietnam War.

A primary effect of mind-altering drugs is that they open people up to new ideas; maybe that's why they're called "mind-altering."

And then, most devastating of all, there was widespread confusion among America's churches and churchgoers over God. Remember *Time* magazine's 1966 "Is God Dead?" issue shockingly quoted top church leaders expressing anxiety and uncertainty over who God is or even *if* He is. With America's traditional Judeo-Christian beliefs and moral standards in doubt or disrepute, alien philosophies and beliefs readily flooded into the vacuum—paganism, occultism, channeling, and New Age practices of every conceivable sort.

Similarly, without a godly paradigm—whereby we comprehend that man's only true freedom is to be a servant of heaven rather than a slave of hell—our whole concept of freedom was transformed. This naturally opened America up to a torrent of "liberation" movements, from sexual liberation to women's liberation to "gay" liberation. In America's morally weakened and confused state, even the most radical and alien ideas exerted an immensely powerful influence on the national mind and mood.

As if all this wasn't enough, there was something else at play—something seldom mentioned in polite circles out of fear of ridicule. And that is the issue of communist influence. We didn't just get high on LSD and fall off the cliff during the 1960s. We were pushed.

Hard as it may be to believe today when communism has been so thoroughly discredited, back during the '30s, '40s, and '50s many people—including some well-known Americans—believed Marxism was a good thing. There was an ideological struggle going on in the world, and the seduction of secular socialism was in its heyday—including in the United States.

During this time the Soviet Union was engaged not only in its very public military and scientific buildup but also in massive espionage and infiltration. And, as the public record undeniably shows, the USSR had direct ties with the Communist Party USA (CPUSA).

The entertainment industry was one area targeted by the communists, which had been active in Hollywood since 1935. Headquartered in New York, the CPUSA had decided to wrest control of the entertainment industry—and therefore of what Americans would see in their movie theatres—by taking over Hollywood's labor unions.

"By the end of the Second World War, [communist] party membership in Hollywood was close to six hundred and boasted several industry heavyweights," revealed Peter Schweizer in his celebrated book, *Reagan's War.* "Actors Lloyd Bridges, Edward G. Robinson, and Fredric March were members, as were half a dozen producers and about as many directors." (Some, it should be noted, later renounced their Communist Party affiliation.)[21]

It was none other than Ronald Reagan who took the leading role in throttling this attempted communist takeover of Hollywood when, as head of the Screen Actors Guild, he very publicly and courageously opposed them. It marked Reagan's entry into the world of politics—and the anti-communist mission he would complete forty years later when, as president of the United States, he took the central role in engineering the end of what he himself had aptly called the "evil empire."

But back in the era immediately preceding the 1960s, there had been many communists infiltrating America's government and institutions. Without a doubt, America came under a direct revolutionary assault—pushed primarily by avowed leftists of every stripe—during the 1960s. Most U.S. college campuses were swept up in the revolutionary fervor, and leftist propaganda and agitation were everywhere. Believe me, I know—I was there.

When all these various national assaults and traumas hit the nation at once—an unpopular war, a presidential assassination, music and drug cultural invasion, a massive erosion of faith—the anti-America subversion that previously had existed below the surface of society seized the moment and burst out into open rebellion.

Looking back, one has to wonder just how successful the radical left was in subverting key American institutions, including government, education, entertainment, the press and the churches. It's hard to say for sure. But it's very sobering to realize that today America's colleges and universities are absurdly to the left of the mainstream. In fact, just about the only place in the world you can find real, bona fide Marxists any more is on U.S. college campuses, where they are insulated from reality as tenured professors. Same with radical feminists, who also tend to be socialists. The National Education Association, which "represents" America's public school teachers, is a leftist organization, as are the National Council of Churches and the World Council of Churches.

Oh, by the way, maybe it's just a coincidence, but guess what Lenin (Vladimir, not John) did right up front to facilitate the communist revolution? He broke up the family by instituting de facto no-fault divorce, as celebrated Soviet expert Mikhail Heller explained:

> It is significant to note that one of the first things V.I. Lenin did when he came to power in the Soviet Union, after the revolution in nineteen seventeen, was to have passed what amounts to our no-fault divorce statutes.
>
> Lenin, and later [Joseph] Stalin, determined that in order to maintain control of the people it would be necessary to completely destroy the family and restructure it.
>
> Thus, on September sixteen nineteen eighteen, a law was passed whereby one could obtain a divorce by simply mailing or delivering a postcard to the local register without the necessity of even notifying the spouse being divorced.
>
> This statute, along with the communist encouragement of sexual immorality during marriage, approval of abortion, and forcing women out of the home into the workforce, accomplished its purpose of destroying the Russian family.[22]

Unlike Lenin, who had guns, gulags, and thugs to enforce his will, America's revolutionaries, including the radical feminists, had no means of forcing their anti-marriage and other agendas on society other than the force of "moral persuasion"—or to put it more aptly, angry intimidation.

Unfortunately, people who aren't strong and sure of their beliefs simply cannot withstand the demands of unreasonable, angry intimidators. They give in, they compromise, and they even adopt the bully's views as their own—to keep the peace. And that's what happened in America.

Now that we've surveyed the sad road to family destruction we as a nation have merrily gone down, let's ask the obvious question: Is there a way back? The answer, of course, is yes. It's uphill all the way, but it's a glorious road. So let's start.

KNIGHTS AND LADIES

TO BEGIN with, we need to look at marriage with fresh eyes. We've heard innumerable slogans about the dynamic between men and women: "Men are from Mars, Women are from Venus." "The shortest books ever written are 'What Men Know About Women' and 'What Women Know About Men.'" "Sign above a saloon: 'Men are fools, and women are devils in disguise." Men and women, it seems, are inscrutable to each other.

Men, until they mature, have a fantasy of how they think women are, or how they *should* be, or how they would *like* them to be. Namely, they believe women were born to love and support insecure, egotistical males—mentally, emotionally, and sexually—and help them feel good about themselves, thus making them "whole." It's the subject of all popular songs from the beginning of time: "Baby I need you, I can't live without you. You make me feel like a king." But that—I hate to break it to you, guys—is *not* how women really are, or even are supposed to be. In fact, being pressured to play that ego-supporting role turns them into liars, full of inner conflict. And when those "male needs" extend to no-limit sexual demands, they turn women into acrobatic prostitutes.

Women, if they're still fairly innocent and uncorrupted, also have a notion of how men are, or at least how they are *supposed* to be, that's actually about right: men are supposed to be knights in shining armor. The problem is, men somehow have lost sight of this higher calling. And of course, when a woman sees her knight fail her in so many ways—and he truly cannot help it, at least in the beginning—she develops contempt and resentment toward him, which profoundly shapes both of their lives for the worse.

At the extreme edges of dysfunctionality, women can become so angry at the men who have failed them—whether fathers, husbands, boyfriends, or strangers—that they look to other women for companionship and love. Hence the major increase in lesbianism today, which is the not-too-well-hidden secret side of radical feminism. (Lesbians have long laid claim to being leaders of the feminist revolution.) How ironic that feminists, fueled by rage and an unconscious desire for revenge against the men who corrupted or failed to protect them, have dedicated their lives to denying other women and children the very happiness they themselves were denied.

In case you haven't realized it before, buried resentment toward those who have hurt us, if the emotion is sufficiently strong, inevitably ends up forming the basis of our thoughts, our feelings, our values—our very identity, who and what we think we are. A cruder way of saying that is that hatred makes us crazy. Maybe that's why we use the word *mad* to mean both "angry" and "insane."

If only we could rise above our anger and our ego and our favorite delusions and search with a sincere intent, we'd easily arrive at the real reason for marriage—the development of strong character, fulfillment of our highest potential, true happiness, and spiritual growth. In other words, all the things feminists led us to believe we would find by *abandoning* marriage.

Think back. Can you remember a time in your life when you used to think men should grow up to be knights in shining armor?

Take my young son Joshua, for example. What do you suppose he likes to watch on TV? Robin Hood, Zorro, Roy Rogers, the Lone Ranger—knights in shining armor all. (Joshua's homeschooled.) Movies? *Ben-Hur, Cromwell, The Ten Commandments, High Noon, El Cid, The Scarlet Pimpernel.* He loves the Jedi knights of Star Wars and the "fellowship" in *The Lord of the Rings.* These are all stories of brave knights. And by knights I don't mean just fighters, but fighters for what's right, possessing great character and nobility—confident, unselfish, mature, wise—faithful in word and deed to the last detail of life.

That's my son's programming, his ideal. That's your son's programming, too. I'm not saying my son acts that way all the time; I'm saying he is powerfully attracted to that way. And I didn't put this attraction in him, nor did it come from TV. It came from God. It's normal. Those classic shows he watches just nourish the inborn ideal that has fascinated generation upon generation of little boys.

The problem is, my son also has another side to him. Christianity calls it "original sin," an inborn nature that tends toward pride, selfishness, laziness, denial, self-gratification, and anger. So how does he—and how do all little boys—grow from the immature mix of latent nobility and compulsive selfishness into a true man? For most men, the answer is marriage.

Marriage comes complete with all the trials, tribulations, obstacle courses, tests, rewards, and consequences necessary to fulfill your highest potential as a human being—the challenge to serve a higher ideal than self. If you fail in that, marriage can crush you.

LOVE AND LUST

WHO REMEMBERS when little girls dreamed of falling in love with and marrying a knight in shining armor?

Oh, get real, you may be thinking. *There's no one like that—except in the movies.*

Let's adjust the zoom of our lens and take a closer look at marriage. Not the storybook, Hollywood fantasy version—but the real thing. Marriage is full of difficulty. And not just because any two people living and working together are going to have their differences and conflicts that need to be resolved. *Uh-uh.* Difficulty because, when you put a man and a woman together, that relationship can lead either to tremendous spiritual growth and fulfillment of their inborn potential, or it can lead to such conflict and hatred between them that they would rather die than be compelled to spend the rest of their lives with each other "in hell."

Truly, when they get married, most newlyweds have no idea what they're getting into. At first, they think their infatuation is love; it's not. Their think their physical and emotional need for each other is love; it's not. He thinks her enthusiasm to have sex is love: it's not. She thinks his giving in to her on every issue is love; it's not.

Fast-forward a few years. Most often children have come along—which logically should help cement the father and mother's relationship. Instead, in half of American marriages, what started as wedded bliss has turned inexorably into the nightmare of hatred and divorce. And of course, for every marriage that actually falls into the abyss, others are teetering on the brink.

So what happens in those few years? What turns heaven into hell? Can't men and women, dads and moms get along anymore? What is so bad, so intolerable, that they have to explode the relationship, break their solemn vows to God and to each other, and devastate their children?

To put it perhaps too plainly, there is something in a man's makeup that is capable of drawing the worst out of women. And there is something about a woman's makeup that is capable of drawing the worst out of men. This is a spiritual inheritance we all share, having roots deep and profound.

Thus, without also a shared love of truth to lead them both into the nobler realm of life, theirs will never be a "marriage made in heaven." And that, again, is the ultimate purpose of marriage—to lead us to a closer relationship with our Creator by developing within us the character traits that befit God's children.

For those sincere enough to embrace this challenge, marriage is *the* arena of life. The willingness to face one's own weaknesses and failings honestly, to suffer gracefully without becoming angry and resentful, to bear with patience the slings and arrows coming from the "crazy" side of your spouse—that's love, *real* love. And out of that slow growth of virtue comes, invisibly (no one else can see where your happiness comes from), the good life you've always wanted. Then come the green pastures, the still waters of marriage, the ever-deepening affection and concern for the other, the comfort of true companionship, the deep reservoir of strength sufficient to deal with any and all adversity—all of the transcendent joys of a long and fruitful life together.

But. Why does this ideal seem so foreign, so unreal?

Why do moral confusion, "me-me-me" instant gratification, cynicism and doubt about anything truly noble seem "real," while selflessness, true moral strength, real masculinity and real femininity seem to be unreal and old-fashioned?

Doesn't this old-fashioned ideal of noble knights and noble ladies have the aroma of a vivid dream you once had when you were young—as though maybe things actually *were* like this once upon a time, long, long ago? Then again, maybe it's not a chronological gulf between then and now. Perhaps instead it's another dimension called heaven on earth we vaguely "remember," the ever-present inner standard we've lost sight of, the higher calling that's gotten drowned out in the din of marketing messages.

Maybe what many of us think of as reality—you know, the pop boy-girl thing that ends in disgust, disillusion, and divorce—is just a "matrix," like in the blockbuster film of that name. And maybe, as in the movie, we need to pull the plug on the comforting but anesthetizing fantasy and face reality—even if it's unpleasant to begin with.

UNTIL DEATH DO US PART

MARRIAGE IS indeed a divine institution—something created by and provided for by God. Not only for the propagation of the species, but so that men and women could discover what real love is—not just the love that brings children into the world, but the love that enables us to experience betrayal and yet not hate, the love that learns to forgive, that learns to be strong and to stand up for what's right, that learns to delay gratification—in other words, the love that makes us fully human.

Therefore, without the matrimonial promise made before God and man to stay together forever—without a lifelong *commitment* inoculating them against hard times—the trials, difficulties, and pain of marriage and raising a family would be too much for many people to handle.

So now, considering this man and woman coming to a committed marriage with different backgrounds, baggage, and problems, and with their imperfect, incomplete natures crying out for all the wrong kind of love from each other, what enables them ultimately to triumph—to have a truly happy long-term marriage and family? One thing only. Both of their lives must revolve around a love of truth. If they have that, they both have the same spiritual father, they're members of the same spiritual family.

They have a shared standard by which to resolve differences. All disagreements ultimately find resolution—not because one knuckles under to the other, the submissive to the dominant, but because they both have placed God's will at the center of the lives, the center of their family. The wife is not threatened by her husband's being the ultimate and natural authority in the family, because she trusts him and his judgment. Nor, however, is the husband threatened by submitting to his wife's guidance when he sees she is clearly right.

I'm talking about a shared, deep understanding of life, obtained by honestly confronting our imperfections, standing up to our own lower nature (instead of running away into denial, distraction, and pleasure), facing up to each painful reality as it presents itself in marriage and in life. This is reality—full-bore and in Technicolor. This is not a matter of rigid dogma but rather the moment-to-moment presence of the Living God shining into our lives and our relationships. Any less than that, and we're failing. This is why God ordained marriage—so we could find Him.

"LET NO MAN PUT ASUNDER"

WHEN A man and woman are married—one of the most joyful days of their lives—the officiating minister traditionally seals the wedding ceremony by warning the rest of the world to keep their hands off: "Those whom God hath joined together let no man put asunder." Yet no-fault divorce laws, which by making divorce so easy have deprived couples of much-need protection of their marriages during periods of conflict and anger, represent an unimaginably broad and destructive policy of government "putting asunder" those whom God joined in *holy* matrimony. So while men and women need to approach marriage with a mature, spiritual paradigm such as we've discussed, it's also critical that the government wake up and learn from the sad legacy of its no-fault divorce laws: a generation of broken homes, broken promises, broken spirits.

Marriage is too important, too wonderful, and too challenging to have the odds stacked against it due to shortsighted and pernicious easy-divorce laws. Enlightened legislators and other leaders must revisit and refashion divorce laws so they serve to preserve marriages, not dissolve them. We must once again realize that marriage really is meant to be forever.

By the way, one last note about my grandfather, Paul M. Paulson. He was an uneducated man, a poor tailor who immigrated to America for a better life, and who barely knew his arranged bride on his wedding day. But decades later he would credit the success of his marriage to "seeking constant guidance from above, because we both love God and assume woman is a gift of God [to man]—the most important gift after God's Son." Grandpop believed that if couples felt this way, they would regard each other with sufficient love, respect, and determination to make any sacrifice necessary to preserve the marriage partnership. His favorite Bible verse? "And above all things have fervent charity among yourselves: for charity shall cover the multitude of sins" (1 Peter 4:8).

Another "poor tailor"—Motel (pronounced "Mottle"), the tailor in *Fiddler on the Roof*—immortalized these same sentiments in song when the reluctant patriarch Tevye finally agreed to let Motel marry his first-born daughter, Tzeitel.

"Wonder of wonders," exclaimed the poor tailor, describing how God had taken him "by the hand" and led him to his heart's desire. Affirming that the Almighty is indeed a Maker of miracles, Motel recounted miracle after biblical miracle, from the supernatural provision of "manna in the wilderness" to David's victory over Goliath.

Yet, he concluded in the beloved song, of all God's dramatic, magical and impossible miracles, the greatest miracle of all "is the one I thought could never be: God has given you to me."[23]

6

OBSESSED WITH SEX

How Fraudulent Science Unleashed a
Catastrophic "Revolution"

W EEEEEEEEEEEEE ARE THE chaaam-pions, mah frehhhhh-und . . ."

To triumphant strains of the Queen rock anthem, the paunchy, middle-aged male actor is jumping up and down in an ecstatic victory ritual—in slow motion yet, to immortalize the transcendent moment—delirious over his newfound sexual potency thanks to Viagra.

"Oh no, not on Fox News?!" *Click.* "Let's see what else is on."

A middle-aged man and woman, presumably naked, reposing in his and hers bathtubs on a mountain bluff, are cozying up to each other to the tender strains of jazz guitar music while the announcer poses the towering question of our age: "When the moment is right, will you be ready?" For Eli Lilly and Company the moment was right during the third quarter of the Super Bowl, when the drug manufacturer paid more than four million dollars to subject ninety million unsuspecting fans to this sixty-second Cialis commercial. (Serendipitously, just a few minutes earlier pop singer Janet Jackson had warmed up the viewers by baring her breast during her strategically naughty halftime show.)

In the fierce battle for market share in what Wall Street analysts project will be a six-billion-dollar-a-year market by 2010, Lilly spent more than one hundred million dollars launching its competitor to Pfizer's Viagra, the market leader. To further penetrate the mass mind, Cialis's marketers even met with sitcom writers and Broadway producers to induce them to incorporate the sexual-potency drug into their scripts.

Click.

An attractive brunette talking directly to the camera asks viewers if they "want to know a secret?" In this racier and more aggressive TV commercial than those of Viagra and Cialis, market underdog Levitra, made by GlaxoSmithKline, presents prime-time viewers—including millions of innocent children—with a sultry seductress reveling in how the drug's effectiveness has increased her partner's desire to "do this more often."

"For him, Levitra works," she coos. "Just look at that smile."

Click, TV off. And all across the nation, from sea to shining sea, children look up at their parents and ask, "Daddy, what's 'an erection that lasts longer than four hours'?"

Such ads are inundating not just TV, but radio, the Internet, newspapers, magazines, and mailboxes nationwide. They've become part of today's "mainstream" cultural landscape, along with *Cosmopolitan* and clones with their "Hot Sex Tips" and in-your-face cleavage screaming from every grocery checkout in the country, not to mention ever-more-explicit TV and movie fare, ubiquitous spam e-mail messages hawking supplements to enlarge one's private parts, salacious condom demonstrations in public school classrooms, Howard Stern, MTV, swimsuits, the fashion industry, cars, children's toys. You name it, and it's been sexualized.

And that's just what's on the surface—the still-"civilized" world of titillation, temptation, and tease—readily visible to all who turn on the television or drive down the street. But scratch just a fraction of an inch beneath that veneer of civilization, and you'll leave the world of entertainment and marketing and enter the world of hardcore sex, perversion, crime, and self-destruction.

SECRET OBSESSION

FIRST, THERE'S the multi-billion-dollar pornography industry, which through the Internet is magically being transported into previously unreachable market territory—namely, the sanctity of millions of middle-class homes. By all accounts, Internet pornography has become a genuine national epidemic, ensnaring millions of people who never had a pornography problem before. Online porn is immediately accessible, almost totally anonymous, inexpensive (or free), and highly addictive. Indeed, it has been called "the crack cocaine of pornography."

According to Internet Filter Review, which analyzes and rates Web content filters, revenues from pornography exceed those of all professional football, baseball, and basketball franchises combined. There are 4.2 million pornographic Web sites—that's 12 percent of all Web sites in the world, totaling 372 million pornographic pages. Pornographic search engine requests total 68 million per day.

Exactly how damaging is pornography? After all, some "scientific studies"—mostly from Scandinavia, of course—claim pornography can actually be beneficial. Not quite. As scientist and adjunct law professor of bioethics Kelly Hollowell points out:

> Studies reveal that acts of sexual violence are commonly linked to pornography and the numbers of victims are massive. According to sworn testimony before the U.S. Senate, experts reveal that by the time a female in this country is 18 years old, 38 percent have been sexually molested. One in eight women will be raped. Fifty percent of women will be sexually harassed on their jobs during their lifetimes. In fact, sexual dysfunction is on such a rampant rise that experts are calling it more than an epidemic. They are calling it a sexual holocaust.[1]

Just hours before he was executed on January 24, 1989, notorious serial killer Ted Bundy was interviewed by Focus on the Family chief Dr. James Dobson, a clinical psychologist. Bundy movingly revealed how pornography had fueled his inner thought world and later his murderous rampages, and he also confirmed the central role porn played in the lives of virtually all the other violent offenders with whom he was incarcerated.

Chillingly, Hollowell disclosed, "When one study group was exposed to as little as five hours of non-violent pornography, they began to think pornography was not offensive and that rapists deserved milder punishments. They also became more callous and negative toward women and developed an appetite for more deviant or violent types of pornography."

Driving it all, of course, is money. Pornography is a lucrative business. As PBS reported in its *Frontline* documentary titled "American Porn," many U.S. companies have profited handsomely from peddling smut. The Marriott, Westin, and Hilton hotel chains, for instance, have enjoyed a nice income stream from making X-rated fare available in their hotel rooms. Many other megacorporations including AT&T, News Corporation, and Yahoo! have earned big bucks over the years from their involvement in cable and Internet distribution of "adult entertainment."[2]

But pornography is just the fuel. A quick survey of the sexual fires now blazing is even more disturbing:

• There is a youthful epidemic of "hooking up"—widespread, casual, recreational sex, often with multiple partners. Turbocharged by President Clinton and Monica Lewinsky's high-profile example—"If it's okay for the president, it must be okay for me"—middle- and high-school children are experimenting with sex in the bathroom stalls at school, behind the gym, and in the back of the school bus. More children, at earlier ages, are engaging in sexual acts than ever before. Often the only way parents and school authorities find out is when confronted by an epidemic of sexually transmitted disease infecting large numbers of kids in the same social group.

• Homosexual sex, a generation ago, was widely considered both immoral and pathological. Today it's enshrined as a constitutional right and the hallmark of a new "protected class." Government schools nationwide teach children as young as five that homosexuality is normal and that disagreeing with this viewpoint brands you as an intolerant "hater." The popular culture *always* portrays homosexuals sympathetically and often as heroes. America's bedrock institutions—from its legal system to the news media, from its schools to its churches—are rapidly reversing millennia of traditional values on homosexuality.

• One by one, the time-honored sexual taboos of Western civilization are crashing down with dizzying speed. When the Supreme Court, in its controversial 2003 *Lawrence v. Texas* decision, struck down that state's anti-sodomy statute, the court opened the legal floodgates not only to homosexual marriage but potentially to the total legitimization of *all* "consensual" sex acts, including polygamy and adult incest. Indeed, polygamists have jumped onto the *Lawrence* bandwagon and are pushing to have marriage with multiple partners legalized in the United

States. After all, they argue, their relationships are consensual and they are adults—so what's the problem?

• Sexual slavery is no longer confined to the Far East, Australia, and other exotic locales. Statistics vary widely, but somewhere between twenty thousand to fifty thousand women and children are trafficked each year into the United States, primarily from Latin America, countries of the former Soviet Union, and Southeast Asia, for exploitation in prostitution and the "sex industry."

• Believe it or not, even child sexual abuse, rape, and incest (which its apologists euphemistically now call "adult-child sex" and "intergenerational sex") are slowly but surely gaining respectability. As far back as 1999 the American Psychological Association, which claims to be the largest association of psychologists worldwide with more than 150,000 members, published in its peer-reviewed journal, *APA Bulletin,* a report disputing the harmfulness of child molestation. Titled "A Meta-Analytic Examination of Assumed Properties of Child Sexual Abuse Using College Samples," the report by Bruce Rind et al. claimed child sexual abuse could be harmless and beneficial.[3]

Many people seem to think having sex with children is a good thing, as one hundred thousand Web sites now offer illegal child pornography, according to Internet Filter Review. Worldwide, child porn generates three billion dollars in revenues every year. And culturally, "adult-child" sexuality is creeping, ever so artfully and gradually, into the public consciousness.

For instance, in the 2004 movie *Birth,* Academy Award–winner Nicole Kidman plays Anna, a young widow who thinks her deceased husband has been reincarnated—into the body of a ten-year-old boy. Thus one scene depicts Kidman tenderly kissing the boy on the lips. Another scene has her asking the boy—played by eleven-year-old Cameron Bright—if he has ever had sex. In still another scene—which elicited boos from the audience when the film was first screened at the Venice International Film Festival—the boy slowly undresses in front of Kidman before joining her in the bathtub.

"The film disturbs some people and it makes them uncomfortable," Kidman admitted in a Hollywood interview, according to the *New York*

Post. "It's meant to do that, but not in a way where you're trying to exploit a young boy."[4]

Well now, what an ingenious way to justify intimacy between an adult female and a male child. The little boy is not your normal kid, you see, but actually the reincarnation of the woman's grown husband. We, the audience, "understand" her behavior since she's not actually seducing a little boy but rather just being intimate with her "husband." In reality of course, she's sexually corrupting a child in front of millions of viewers.

How on earth did America get to this point where we're literally drowning in sex and corrupting each other right and left? How can we return to a more innocent time, to a culture of morality and of real respect between men and women? Is it even possible?

Maybe the first question we have to answer is: Exactly how and when did we "buy into" wanton sexual anarchy disguised as freedom?

OZZIE, HARRIET . . . AND KINSEY

LET'S TURN the clock back a few decades—before the days of the Internet and instant, anonymous and free online porn. Back before the 1990s with Bill and Monica, before the 1980s with its major growth in sex education and birth-control clinics in government schools. Back before the high point of the sexual revolution—the 1973 *Roe v. Wade* abortion decision. Back even before the tumultuous 1960s and its "make love, not war" and "sex, drugs, and rock 'n' roll" youth counterculture. Let's go back to the era most Americans still remember fondly as the golden age of traditional values and national sanity—the 1950s.

Divorce was rare, abortion and homosexuality were "in the closet" and out of view of polite society. It was the age of *Ozzie and Harriet, Father Knows Best,* and *Leave It to Beaver.* Classics like *Ben-Hur* and *High Noon* were box-office favorites, and C. S. Lewis was publishing his beloved adventure book series, the Chronicles of Narnia.

It was a more innocent and naïve time than now. We were at peace. John F. Kennedy hadn't been assassinated. Americans trusted their government, schools, and news media. They bought whatever caught their fancy at the supermarket without reading the labels—it was before the era of *caveat emptor* ("buyer beware"). We'll stop our time machine at the very beginning of this era—around the start of the baby boomer generation—in 1948, a pivotal year.

Harry S. Truman was president of a nation greatly relieved to be home from war. Traditional values were intact, and hope for a prosperous and peaceful future was everywhere in the air.

Then, on January 5, 1948, a bomb was dropped on America. Indiana University zoologist Alfred C. Kinsey released the book *Sexual Behavior in the Human Male*. Today, more than five decades later, Kinsey is universally referred to as the "father of the sexual revolution."

The respected National Research Council says the science of sex "can be divided somewhat crudely into the pre-Kinsey and post-Kinsey eras." Scott McLemee in *Salon* writes, "The history of sex in America falls into two large, unequal, yet clearly defined periods. The first era belonged to the Puritans, the Victorians. . . . This epoch of libidinal prohibition lasted until Jan. 4, 1948. The following day, Professor Alfred C. Kinsey of Indiana published 'Sexual Behavior in the Human Male.' Whereupon, as the expression has it, the earth moved."[5]

What, exactly, did Kinsey's research reveal?

Funded by the prestigious Rockefeller Foundation and based on thousands of interviews, Kinsey had "discovered" that while American men of the World War II "greatest generation" pretended to be faithful and monogamous, virtually all of them—95 percent—were, according to 1948 law, sex offenders. Specifically, Kinsey claimed that 85 percent of males had intercourse prior to marriage, nearly 70 percent had sex with prostitutes, and 30–45 percent of husbands had extramarital affairs. Moreover, from 10 to 37 percent of men had engaged in homosexual acts, according to Kinsey. In fact, the oft-repeated claim that one in ten human beings is homosexual—a cornerstone of the "gay rights" movement until it was debunked—came directly from Kinsey's published research.[6] In endless and graphic detail, Kinsey painted a picture of Americans as being amoral sexual animals in search of constant gratification.

If Kinsey had discovered the cure for all diseases, his press coverage could not have been more extensive or enthusiastic. *Time, Life, Look,* and most of the rest of the mainstream press reported that Kinsey—whom they portrayed as a conservative Republican academic and devoted family man—had conducted the most exhaustive scientific survey ever of Americans' sexual habits. The previously unknown zoologist—whose only prior claim to fame had been his comprehensive and painstaking research into the gall wasp—was catapulted overnight to the status of national hero, in keeping with Americans' postwar near-worship of science.

The revolutionary *Kinsey Reports*, as they came to be known—including his companion volume released in 1953, *Sexual Behavior in the Human Female*—rocked the nation's beliefs about itself. But perhaps most shocking of all were his "findings" on childhood sexuality. The *Kinsey Reports* came to the stunning conclusion that children are sexual from birth, and that youngsters as young as a few months of age have the capacity for a pleasurable and healthy sexual life.

Despite the radical nature of Kinsey's findings, he was honored as a heroic scientific pioneer, pushing back the dark boundaries of ignorance and delivering new knowledge that would guide America in a brave, new world of sexual enlightenment. That is, until 1981, when a sole researcher—a Ph.D. and scholar named Judith Reisman—came along and raised the question of "Table 34."

Toddler Sex

WARNING: The next section is extremely disturbing and involves graphic descriptions of child sexual abuse on which Kinsey admittedly relied in tabulating his "data" on childhood sexuality.

TABLE 34 in Kinsey's first report purports to be a scientific record of "multiple orgasm in pre-adolescent males." Reisman wondered: How did Kinsey and his associates obtain this "research" that infants as young as five months of age enjoyed sex? Child sexual abuse is a felony—how could such research be conducted legally? Why had nobody raised this issue before?

Get ready for a shock. According to Reisman, whose heartbreaking findings were corroborated subsequently by other researchers:

Kinsey solicited and encouraged pedophiles, at home and abroad, to sexually violate from 317 to 2,035 infants and children for his alleged data on normal "child sexuality." Many of the crimes against children (oral and anal sodomy, genital intercourse and manual abuse) committed for Kinsey's research are quantified in his own graphs and charts.

For example, "Table 34" on page 180 of Kinsey's "Sexual Behavior in the Human Male" claims to be a "scientific" record of "multiple orgasm in pre-adolescent males." Here, infants as young as five months were timed with a stopwatch for "orgasm" by Kinsey's "technically trained" aides, with one four-year-old tested 24 consecutive hours for an alleged 26 "orgasms." Sex educators, pedophiles and their advocates commonly quote these child "data" to prove children's need for homosexual, heterosexual and bisexual satisfaction via "safe-sex" education. These data are also regularly used to "prove" children are sexual from birth.[7]

Whoa! Wait a minute. This seems too horrible to be true. You're got to be thinking, *Why haven't I heard about this before? If this actually happened, Kinsey would have been arrested and locked up. This must be some hysterical anti-sex researcher jumping to conclusions.*

Sorry. For the sake of the children "experimented" upon, one wishes that were true. But Reisman is a world-renowned expert and scholar on this subject, has been a consultant to four U.S. Department of Justice administrations, the Department of Education, and the Department of Health and Human Services, and is sought worldwide to lecture, testify, and counsel regarding fraudulent sex science. She is speaking the awful truth here.

Reisman reveals that in *Sexual Behavior in the Human Male,*

Kinsey defined children's torment ("screaming," "writhing in pain," "fainting," "convulsions") as "orgasms" for infants too young to speak. Who sexually tested these children? Where were the parents? Among thousands of international reviews of the Kinsey reports, no one asked these questions of the man who, as Gore Vidal declared, was "the most famous man for a decade," and who is the one man the homosexual and pedophile movements today thank most for their advances.[8]

Before we answer these questions, you need to know a little more about Kinsey. Indiana University portrayed Kinsey as a conservative Republican and family man, and the press totally and uncritically bought into this image. "An article in McCall's," writes Salon's McLemee, "assured its readers that 'Yes, There Is a Mrs. Kinsey.'"

The wife of the scientific pioneer had "a wholesome, girlish air." Being married to "Prok" (as she affectionately called Prof. K) meant sacrifice, including quite a bit of loneliness, for her husband kept a busy schedule. He was determined to collect 100,000 interviews. Even so, they led a homey enough private life. Mrs. Kinsey made clothes for their children. There was a photograph of the professor's daily bag lunch. Returning from the lab, he enjoyed "persimmon pudding, highly spiced and topped with whipped cream." His research might be controversial, but Kinsey himself was an old-fashioned guy.[9]

Well, not quite so old-fashioned.

First there were rumors that Kinsey had interviewed a lot of prisoners and sex-offenders, casting doubt on the integrity of his population sample. Then there were whispers about his own unorthodox sexual practices and obsessions. But never did these untidy personal foibles seem sufficient to undermine the vaunted reputation of Kinsey's research—or its radical conclusions.

PSYCHOPATH

ALFRED C. KINSEY—the universally proclaimed "father of the sexual revolution," the supposedly conservative family man, the objective scientific researcher and amiable academic—was a sexual psychopath. Summarizing *Alfred C. Kinsey: A Public/Private Life,* the 1997 biography of the scientist by pro-Kinsey author James H. Jones, Salon's McLemee writes:

> He did date a woman, once, and very shortly thereafter asked her to marry him, which she did. Consummation was delayed for quite a while, because of their mutual ignorance of the mechanics involved. At some point in adolescence, Kinsey developed a taste for masochistic practices of a really cringe-inducing variety. (Two words here, and then I'm changing the subject: "urethral insertion.") He also had some pronounced voyeuristic and exhibitionistic tendencies. On bug-hunting field trips in the 1930s, he liked to march around the camp in his birthday suit, and he interrogated his assistants about masturbation. That his career was not destroyed by such behavior is, in itself, pretty remarkable.[10]

As Jones, Kinsey's key biographer, tells it: "On one occasion when his inner demons plunged him to new depths of despair, Kinsey climbed into a bathtub, unfolded the blade of his pocketknife, and circumcised himself without the benefit of anesthesia." But Jonathan Gathorne-Hardy, who published another Kinsey biography, *Sex, the Measure of All Things: A Life of Alfred C. Kinsey* in 1998, said the scientist's gruesome self-circumcision was part of his ongoing exploration of the relationship between pain and sexual pleasure. Ah, always the diligent scientist.

Reisman adds: "An early adherent and advocate of masturbation, Kinsey suffered an untimely death due, at least in part, to 'orchitis,' a lethal infection in his testicles that followed years of sadistic, orgiastic 'self-abuse.' Kinsey's obsessive, brutally masochistic masturbation methods appear to have assisted in his early demise."[11]

And Caleb Crain, reviewing the 2004 Hollywood film, *Kinsey*—created to whitewash and popularize the father of the sexual revolution—wrote in the *New York Times:*

> Mr. Jones's book revealed that Kinsey had had affairs with men, encouraged open marriages among his staff, stimulated himself with urethral insertion and ropes, and filmed sex in his attic. But Mr. Jones did not feel he was debunking Kinsey. "What I told myself, and I still think this, was that I was writing a biography of a tragic hero," he says. "It shouldn't surprise us that pleas for sexual tolerance would come from a person who couldn't be himself in public."[12]

"Both of Kinsey's most recent admiring biographers," summarizes Reisman, somewhat less euphemistically, "confessed he was a sadistic bi/homosexual, who seduced his male students and coerced his wife, his staff and the staff's wives to perform for and with him in illegal pornographic films made in the family attic. Kinsey and his mates, Wardell Pomeroy, Clyde Martin and Paul Gebhard, had 'front' marriages that concealed their strategies to supplant what they saw as a narrow procreational Judeo-Christian era with a promiscuous 'anything goes' bi/gay pedophile paradise."[13]

"Okay," you're saying, "Okay. So he was a sexual nutcase. But wasn't his research still solid?"

Uh, no. Kinsey's "research" team, reveals Reisman:

1) "forced" subjects to give the desired answers to their sex questions, 2) secretly trashed three quarters of their research data, and 3) based their claims about normal males on a roughly 86 percent aberrant male population including 200 sexual psychopaths, 1,400 sex offenders and hundreds each of prisoners, male prostitutes and promiscuous homosexuals. Moreover, so few normal women would talk to them that the Kinsey team labeled women who lived over a year with a man "married," reclassifying data on prostitutes and other unconventional women as "Susie Homemaker."[14]

By now, you may have been wondering just how today's Kinsey Institute at Indiana University explains things like Table 34 with its "data" derived from the criminal sexual abuse of hundreds of infants and children. Here's how the official Kinsey Web site answers this seemingly unanswerable question:

"WHERE DID THE CHILDHOOD SEXUAL DATA COME FROM?"

Reports of childhood sexual behavior were mostly from interviews of adults recalling their early experiences. Parents and teachers were also asked if they had noticed sexual reactions in their children, and some children were interviewed in the presence of a parent or teacher. Among more than 5,000 men interviewed for "Sexual Behavior in the Human Male," there were 9 who reported having had sexual relations with children. One in particular, with an extensive sexual history, is the source of the childhood response tables in the Male book. Dr. Kinsey and his staff never conducted experiments with children.[15]

Although Kinsey claimed the child-sexuality information came from multiple sources, in 1995 then-Kinsey Institute director John Bancroft insisted it all came from serial pedophile Rex King, speculating that Kinsey might have "invented" the other purported sources for his child sexual response data as a way of protecting King.

In fact, not only did Kinsey use data from Rex King—whom Kinsey encouraged, in writing, to continue with his "research"—but also from

Nazi criminal Fritz von Balluseck, who was arrested and investigated for the murder of a ten-year-old girl and ultimately convicted of sexual abuse of up to two hundred children. As a *Times* of London story notes, Kinsey and von Balluseck corresponded, with Kinsey once warning the Nazi pedophile to "watch out" so as to avoid being caught.

Today, writes Crain in the *New York Times*, as a matter of policy "the institute will not—to the frustration of defenders and accusers alike—answer questions about King, Balluseck or anyone else who may have confided in Kinsey."[16]

Obligated to deal in some way with Kinsey's cozy relationship with child molesters, the *Kinsey* feature film includes a brief scene depicting Kinsey's June 1944 meeting with the sixty-three-year-old King, whose diaries included meticulous notations of sexual encounters with boys. What isn't shown in the film, however, is the letter Kinsey sent King urging him to send the diaries. According to Kinsey biographer Jones, on November 24, 1944, Kinsey wrote to King: "I rejoice at everything you send, for I am then assured that much more of your material is saved for scientific publication."

Rejoice at the sexual torture of hundreds of innocent children?

The North American Man-Boy Love Association (NAMBLA), the world's largest pedophile group, credits Kinsey to this day as its scientific standard bearer. "Gay liberationists in general, and boy-lovers in particular, should know Kinsey's work and hold it dear," says one NAMBLA publication. "Implicit in Kinsey is the struggle we fight today."[17]

So the "heroic scientist"—whose "research" launched the sexual revolution and provides the "scientific" basis for it to the current day—was actually a sexually depraved human being who "rejoiced" at pedophiles' conducting horrifying, Joseph Mengele–like sexual experiments on hundreds of children.

WHY NO MASS OUTCRY?

"BUT," YOU say, "something still stinks here. If all this is really true, how come Kinsey hasn't been more widely discredited? Why has Hollywood made a feature movie glorifying him?"

To be sure, after almost a quarter century of Reisman's tireless whistleblowing research, her discoveries about Kinsey have been corroborated and augmented by others. In fact, in April 2004, with Reisman's help as science adviser, the American Legislative Exchange Council (ALEC), an organization of twenty-four hundred state legislators, issued a "State Factor" report titled "Restoring Legal Protections for Women and Children: A Historical Analysis of the States' Criminal Codes." The number-one focus of this in-depth report was the fraudulent "junk science" of Alfred Kinsey.

But when it comes to America's culture, laws, beliefs, and attitudes regarding sex, Kinsey is still king—revered to this day by the vast majority of academics and "experts." Why?

In his book *Libido Dominandi: Sexual Liberation and Political Control*, E. Michael Jones sheds some light on why Reisman's research—even that exposing mass sexual torture and experimentation on young children in the name of science—has met with such a tepid response. He writes:

> On July 23, 1981, Reisman delivered a paper entitled, "The Scientist as a Contributing Agent to Child Sexual Abuse: A Preliminary Study," in which she brought up for the first time in the 32 years since it had been published, the material on child sexuality in Tables 30–34 of the Kinsey Male volume and wondered how this data could have been obtained without involvement in criminal activity. Before giving her report, Reisman had written to Male volume co-author Paul Gebhard to ask about the data in Tables 30–34. Gebhard wrote back saying that the data had been obtained from parents, school teachers, and some male homosexuals, including "some of Kinsey's men" who had used "manual and oral techniques" to catalogue the number of orgasms they said they could stimulate in infants and children. Virtually the entire sex industry/sex research establishment worldwide was in attendance at the meeting in Jerusalem, but the reaction to the talk was silence, stunned or sullen or otherwise, until a Swedish reporter wondered out loud why the assembled experts had nothing to say.
>
> The silence was understandable. Just about everyone in attendance had cited Kinsey as their mentor, and some even knew about the criminal activity involved in Kinsey's research. They all knew that Kinsey's research was the basis of their "science," which is to say, the legitimizing basis for everything they did. Kinsey was the foundation of that house of cards. If what he had done could be discredited, it threatened the sexual empire

that had been built since his death and upon which they all depended for a livelihood."[18]

"Sexual empire" is right. Indeed, Reisman documents Kinsey as the inspiration and mentor for two men who carried forward the torch of sexual liberation: Hugh Hefner and Harry Hay.

In high school, Hefner had written an essay bemoaning the lack of explicit discussion of sex in 1950s *Ozzie and Harriet* America. A few years later he read Kinsey's *Sexual Behavior in the Human Male* and praised it in his college newspaper. Fortified, liberated, and energized by Kinsey's newly discovered "scientific truth" about human sexuality, Hefner didn't wait long before creating *Playboy* magazine, the clubs, and most of all, the "Playboy philosophy" that has so profoundly influenced the American psyche.

When Harry Hay, who was sexually molested as a fourteen-year-old boy, read Kinsey's claim that 10 to 37 percent of men have had homosexual experiences, he left his wife and children and began the campaign to legitimize sodomy. He formed the Mattachine Society, urging that homosexuals be regarded as a 10 percent minority class. Hay was the father of the modern "gay rights" revolution that began in the 1960s.

. To this day, Kinsey is still the gold standard in sex research. In fact, in the more than two decades since she first exposed the Kinsey fraud in 1981, Reisman notes that the comprehensive Westlaw electronic legal database has cited Kinsey positively around 650 times—"on issues from hate crimes and homosexual marriage to child custody and rape." And the Social Science and Science Citation Indices, she adds, "reference Kinsey roughly 6,000 times over this same period. On the evidence, Kinsey is far and away the most influential sex scientist in the law. Fully 100 percent of the sex science citations in the original 1955 American Law Institute's 'Model Penal Code' cite Kinsey's bogus data on 'normal sexuality'—alive today in courts and legislatures."

Changing America's sex laws was exactly what Kinsey had intended, as biographer Jones revealed in 1997:

The man I came to know bore no resemblance to the canonical Kinsey. Anything but disinterested, he approached his work with missionary fervor. . . . He wanted to undermine traditional morality, to soften the rules of restraint. . . . Kinsey was a crypto-reformer who spent his every waking hour attempting to change the sexual mores and sex offender laws of the United States.[19]

To sum it up, today virtually everything having to do with sex—from attitudes toward extramarital affairs and homosexuality to the nation's sex-education curricula, to the ways medicine, psychiatry, psychology, and even the criminal justice system define and deal with sexual pathology—is rooted firmly in the ludicrously fraudulent "data" of Kinsey and his cult of criminally deviant sex "researchers."

WAR ZONE

TIME OUT. Take a breath. It's time to pause and look deeper, beyond all the horror and depravity of Kinsey, even beyond the malignant "sexual revolution" that has metastasized throughout the West in the last half century. It's time to simply ask ourselves honestly why we ever bought into the big lie of sexual freedom.

Could it be, when all is said and done, that we believed it because we wanted to believe it? That this fascinating new scientific "truth," which seemed to bless and sanctify our darkest sexual tendencies, was too much to resist?

Sex has always been a war zone. Sexual purity—living within certain behavioral confines deemed wholesome and moral, even if it means denying or delaying gratification of one's own powerful drives—has always been a major dividing line between those attempting to obey God's laws and those rebelling against them (or denying they exist).

This chasm between Judeo-Christian sexual morality and, basically, the rest of the world becomes stunningly clear in Dennis Prager's award-winning essay, "Judaism, Homosexuality and Civilization":

When Judaism demanded that all sexual activity be channeled into marriage, it changed the world.

It is not overstated to say that the Torah's prohibition of non-marital sex made the creation of Western civilization possible. Societies that did not place boundaries around sexuality were stymied in their development. The subsequent dominance of the Western world can largely be attributed to the sexual revolution initiated by Judaism, and later carried forward by Christianity.

The revolution consisted of forcing the sexual genie into the marital bottle. It ensured that sex no longer dominated society, heightened male-female love and sexuality (and thereby almost alone created the possibility of love and eroticism within marriage), and began the arduous task of elevating the status of women.

By contrast, throughout the ancient world, and up to the recent past in many parts of the world, sexuality infused virtually all of society.

Human sexuality, especially male sexuality, is utterly wild. Men have had sex with women and with men; with little girls and young boys; with a single partner and in large groups; with total strangers and immediate family members; and with a variety of domesticated animals. There is little, animate or inanimate, that has not excited some men sexually.

Among the consequences of the unchanneled sex drive is the sexualization of everything—including religion. Unless the sex drive is appropriately harnessed (not squelched—which leads to its own destructive consequences), higher religion could not have developed.

Thus, the first thing Judaism did was to de-sexualize God—"In the beginning God created the heavens and the earth" by His will, not through any sexual behavior. This broke with all other religions, and it alone changed human history.[20]

Prager goes on to catalog the various gods of the ancient world, showing that virtually all of them were depicted as engaging in sexual relations. Thus, "given the sexual activity of the gods, it is not surprising that the religions themselves were replete with all forms of sexual activity," he explains, citing numerous examples of ancient and even more recent religious traditions that included "sacred" ceremonial sex of various sorts and ritual prostitution within religious sanctuaries, such as sex between Hindu monks and nuns and even sex with children.

Judaism placed controls on sexual activity. It could no longer dominate religion and social life. It was to be sanctified—which in Hebrew means "separated"—from the world and placed in the home, in the bed of husband and wife. Judaism's restricting of sexual behavior was one of the essential elements that enabled society to progress.

Along with ethical monotheism, the revolution begun by the Torah when it declared war on the sexual practices of the world wrought the most far-reaching changes in history.[21]

Clearly the spiritual view of sex—particularly the Judeo-Christian view—is radically different from the mechanistic, secular, or pagan view of sex. Kinsey epitomized the latter. Like the socialists, progressives, Darwinists, atheists, humanists, and assorted other God-deniers that paved the way for him, Kinsey regarded man as an animal—and *only* an animal.

Remember, Kinsey was a zoologist. He liked to film the mating habits of animals. When he moved on to studying human beings, he regarded this new sex research as just a continuation of his previous work.

Think about it. If humans are just animals, without soul, spirit, or afterlife, without accountability to God and His laws, without an obligation to wrestle with their own lower, fallen nature so their noble, higher, godly nature can bloom—if none of this is real—then there's just not much problem with Kinsey and his data. In that case, we are just animals, and whatever comes "naturally" to animals, whatever impulses and drives they experience, even if they seem bizarre, cruel or predatory, are *right* for that animal.

But in reality, human beings are born with what amounts to a dual nature—a lower, prideful, selfish, hell-bent animal nature we inherit (rooted in what Christianity calls original sin), but also a higher, nobler, conscience-driven, heaven-oriented nature. And these two parallel worlds war for ascendancy over the mind and body of each and every one of us. Thus, when it comes to sex, despite the unruly sexual urges we discover within, they need to be restrained, according to the Judeo-Christian spiritual world view that has shaped Western society. Specifically, sex needs to be confined to an honorable, committed, lifelong heterosexual marriage. Only there do we find its true joy.

The problem is, because this sex drive is so powerful and compelling, it "has a mind of its own" and is known to impel us urgently toward sexual expression rather than restraint. In fact, for most of us—and men in particular—regardless of whatever good character traits we may possess, there's also a part of us that is vulnerable to some sufficiently persuasive rationale that would set free the sexual genie within us from any limitations.

This was exactly the dark reassurance that Kinsey delivered. He provided a "documentable" scientific cover for the latent rebellion against God's laws that is never too far from most of us. That's why the *Ozzie and Harriet* generation could be taken in—because, just as with all con jobs offering wealth, riches, fame, love—some part of every person *wanted* to believe it.

HIGH PRIEST

THE IMPLICIT message regarding sexuality coming from the secular, mechanistic world view—if we were to verbalize it—would be this: Mankind, you have evolved powerful sexual desires. There is no need to suppress them. If your activity is consensual, why should you be compelled to refrain from indulging whatever your sexual desires are, whenever you wish, regardless of how abnormal or strange those desires may seem to others? As long as you don't hurt little children and confine your behavior to consenting adults, there is nothing immoral, unethical, wrong, or forbidden in doing *whatever* you want with *whomever* you want.

Do you agree with this view? Does part of you agree with it? Many people do.

Considering how widespread this view is today, it may be unnerving to realize this is also precisely the world view and philosophy of the Church of Satan—including the part about not victimizing children. Essentially, Satanist philosophy teaches that God is cruel and capricious—that although He created man with these powerful drives and lusts, He then unfairly denies His creatures their full and free expression without risking eternal damnation.

"It has become necessary for a *new* religion, based on man's natural instincts, to come forth," proclaims *The Satanic Bible* by Anton Szandor LaVey, high priest of the Church of Satan from its founding by LaVey in 1966 until his death in 1997.[22] "Satan represents man as just another animal, sometimes better, more often worse than those that walk on all-fours, who, because of his 'divine spiritual and intellectual development,' has become the most vicious animal of all!"[23]

Read what the *Satanic Bible* says about man and sex and note how familiar and mainstream it sounds:

The basics of Satanism have always existed. The only thing that is new is the formal organization of a religion based on the universal traits of man. For centuries, magnificent structures of stone, concrete, mortar, and steel have been devoted to man's abstinence. It is high time that human beings stopped fighting themselves, and devoted their time to building temples designed for man's indulgences.

Even though times have changed, and always will, man remains basically the same. For two thousand years man has done penance for something he never should have had to feel guilty about in the first place. We are tired of denying ourselves the pleasures of life which we deserve. . . . Why not have a religion based on indulgence? Certainly, it is consistent with the nature of the beast. We are no longer supplicating weaklings trembling before an unmerciful "God" who cares not whether we live or die. We are self-respecting, prideful people—we are Satanists![24]

"Gosh!" you might wonder. "Satan? I mean, what does a little 'free sex' have to do with the devil and hell and all that?"

You see, Satanism simply champions our prideful, lower nature—in rebellion against the Creator and His plan for mankind. But that's exactly the same mode in which a great many of us are already operating, having bought into a phony notion of freedom that really delivers exactly the opposite—bondage, addiction, and misery.

LOVE

WHEN ALL is said and done, what your grandmother told you is true: sex outside of marriage is wrong. But how do we really know this for ourselves?

The Good Book says, "I will put my laws into their mind, and write them in their hearts: and I will be to them a God, and they shall be to me a people" (Hebrews 8:10). God's truths are written in our hearts and minds. That's why a three-year-old knows it's wrong to steal. Nobody told him—he just knew. In the same way, we know extramarital sex is wrong. Just the fact that sex leads to having children—who need the love and security that parents provide—makes it crystal clear to the unconfused mind that God intends for only married people to have sex.

As the brilliant twentieth-century writer G. K. Chesterton put it,

> Sex is an instinct that produces an institution; and it is positive and not
> negative, noble and not base, creative and not destructive, because it
> produces this institution. That institution is the family; a small state or
> commonwealth which has hundreds of aspects, when it is once started,
> that are not sexual at all. It includes worship, justice, festivity, decora-
> tion, instruction, comradeship, repose. Sex is the gate of that house; and
> romantic and imaginative people naturally like looking through a gate-
> way. But the house is very much larger than the gate. There are indeed a
> certain number of people who like to hang about the gate and never get
> any further.[25]

Sex and love. The desire to have sex does not come from love anymore than the desire to eat comes from love. Both are basically animal
functions. But the love part of sex has to do with everything else surrounding us in marriage—the commitment, caring, unselfishness, restraint, hard work, planning, sacrifice, affection, and endless patience.
These provide the virtue that infuses an animal act with love.

So, borrowing Chesterton's metaphor, what happens if we get
"hung up" about the gate and never enter the house? What happens if
we go Kinsey's way and indiscriminately indulge every appetite?

Let's take it to the extreme and ask whether a king with his harem of
dozens of concubines is happy and satisfied? No way. He's guiltier, more
sensitive to stress, more conflicted and easily disturbed, more haunted by
his own demons than you can imagine.

Any illicit desire—even when fulfilled—is satisfied only temporarily.
Before long the appetite returns—with a vengeance. This is the nature of
addiction—the craving never ends, but the fix needed is always greater.
That is, when we fulfill ourselves in a wrong way, the original high is no
longer attainable just by having the same sexual experience, the same
drug, the same hit as before.

To put it perhaps too plainly, men are born all but addicted to
women. Men compulsively look at women in terms of gratification.
Women, who quickly catch on to this terrible weakness men have for
them—a weakness not only for physical gratification, but for the ego
support and reassurance that usually come with it—in turn discover they
have a tremendous power over men they never asked for. If they're not
careful, they can easily become as addicted to men's need for them as

their men are to sex, and then they'll compulsively promote their man's weaknesses for the sake of power over him.

This basic sexual dynamic can easily become a serious problem. That's why, without real virtue—not the phony kind, but real maturity on the part of married men and women—we just can't relate to sex properly. The games that develop around this syndrome give rise to enormous resentments, intrigues, and conflicts—and ultimately hatreds—which in turn are a major reason half of today's marriages, even among Christians, end in divorce.

We need to rediscover, or discover for the first time, unselfish love for each other. If we do, we will relate to sex properly. If we don't, we are destined to drive each other into terrible conflict. Men don't need to be "addicts." And women don't need to be "liars." But these are the roles we tend to foster in each other when our relationship is based on anything other than true, godly caring for each other.

When all is said and done, Alfred Kinsey led the nation in the ultimate devaluation of something precious—love, marriage, children, and the difficult but fantastically rewarding personal growth that couples experience when they walk down that road of love and fidelity together.

In truth, sex is a great mystery—a *mysterium magnum*. We constantly degrade sex into far less than it really is, but then we also build it up to be far more than it really is. To get it right, we just need to remember to Whom we belong. "Know ye not that your body is the temple of the Holy Ghost which is in you, which ye have of God, and ye are not your own? For ye are bought with a price: therefore glorify God in your body, and in your spirit, which are God's" (1 Corinthians 6:19–20).

SABOTAGING OUR SCHOOLS

How Radicals Have Hijacked America's Education System

WHEN I WAS A little boy, about nine or ten, I had a recurring dream. It didn't come at night, however, but during the daytime. It would happen when, on occasion, I found myself lying on my parents' bed, not doing much of anything or thinking about much in particular.

I would gaze up at the ceiling—I don't really remember if I had my eyes closed, but I don't think so—and I would visualize outer space, with its multitude of worlds and heavenly bodies orbiting and streaming through limitless space. I would extend the expanse of space farther and farther out, in my mind, and then farther still, as though I wanted to see what came next, what lay beyond it all. Of course, all I saw was more and more of the same galactic landscape.

Each time I had this "dream," a wordless question would arise in my mind as I mentally searched out the ends of the universe:

Is that all there is?

Somehow, despite the infinite expanse of the universe and its spectacular cosmic events, I felt as though it were just so . . . one-dimensional. All I could see in my mind's eye was more space, more worlds, stars, galaxies, and such, and beyond them more and more and ever more of the same.

I was searching, it seemed, for something more, for something beyond the final outer wall of space and matter and time. What lay on the other side of that wall?

Pretty soon I would wake up from my daydream and go play, eat, watch TV, do homework or fight with my older brother.

Decades later, I can more readily appreciate my recurring childhood dream. In those special moments, some part of me was looking for God. For some strange reason, even though I lived in a fog like many young people, I was graced on occasion with magical, faith-giving moments of wonderment. I was searching, at least during those brief flights of fancy, for meaning, for purpose—for the spiritual dimension of life.

Actually, far from being daydreams, I would say those infrequent but soulful inner explorations of mine were probably my most awake moments as a child.

Indeed, for most of us, childhood itself is something of a dream. We float along in the world of our parents, for better or for worse, and we grow up pretty much shaped by the most powerful forces around us—home and school.

Fast-forward a dozen or more years. The next time I remember brushing up against the Infinite was after I had graduated from college. Taking an extended and much-needed break, it was the first time in years I didn't have the demands and anxieties of school hanging over me. There was an unaccustomed absence of pressure. I could breathe. My future was not mapped out for me as it had been during all previous years, when I always knew I'd be moving up the next grade when September arrived.

I went into neutral. My mind relaxed. Reflection and introspection set in, and I found myself taking nature walks and gazing up at the sky and looking for God—again. I hadn't thought much about Him during all my school years.

And where had God been during my education?

To put it more precisely, during those critical years of youthful metamorphosis—the seventeen years I spent in public school and college—where was that deeper part of me, the real me?

ANXIETY SPELL

"Our schools are not teaching students to think."—*Thomas Alva Edison*[1]
"It is nothing short of a miracle that modern methods of instruction have not yet entirely strangled the holy curiosity of inquiry."
—*Albert Einstein*

THE TRUTH is, during all those formative years when I was being "educated" and supposedly prepared for adulthood and a career, my life was basically one long anxiety spell. I discovered—or maybe I should say rediscovered—God and meaning and purpose only when I was free of school. Moreover, though I was a high achiever as a student, I can say honestly that 95 percent of what is really useful in my life today, both in my career and as a husband, father, and citizen, I learned apart from school. In this I am far from alone.

But why do I open a chapter on public education with a bunch of talk about God?

Public education today doesn't honor God, doesn't recognize God, in truth doesn't really want there to *be* a God, and therefore doesn't acknowledge the sacred little flame—Einstein's "holy curiosity of inquiry"—within each student.

Understand, I'm not talking here about whether prayer or Bible reading should be permitted in the classroom or whether the Ten Commandments should adorn a hallway display or things like that. Rather, I'm saying the government's school system has been cultivated to indoctrinate, to mold, to socialize children, and even to prepare them for the work force, but not to bring forth from within them the noble character and understanding of truth that lie buried within each child.

In this chapter we're going to explore how the radical transformation of education in America—in pursuit of a private agenda utterly alien to traditional core American ideals—has been "job one" for a wild assortment of elitists, marketers, and "hidden persuaders." But before we look at school, let's look first at children.

In a riveting speech at the National Religious Broadcasters annual convention in 2002, Focus on the Family's Dr. James Dobson, a clinical psychologist, asked the crowd of thirty-five hundred people a provocative question about children:

Do you understand what a stem cell is? A stem cell is a cell—in the human being at least—that in the very early stages of development is undifferentiated. In other words, it's not yet other kinds of tissue, but it can go any direction depending on the environment that it's in.

The stem cell, if it's in the brain, develops into a nerve cell or into the substances between the nerves. Or if it's in the heart, it becomes a heart cell, or if it's in the eye, it becomes an eyeball cell. Wherever it is, it takes on the characteristic of the surrounding area.

Do you understand that children are the stem cells for the culture? The environment that you put them in is what they grow up to be. And if you can control what they hear, if you could control what they're told, if you have access to their minds . . . you can make them into just about whatever you want them to be.[2]

Hold that thought while we take a quick romp through the government's school system.

ACT OF WAR

"IF AN unfriendly foreign power had attempted to impose on America the mediocre educational performance that exists today, we might well have viewed it as an act of war." The rantings of a right-wing anti-public-school fanatic? No, it's the conclusion of the National Commission on Excellence in Education convened at the outset of the Reagan administration by U.S. Education Secretary Terrence Bell and concerned over "the widespread public perception that something is seriously remiss in our educational system."

After eighteen months of thoroughly examining America's schools, the commission presented its dismal conclusions in its April 1983 report titled *A Nation at Risk*, which focused on America's loss of competitive edge in the post-Sputnik era. That report has been joined by scores of books before and since, sounding the alarm over the corruption—some say intentional subversion—of America's government schools.

Some of the analyses sound downright sinister. "Change agents," we are told, are attempting to reprogram Johnny into a drone carefully groomed for service in a future utopian socialistic state. Others speak of the "deliberate dumbing-down" of educational standards and practices. Are these characterizations accurate or exaggerations—or just paranoid fantasies?

The educational Paul Reveres warn of bizarre curricula that have evolved in our lifetimes. There's "death education," during which the class takes a field trip to a mortuary and children are required to discuss how they might commit suicide. And there's "values clarification," forcing students to decide who should live and who should die in controversial group mental exercises.

No matter how far out of the mainstream, it somehow seems to qualify as the basis of public school curriculum, we're told, from New Age rituals to Islamic jihad. That's right, some California middle schools teach a major unit on Islam as a required part of their curriculum, compelling students to dress up as Muslims, memorize portions of the Koran and participate in "jihad games."[3]

And then there's sex. We've heard for years about pornographic, co-ed sex-education classes in public schools, about school counselors eagerly dispensing birth-control devices to vulnerable teens, and even referring them out for abortions during school hours—no need for mom or dad to know. Today the nation's middle schools are the focus of major national news stories decrying an epidemic of sexual activity on the part of twelve-, thirteen-, and fourteen-year-olds. And of course, homosexual proselytizing has become so rampant in government schools—in some states, like California, it's even mandated by law, starting in the earliest grades—that major cultural icons like James Dobson and talk radio's Dr. Laura Schlessinger have publicly urged parents to remove their children from public schools altogether.

We hear a lot about the American Civil Liberties Union suing government schools over alleged violations of the separation of church and state. As a result, public schools are now so intimidated they go to absurd lengths to censor the slightest reference to God. A recent example was a California school that prohibited a teacher from giving his history students excerpts from the Declaration of Independence, the diaries of George Washington and John Adams, the writings of William Penn, and various state constitutions because of the documents' references to God.[4]

And since the April 20, 1999, Columbine school massacre, another bizarre phenomenon revealing widespread abandonment of common sense on the part of school administrators is repeating itself from coast to coast:

• Four kindergartners in Sayreville, New Jersey, were suspended from school for three days for playing "cops and robbers" on the playground during recess. The boys were found guilty of using their fingers as guns and shouting words like "bang" while running around the school yard.[5]

• An eighth-grader at Blue Ridge Middle School in Loudoun County, Virginia, received a note in class from a friend who said she was contemplating suicide and had brought a knife to school in her binder. Aware that the girl had been hospitalized for psychiatric problems, the boy took the knife away from her and locked it in his locker. As thanks for the boy's heroism, the school board decided he should be suspended for four months.[6]

• Three boys were suspended from Bemiss Elementary School in Spokane, Washington, for bringing to school miniature toy guns from G.I. Joe action figures. The toys were about one to three inches, but the school said it stands by its zero-tolerance policy on "weapons."[7]

• A thirteen-year-old boy was suspended for violating Kansas's Derby Unified School District's zero-tolerance policy against racial harassment and intimidation when he drew a replica of the Confederate flag on a scrap of paper. The flag was listed as a prohibited symbol of racial hatred.[8]

• In New Jersey, a nine-year-old student was suspended from school for a day and ordered to undergo a psychological evaluation after mentioning to a friend his intent to "shoot" a classmate with a wad of paper. The fourth-grader had planned to launch spitballs at the girl using a rubber band. Local police went to the boy's home after midnight and questioned him about the "shooting" incident.[9]

• A Louisiana high-school student was expelled for one year because she had Advil pills in her purse. She carried the over-the-counter medicine because of frequent headaches, but the Bossier Parish School District maintained it was following a state law barring drugs on campus.[10]

• In Florida, a female high-school sophomore with a good academic record and no disciplinary problems was suspended for possession of a nail clipper. She had lent the clipper to a friend, who used the two-inch file attachment to clean underneath her nails, but a school officer deemed the attachment to be a "knife blade."[11]

In a grotesque overreaction to the rash of school shootings and prevalence of illegal drugs on campus, administrators' solutions have turned many schools into *Alice in Wonderland* environments where nothing makes sense and the Queen of Hearts shouts "Off with their heads!" for the slightest perceived offense.

"MY KID'S SCHOOL IS FINE"

DESPITE OVERWHELMING evidence that government schools have become increasingly hazardous to America's children, for most people there remains an air of unreality about all these dire claims. After all, such unsavory episodes must be the exception, not the rule—mustn't they? For every parent who is troubled by these things, there are evidently hundreds who say, "I haven't heard any of this sort of nonsense going on at *my* children's school. In fact, they *love* their school; they've made so many friends. I know there are some bad schools out there, but my kid's school is fine. I've met their teachers at back-to-school night, and they're just great!"

It's easy to sympathize with this attitude. For one thing, the notion that someone has *intentionally* subverted our schools is not only disturbing, it's difficult to believe. Almost any other explanation is preferable. Even if our educational system *has* been sabotaged, hasn't it been by accident? Who would purposely hurt children?

This aura of unbelievability has prevented all these grim reports from being taken too seriously by a wide audience, mostly because the establishment press apparently hasn't found them newsworthy. And yet, not only are most of these claims of educational subversion essentially true, but the reality is often far worse than the words convey. After all, isn't reality always more than what words can describe? Heaven and hell both must be far better and far worse than what mere words can conjure up in the mind.

The truth is, the Reagan-era commission was on the mark—perhaps more than it even realized at the time—when it characterized the dismal state of government schools as equivalent in seriousness to "an act of war." Indeed, it *was* an act of war. Or maybe *revolution* is a better word.

Let us travel back to the war rooms of educational reform and behold the astounding transformation of American education—and thereby of the nation's children and ultimately American society—which has been dreamed up, planned, and executed by people with values and agendas profoundly at odds with those of most Americans.

REVOLUTIONARIES

YOU'D NEVER guess it from the way today's government learning centers have been surgically scrubbed clean of any vestige of Christian influence, but America's earliest schools were originally established to ensure biblical literacy. The Puritan founders of New England saw their settlement as a once-in-a-lifetime chance to create a biblically based society free of the corrupting influences of the Old World. To make this dream of a "Bible commonwealth" a reality, the Puritans recognized the need to pass the torch of biblical knowledge on to the next generation. Thus, in the 1630s, Calvinists—that's what most of the Puritans were—founded Harvard College as a seminary for educating a learned clergy and organized grammar schools to prepare young scholars for Harvard.

To give you the flavor of the original Harvard, here's a snippet from its Rules and Precepts of 1642:

> Let every Student be plainly instructed, and earnestly pressed to consider well, the maine end of his life and studies is, to know God and Jesus Christ which is eternal life, John 17:3 and therefore to lay Christ in the bottome, as the only foundation of all sound knowledge and Learning. And seeing the Lord only giveth wisedome, Let every one seriously set himself by prayer in secret to seeke it of him Prov. 2, 3.[12]

This Calvinist utopian experiment didn't last long, however. After a long rivalry, in 1805 the Unitarians took control of the college and kicked out the orthodox Calvinists. What was this controversy all about? Essentially, the Unitarians rejected the strict Calvinist view that man is innately depraved—"born in sin." Rather, the Unitarians were convinced that man not only was born good but was perfectible. Therefore the Unitarians practiced their religion mostly in the area of social progress and good works. Evil, they contended, entered our lives, not because of man's fallen and sinful nature as the Calvinists believed, but rather because of poverty and lack of education. By eradicating ignorance through universal education, the Unitarians believed they could end poverty and social injustice. Moreover, they were confident that the ideal educational system should be secular—and directed by government.

Thus, led by Horace Mann, the Unitarians paved the way for the establishment of America's "public" school system. Although the early government schools still maintained high academic standards as well as Judeo-Christian morality, all that started to change during the post–Civil War era, when education came under the sway of a fantastic revolution then brewing.

John Taylor Gatto, one of America's most celebrated public school teachers (he was voted both New York City and New York State teacher of the year) describes what happened to America's schools in the late nineteenth century. In *The Underground History of American Education,* Gatto tells how "progressive educational leaders" hijacked America's school system and recreated it according to strange new philosophies— all with the apparent best of intentions, believing they were doing the great work of advancing civilization.

Transporting readers back to the smoke-filled rooms of the late nineteenth century, Gatto writes:

> Somehow out of the industrial confusion which followed the Civil War, powerful men and dreamers became certain what kind of social order America needed. This realization didn't arise as a product of public debate as it should have in a democracy, but as a distillation of private discussion. Their ideas contradicted the original American charter but that didn't disturb them. They had a stupendous goal in mind—the rationalization of everything. The end of unpredictable history and its transformation into something orderly. . . .
>
> The first goal, to be reached in stages, was an orderly, scientifically managed society, one in which the best people would make the decisions, unhampered by democratic tradition. After that, human breeding, the evolutionary destiny of the species, would be in reach. Universal institutionalized formal forced schooling was the prescription.[13]

If your head is already spinning, and you're tempted to relegate this to the conspiracy bin, don't. Truth is sometimes stranger than fiction. Gatto goes on to name names:

> In the first decades of the twentieth century, a small group of soon-to-be-famous academics, symbolically led by John Dewey and Edward Thorndike of Columbia Teachers College, Ellwood P. Cubberley of Stanford, G. Stanley Hall, and an ambitious handful of others, energized and financed by major corporate and financial allies like Morgan, Astor, Whitney, Carnegie, and Rockefeller, decided to bend government schooling to the service of business and the political state—as it had been done a century before in Prussia.[14]

And what were the motives of this group?

> After the Civil War, utopian speculative analysis regarding isolation of children in custodial compounds where they could be subjected to deliberate molding routines began to be discussed seriously by the Northeastern policy elites of business, government, and university life. These discussions were inspired by a growing realization that the productive potential of machinery driven by coal was limitless. Railroad development made possible by coal, startling new inventions like the telegraph, seemed suddenly to make village life and local dreams irrelevant. A new governing mind was emerging in harmony with the new reality.
>
> The principal motivation for this revolution in family and community life seems on the surface to be greed, but appearance concealed philosophical visions approaching religious exaltation in intensity—that effective early indoctrination of all children would lead to an orderly scientific society, one controlled by the best people now freed from the obsolete strait-jacket of democratic traditions and historic American libertarian attitudes.
>
> Forced schooling was the medicine to bring the whole continental population into conformity with these plans so it might be regarded as a "human resource." Managed as a "workforce." No more Ben Franklins or Tom Edisons could be allowed; they set a bad example.[15]

Wait a minute! Where do God, the Bible, the Ten Commandments, and good old American independence fit into this scheme? They don't.

A core change in American values—one that didn't involve God or absolute values—was being birthed in secret. That's right, in secret. For while most of us are at least somewhat familiar with America's history as it encompasses politics and elections, medical and scientific advances, fashions and cultural trends, wars and revolutions, we are only dimly aware of the most important modern revolution of all. That is, the overthrow by a self-anointed leader class of Western Judeo-Christian values and beliefs in favor of a de facto atheistic, "scientific" world view. Scientific? Let's take a closer look at what that code word actually meant to these revolutionaries.

THE HUMAN ANIMAL

IS THERE really a God? Does man have an immortal soul? Is our primary responsibility in this life to be obedient and faithful to God and to His laws of life? Or are we just animals—highly evolved mammals without higher purpose, except whatever purpose we decide upon, whose ultimate goal is to live comfortably and pleasurably and to interact in maximum harmony with the rest of "society"?

This battle of world views, of course, rages endlessly just below the surface of many of today's most contentious issues. Although many have been powerfully attracted to the latter, humanistic world view throughout history, it wasn't until the nineteenth century that a "scientific" justification emerged for rejecting the spiritual nature of man—literally for denying God.

Of course, Charles Darwin's evolutionary theory, since it offered a way to explain creation without the need for a Creator, provided the philosophical underpinning for an atheistic world view. But it was people like German psychologist Wilhelm Wundt, the founder of experimental psychology, who created the "scientific" basis not only for denying God but for transforming society.

Wundt and his followers believed man was just an animal that could be analyzed, understood, and reprogrammed for the betterment of society. They contended this could be done first by careful observation and measurement of psychological and physical reactions, sensations, perception, attention, feelings, associations, and so on, and then by inducing appropriate stimulation to reeducate humans in the desired way.

So influential was Wundt—to this day he is referred to as the "father of experimental psychology"—that the redefinition of education was inevitable. As Wundt observed:

> Learning is the result of modifiability in the paths of neural conduction. . . . The situation-response formula is adequate to cover learning of any sort, and the really influential factors in learning are readiness of the neurons, sequence in time, belongingness, and satisfying consequences.[16]

What this technical jargon means is that man is an animal and can be trained like one. Wundt's work provided scientific cover for the revolutionary reformist views of the intellectuals of his day. Basing their new approach to governance on science, evolution and psychology, their number-one goal was to transform America through its education system, which they did by taking control of teachers' colleges, textbook publishers, and other institutions.

Educational historian Samuel L. Blumenfeld describes a few of the main revolutionaries on the education front:

> They were men like G. Stanley Hall, James McKeen Cattell, Charles Judd and James Earl Russell, all of whom had studied the radical new evolution-based psychology under Wundt at Leipzig. Hall eventually became president of Clark University in Worcester, Mass.; Cattell became an advocate of eugenics (scientific racism) and became head of educational psychology at Columbia University; Charles Judd became head of the education department at the University of Chicago; and James Earl Russell became head of Teachers College, Columbia.
>
> [John] Dewey didn't go to Leipzig. Rather, he received his training in the new psychology from G. Stanley Hall at Johns Hopkins University. In 1894, Dewey was appointed head of the department of philosophy, psychology and education at the University of Chicago, which had been established two years earlier by a gift from John D. Rockefeller. In 1896, Dewey created his famous Laboratory School, in which he could test the new psychology and the new curriculum on real live children.
>
> The results of his experiments were summed up in 1899 in his book, "School and Society," which has become a bible of sorts among progressive educators. In it, he said: "[T]he tragic weakness of the present school

is that it endeavors to prepare future members of the social order in a medium in which the conditions of the social spirit are eminently wanting. . . . The mere absorbing of facts and truths is so exclusively individual an affair that it tends very naturally to pass into selfishness. There is no obvious social motive for the acquirement of mere learning, there is no clear social gain in success thereat."

In other words, the traditional school promoted individualism, which Dewey and other progressives equated with "selfishness." What were needed were schools that promoted the *collectivist* spirit of socialism.[17]

SABOTAGE

ONE OF the first casualties was literacy. I'll skip the gory details of how phonics—the simple, logical, and proven method of teaching reading used successfully for centuries—was abandoned in favor of a new system dreamed up by progressive reformers. Variously called the "look-say" or "whole word" method, it has been responsible for an epidemic of poor readers in our lifetime and prompted Rudolf Flesch's 1955 national best seller *Why Johnny Can't Read*. "The teaching of reading—all over the United States, in all the schools, in all the textbooks—is totally wrong and flies in the face of all logic and common sense," charged Flesch in one of the most talked-about books of that decade.

Blumenfeld summarizes the book's impact:

Flesch explained to the American people, most of whom were hearing this for the first time, that the professors of education had changed the way reading was taught in American schools. They got rid of the traditional alphabetic phonics method and replaced it with a look-say, whole-word method that taught children to read English as if it were Chinese—that is, composed of characters instead of phonetically structured words. He explained that when you impose an ideographic teaching method on an alphabetic writing system, you cause reading problems. He also explained why it would be so difficult to get phonics back in the schools:

"It's a foolproof system all right," wrote Flesch. "Every grade-school teacher in the country has to go to a teachers' college or school of education; every teachers' college gives at least one course on how to teach reading; every course on how to teach reading is based on a textbook; every one of those textbooks is written by one of the high priests of the word method. In the old days it was impossible to keep a good teacher from following her own common sense and practical knowledge; today the phonetic system of teaching reading is kept out of our schools as effectively as if we had a dictatorship with an all-powerful Ministry of Education."

Flesch's book aroused tremendous indignation among parents. They clamored for a return to phonics. But the educational establishment circled the wagons and created the International Reading Association, which became the citadel of the whole-word method.[18]

Question: What makes "experts" throw out something logical, effective, and proven, and substitute something else that is confusing, defies common sense, and doesn't work?

The truth is, the "progressive" education elite forfeited their common sense way back when they were first seduced into the secular world view that said man is an animal that needs to be controlled and directed by others—namely them. If there is no awareness of God, truth becomes relative, socialism becomes attractive, immorality becomes acceptable, and philosophies become bizarre. Human relationships are no longer based on mutual honor for another child of God, but rather on exploitation and domination, either obvious or subtle. Everything changes. Reading methodology, therefore, is only one of a great many areas of education that were transformed by deluded educational reformers from something that worked to something that didn't work.

Today the theory of evolution is taught as fact while mere mention in the classroom of real-world scientific disputes over the theory is often censored. Differing moral codes are presented as having equal validity according to situational ethics and multicultural studies. Sex education teaches that premarital sex is okay as long as you don't get a sexually transmitted disease or become pregnant. "Outcome-based education" transforms traditional schooling into vocational schooling. Widely established homosexual programs teach kids that the "gay" lifestyle is normal and that thinking otherwise is bigotry and hatred. Meanwhile, with every passing school year the traditional American values and sensibilities that previous generations were raised on become a fainter memory.

If the government's education system—like so much of what the federal bureaucracy touches—is such a disaster, then why do we turn our children over to it for their entire youths? Lots of reasons, starting with the name—"public school." They are government schools, but we call them "public." What a difference a word makes! *Public* sounds open, transparent, free, and wholesome, while *government* sounds compulsory, bureaucratic, wasteful, and hostile to freedom. The mere use of the word *public* is a powerful and deceptive marketing tool of governments all over the world. *Public land* sounds inviting while *government land* makes us feel like serfs.

In truth, the most wretched communist dictatorships on earth—like the People's Republic of China or, worse, the Democratic People's Republic of Korea (North Korea)—have used this ploy for decades. They steal everything from their miserable populations—including their freedom—and then pretend to give it back to them by calling it *public* or *the people's*.

Of course, the main factor keeping most American children in government schools is that they're free. So isn't free schooling a good thing? Sure. Free food is great too, but not if it's been poisoned.

The government's schools are free in the same way everything else the government does is free—you're forced to pay for it with your hard-earned taxes or you go to prison. Still, it costs a lot to raise kids these days, and if you've had thousands of dollars extracted from you in taxes to pay for these schools, shouldn't you get your money's worth by sending your children there—for "free"? Although that's a powerful magnet, there's also a hidden cost, as John Taylor Gatto points out.

The Attention of a Stranger

Beyond all the other reasons it might be unwise to entrust your children to the government, Gatto points to one more, which he considers the core problem. When all is said and done, he doesn't dwell on the grotesque psychological experiments and failed pedagogic approaches, and school crime sprees that steal headlines. Rather, Gatto points to the subtle, soul-killing power of forced government schooling, the devastating effect on each child's not-so-hidden genius of sitting at a desk in a classroom all day for one's entire youth.

The strongest meshes of the school net are invisible. Constant bidding for a stranger's attention creates a chemistry producing the common characteristics of modern schoolchildren: whining, dishonesty, malice, treachery, cruelty. Unceasing competition for official favor in the dramatic fish bowl of a classroom delivers cowardly children, little people sunk in chronic boredom, little people with no apparent purpose for being alive.

The net effect of holding children in confinement for twelve years without honor paid to the spirit is a compelling demonstration that the State considers the Western spiritual tradition dangerous. And of course it is.

The bottom line, says Gatto:

Spiritually contented people are dangerous for a variety of reasons. They don't make reliable servants because they won't jump at every command. They test what is requested against a code of moral principle. Those who are spiritually secure can't easily be driven to sacrifice family relations.[19]

Please understand. The people responsible for this disaster—both then and now—are not deliberately trying to hurt children. They are people who fervently believe, with a religious zeal, in a radically different world view than the one in which most Americans believe—indeed, radically different from the one on which this nation was founded.

If the government's education system is dangerous to our children's freedom and happiness, how then are we to educate them?

SPIRITUALLY CENTERED EDUCATION

"AND THOU shalt love the LORD thy God with all thine heart, and with all thy soul, and with all thy might. And these words, which I command thee this day, shall be in thine heart: And thou shalt teach them diligently unto thy children, and shalt talk of them when thou sittest in thine house, and when thou walkest by the way, and when thou liest down, and when thou risest up" (Deuteronomy 6:5–7).

There are many private schools and other alternatives to government schools, some with impressive and honorable track records. But there is one educational solution I personally believe to be the best—since it has the unique potential not only of providing children the education they need but also of transforming entire families. I'm talking about homeschooling, which is the avenue my wife and I have chosen for our children.

The simple truth is, we love our kids more than any teacher could possibly be expected to love them. That's not to our credit; it's just a fact of life—they're *our* children, whom God has given to *us* to "teach diligently" as it says in Deuteronomy.

While not all homeschoolers are religious, evangelical Christians are unquestionably the driving force behind the rapidly growing homeschool movement in America today. Virtually all of the curricula and moral support groups, the networking organizations, the legal battles, the publications, and curriculum fairs are the passionate work of Christians who fiercely believe a de facto atheistic government school system is no place for their children.

In fact, the motivation and intensity of many committed Christian homeschoolers is strikingly reminiscent of the Pilgrims. Everyone knows the Pilgrims left England for Holland because of religious persecution. But why did they leave Holland and make the incredibly dangerous trip across the Atlantic to America?

William Bradford, one of the Pilgrims who established the Plymouth Colony and later served as its governor for more than thirty years, explained what motivated them to leave Holland, despite the freedom from religious persecution they had found there. "Many of the children," wrote Bradford of the English transplants, "influenced by the great licentiousness of the young people of the country, and the many temptations of the cities, were led by evil example into dangerous corners, getting the reins off their neck and leaving their parents."[20]

The Pilgrims saw their children were in danger of being corrupted, and for this reason they left for uncharted territory—America—where they would have the chance to create a new civilization in which their posterity could flourish, uncorrupted by a decadent and perverse culture. They came to America at great cost and sacrifice for the same reasons many Christians, Jews, and other people of conscience today homeschool their children—to protect them from corruption and to give them a powerful grounding in proven principles of life.

One of the blessings of parenthood is that the Good Lord mercifully seems to grant us a second chance to relive our childhood in some ways—to re-experience traumas, to forgive, to gain experiences and knowledge we missed, to heal the wounds of our youth, to become whole. Homeschooling offers an exquisite opportunity for this healing.

My wife, Jean, while growing up in South Africa, was sent to a Catholic boarding school at the tender age of five, where she grew up for the next five years in the hands of what she recalls were overly strict and impatient nuns. Her memories are mostly of outrages and injustices—like being forced to stand in a spider-infested corner if she didn't finish her meal or committed some other imagined offense. As she grew up, those convent years receded from her memory, but they had of course left their mark on her soul.

Years ago, while discussing whether to send our kids to private school or to homeschool them—public school was never on the table—Jean looked at me and said with memorable conviction: "I am these children's mother. Who has a better right to teach them than I?" The truth of that simple logic penetrated my mind and pierced my heart. Today, many years later, I can say that homeschooling has been a journey—sometimes bumpy, occasionally tumultuous—but overall a wonderful, difficult, well-planned, spontaneous, serene, and rollicking adventure.

But it's not just about better curriculum and protecting your kids from school shooters, gender bending, and jihad studies. It's a way of life for the entire family. I've watched as every family member has grown in character, as Jean and I have both filled in gaps in our own educations by teaching—and learning—history, geography, literature, science, math, and much more. (Jean has even forgiven the nuns for their thoughtless and cruel discipline!) Most important, the homeschooling experience is sewing our family together as a unit. For the family that learns to learn together, work together, and play together is the family where the siblings become best friends for life. In short, their family becomes a rock—a powerful subculture—to which they can always return for guidance and rest.

As for my boyhood question—"Is that all there is?"—it has been answered most graciously. No dramatic visions, no three-hundred-foot statues of Jesus—just a gentle and progressive unfolding of understanding from that "other dimension" beyond time and space. With the Holy Spirit as my compass, and guided by the Scriptures—the blueprint for our character, shown with exquisite clarity in the life and words of Jesus

Christ—I hope, like every conscience-driven dad hopes, to lead my wife and children safely to that distant shore. After all, we're all pilgrims.

As the author of Deuteronomy observed: "And thou shalt teach them diligently unto thy children, and shalt talk of them when thou sittest in thine house, and when thou walkest by the way, and when thou liest down, and when thou risest up."

THE MEDIA MATRIX

*How the Press Creates a World of
Illusion We Think Is Real*

WHEN RONALD REAGAN FINALLY slipped away from this earthly life in June 2004, most Americans were swept up in the week-long memorial, full of poignancy and praise, eulogies and processions, stories and jokes—all sustained by a deep wellspring of love for the fortieth president.

Joining in the pageantry were all of the familiar stars of the news media. With "Hail to the Chief" trumpeting in the background, they memorialized Reagan's paramount role in ending the cold war, his revitalization of America's stagnant economy after Jimmy Carter's "malaise," his rekindling of Americans' faith in their country and its enduring values. And they took obvious pride in sharing stories of their personal experiences with "the Gipper."

It continued all week. Gushing references to the "Great Communicator," the "shining city on a hill," "morning in America," and "Mr. Gorbachev, tear down this wall" flowed effortlessly from silver-tongued media orators echoing the deepest sentiments of the vast majority of Americans.

Yes, the big media loved Reagan in death. Just as they reviled and mocked him in life.

Here's what these same media icons were saying just a few short years ago, at the end of Reagan's second term as president:

"I predict historians are going to be totally baffled by how the American people fell in love with [Ronald Reagan] and followed him the way we did."—CBS News reporter Lesley Stahl, January 11, 1989

"Ronald Reagan presided over a meltdown of the federal government during the last eight years. Fundamental management was abandoned in favor of rhetoric and imagery. A cynical disregard for the art of government led to wide-scale abuse."—CBS News reporter Terence Smith in the *New York Times,* November 4, 1989

"On behalf of [the Nicaraguan Contras'] cause, Reagan sold out his oath of office and subverted the Constitution. Oliver North presented himself as the immortal boy in the heroic green uniform of Peter Pan. Although wishing to be seen as a humble patriot, the colonel's testimony showed him to be a treacherous and lying agent of the national security state, willing to do anything asked of him by a president to whom he granted the powers of an oriental despot." —PBS series *America's Century,* narrated by *Harper's* editor Lewis Lapham, November 28, 1989

"A hundred years from now—long after Ronald Reagan has been lumped with other ineffectual Dr. Feelgoods like William McKinley and Calvin Coolidge who swam with the tide of their times—the last fourth of the 20th century will be remembered for the demise of imperial communism, and the Soviet Union's president will be remembered for both making and letting it happen."—*Boston Globe* Washington reporter and columnist Tom Oliphant, December 28, 1989

"Ronald Reagan and Madonna. On the surface, he stood for the fundamental American values that she parodied. But underneath, they conveyed the same Horatio Alger myth: Self-image over reality. Say it or sing it enough, and any dream of yourself might come true, at least in the public's perception."—*U.S. News & World Report* senior editor Donald Baer, December 25, 1989

"The '80s were the years of excess. We swaggered through the portals and grabbed as much as we could. We were greedy and gluttonous. As long as we wore starched shirts, we could belch at the dinner table. And Ronald Reagan led us."—*USA Today's* Debbie Howlett, November 27, 1989

"The decade had its highs (Gorbachev, Bird) . . . and the decade had its lows (Reagan, AIDS)"—*Boston Globe* headlines over '80s reviews by the paper's columnists, December 28, 1989[1]

"Reagan, AIDS"? Whoa, hit the pause button.

The mainstream press hated Reagan, his values, his policies, and his influence on the nation. The nation, meanwhile, *loved* Reagan. What does this tell us? It tells us the so-called mainstream press is radically *outside the mainstream*.

But this chapter is not about how the press is too "biased" or "liberal" or "left-wing." That's old news—very old. Every objective study for the past three decades has proven conclusively the profound bias that is obvious to almost everyone.

No, the scary fact is that the media—both news and entertainment—are literally the creators and sustainers of what most of us *perceive* as reality, reminiscent of the malevolent computer program in *The Matrix* film trilogy. In *The Matrix,* humans are born into a slave state in which what they think of as reality is actually a powerful computer-generated virtual-reality program. They live in constant and deep delusion. Without realizing it, these humans have been reduced to the lowest form of servitude, their life energies literally sucked out of them to fuel the insatiable needs of their rulers.

"Wait a minute," you're probably thinking. "I know the media are biased and out of touch with the mainstream. But what's this have to do with *The Matrix?*" Let's find out.

READY TO SWALLOW THE RED PILL?

Remember the moment when the hero, a young man named Neo, meets Morpheus for the first time? Morpheus is the leader of the tiny remnant of rebels who know the truth about the matrix and are fighting to free mankind from its enslavers:

MORPHEUS: Let me tell you why you're here. You're here because you know something. What you know, you can't explain. But you feel it. You've felt it your entire life. That there's something wrong with the world. You don't know what it is, but it's there. Like a splinter in your mind—driving you mad. It is this feeling that has brought you to me. Do you know what I'm talking about?

NEO: The matrix?

MORPHEUS: Do you want to know what it is? *(Neo nods his head.)* The matrix is everywhere, it is all around us. Even now, in this very room. You can see it when you look out your window, or when you turn on your television. You can feel it when you go to work, or when you go to church or when you pay your taxes. It is the world that has been pulled over your eyes to blind you from the truth.

NEO: What truth?

MORPHEUS: That you are a slave, Neo. Like everyone else, you were born into bondage, born inside a prison that you cannot smell, taste or touch. A prison for your mind. *(Long pause, sighs)* Unfortunately, no one can be told what the matrix is—you have to see it for yourself. This is your last chance. After this, there is no turning back. *(In his left hand, Morpheus shows a blue pill.)* You take the blue pill and the story ends. You awake in your bed and believe whatever you want to believe. *(A red pill is shown in his other hand.)* You take the red pill and you stay in Wonderland and I show you how deep the rabbit-hole goes. *(Long pause; Neo begins to reach for the red pill.)* Remember—all I am offering is the truth, nothing more.

(Neo takes the red pill and swallows it with a glass of water.)[2]

"A PRISON FOR YOUR MIND"

EVERYONE HAS heard about mass manipulation, mind control, brainwashing, suggestion, hypnosis, and Pavlovian conditioning—the scary stuff of far-off communist operatives, religious cults, and movie thrillers like *The Manchurian Candidate*. It pops up in the news now and then, as when the Symbionese Liberation Army kidnapped and brainwashed Patricia ("I am Tanya") Hearst, or more recently in Stockholm syndrome cases, where terrified hostages come to sympathize, and in some cases actually fall in love, with the terrorists threatening their lives.

Nevertheless, we're never quite sure how much of this mind-control stuff is objectively real and how much is just psychobabble or science fiction. Right? The truth is, if we look at it closely enough, we'll discover it's not only real but it's the fabric of our lives.

To demonstrate the real-life "matrix programming" we consider our reality, let's momentarily set aside the news media and focus on one of the most stunning and powerful matrix programs currently running. I'm referring to "evolution."

In the days *prior* to the evolution matrix program—that is, from the beginning of human life until Charles Darwin came along in the mid-nineteenth century—human beings would step outside their homes and survey with their eyes and minds the wonders of nature. They'd see majestic four-hundred-year-old redwood trees, hummingbirds that were able to hover, and honeybees that somehow knew how to do a special figure-eight dance that would communicate to the other worker bees the precise location of the dancer's newly discovered nectar source.

Looking in every direction, we humans beheld not only fantastic complexity, diversity and order, but also the *supreme intelligence* behind creation, as brashly evident and unavoidable as the noonday sun. This ubiquitous natural wonderland caused man to acknowledge and honor the Creator of creation, as Nicolaus Copernicus did when he wrote, "[The world] has been built for us by the Best and Most Orderly Workman of all." Or as Galileo wrote, "God is known . . . by Nature in His works and by doctrine in His revealed word." Or as Louis Pasteur confessed, "The more I study nature, the more I stand amazed at the work of the Creator." Or Isaac Newton: "When I look at the solar system, I see the earth at the right distance from the sun to receive the proper amounts of heat and light. This did not happen by chance."

Did not happen by chance?

Ever since Darwin and his successors succeeded in loading the evolution matrix program on mankind—a fantastic theory for which there is no actual proof and many serious problems—when we *now* walk outside and look at the created universe, what do many of us see? Chance!

Although our eyes survey the same wonders of God's creation that inspired faith in our forefathers, in our minds today we see only the meaningless result of millions of years of random-chance mutation. That's what our minds "see"—the eternal dance of purposeless recombination of ever-more-complex forms, but all without meaning, without spirit, without love. And by direct implication we also "see" that man is not a fallen being needful of God's saving grace but merely the cleverest, most evolved of all the animals.

And since evolution by definition always results in improvement and advancement, all of man's violent, lustful, and selfish drives are perfectly normal and natural and . . . advanced. There is no good and evil, no heaven and hell—and man, as a highly evolved monkey, has no sin and no guilt, as these are logical impossibilities from the evolutionary point of view.

Get the idea? And that's just one real-life matrix program. Our eyes, our senses work just fine. But we've been lied to so thoroughly and consistently that we no longer perceive the meaning of what we see nor understand what we hear.

Now let's turn our attention to the news media and examine some of the interesting "programs" currently running.

WHO SHOULD BE PRESIDENT?

"LET'S TALK about media bias here. The media, I think, want [John] Kerry to win."

That was *Newsweek*'s Evan Thomas candidly admitting the obvious on PBS's *Inside Washington*. In fact, during the 2004 Democratic convention, *New York Times* columnist John Tierney asked 153 journalists whether they thought John Kerry or George W. Bush would make a "better president." Reporters from outside the beltway favored Kerry three to one, while the approximately 50 Washington-based journalists polled favored Kerry over Bush by a stunning twelve-to-one margin!

This bias, of course, reached absurd levels when Dan Rather and CBS News pathetically stonewalled the entire world—even the rest of the "mainstream media"—arrogantly defending the obviously bogus documents Rather and *60 Minutes* had featured for the intended purpose of bringing down a U.S. president.

But that was just the time they got caught. What about the other thousands of news stories that form the fabric of confusion, spin, and deceit that passes for "political analysis" in the establishment press? The net result of this syndrome, as regards the 2004 election, is that somehow the truth about John Kerry never took root in the public mind.

Let's unplug the Kerry matrix program for a few minutes and look with real eyes at the man who was almost elected to the most powerful position in the world. Kerry told Americans he believes human life begins at conception, but he supports unrestricted abortion-on-demand up until the very moment of birth, opposes bans on the horrific partial-birth abortion procedure, and opposes parental-notification laws.

Kerry said he wanted to balance the budget, but he had opposed a balanced-budget amendment five times.

Kerry said he'd cut taxes on "working people," but he has a long record of supporting tax increases and opposing tax cuts.

Kerry said he would make a "stronger America" and win the war on terror, but he is profoundly anti-military, having voted for at least seven major reductions in defense and military spending.

Kerry said he opposes same-sex marriage—but he was one of only fourteen senators to vote against the Defense of Marriage Act, which was signed into law by President Bill Clinton.

These impossible contradictions are all easily provable—they're Kerry's Senate voting record—and yet the public never heard them. Because the press, which wanted Kerry to win, wouldn't report the truth, at least not so it would sink in.

Kerry made his four-month tour of duty in Vietnam the centerpiece of his campaign, but the best-selling book *Unfit for Command,* giving voice to dozens of decorated Vietnam vets who served alongside Kerry, painted a grotesquely disturbing picture of a budding sociopath. Overwhelmingly, Kerry's Vietnam colleagues portrayed him, writes columnist David Limbaugh, "as a ruthless, self-promoting egomaniac who systematically placed his own interests above his fellow soldiers and who was obsessively involved in building his résumé at all costs during the entirety of his short tour in Vietnam." Author John O'Neill, Limbaugh added, "depicts Kerry—with mountains of documented evidence—as a pathological, unconscionable liar whose penchant for dishonesty in Vietnam was only exceeded by his brutal, unmitigated slander of his fellow soldiers when he rushed stateside to lobby against them, their superiors and the entire military establishment."[3]

In sum, John Kerry was a fraud whose election as president would have caused incalculable national harm. It was only the combined testimony of the Swiftboat vets—scores of bona fide war heroes who were actually there in Vietnam with John Kerry and knew the truth—that ultimately persuaded the public, despite the media's pro-Kerry spin, that the Massachusetts senator was "unfit for command."

So where were the media? Same place they were when Bill Clinton was allegedly trading sensitive weapons technology to the Communist Chinese in return for campaign contributions, when they learned he was having a sexual affair in the Oval Office with a woman barely older than his own daughter, when a credible allegation of forcible rape was made public, when he was subverting America's intelligence capability that later allowed 9-11 to happen, when he committed outrage after impeachable outrage right under the media's noses. The press looked the other way.

You see, corruption and even criminality on the part of a candidate don't matter with the establishment media nearly as much as that candidate's support for legalized abortion on demand, the activist homosexual agenda, and the rest of the secular, big-government agenda. Indeed, the press today share none of the concern and skepticism the Founding Fathers had over government. Rather, the media—and because of them a good deal of the population—have come to look to government as the primary problem solvers. This is simply because the more God diminishes in our lives, the more government has to rise to take His place. As William Penn said, "Men must be governed by God or they will be ruled by tyrants."

Thus the media tend always to favor the Democratic Party and big-government solutions to all problems precisely because God isn't real to them. Please don't tell me some of them "go to church" or that this one's a Catholic or some other nonsense. I'm saying that when people have a real moment-to-moment relationship—with "fear and trembling," as the Good Book says—with the Living God, they do not look to government to solve all of their problems.

One detrimental result of having such a subversive press is that it generates a subtle but powerful pressure on the president and other leaders. Put yourself in the president's place. You're basically always surrounded by the press corps—professional on the surface but secretly hostile to you and, in fact, hostile to the foundational values underlying Western civilization. They're watching every move you make, recording every word that comes out of your month, looking for ways to undermine you. Remember—they wanted someone else to win the office you hold.

Clearly this dynamic exerts a powerful subconscious pressure on the president (and other leaders) to please the media, and thus to bow to the agenda championed by the media. After all, the media determine what much of the public will see, hear, and *think* about the issues of the day and about the president himself. Any president obviously wants the public's approval of what he's doing (otherwise he can't be reelected), and this depends to a significant extent on his favorable portrayal by the press. Thus there is a constant and powerful pressure on elected leaders to bend, to compromise their principles, and to betray the public trust, fearing that not to do so will result in disastrously negative media coverage and their ultimate defeat.

Why did candidate George W. Bush come up with a budget-busting prescription drug benefit program before the 2000 election? Because candidate Al Gore had promised a budget-busting prescription drug benefit program, and the media made the public feel that any candidate who didn't offer a prescription drug benefit program hated old people and shouldn't be elected president. Honest reporting would have relieved Bush of the election-year pressure to mirror Gore's vote-buying giveaway promises.

In short, politicians always have the temptation to abandon their principles and fall to corruption in any of a thousand ways. The media, if they were doing their job, would not only keep politicians honest through watchdog reporting but would also reduce leaders' temptation to stray from the Constitution by not making evil and corruption look so reasonable and attractive, and by not making the Constitution and biblical principles look so unfair and mean-spirited.

But it gets much worse. Let's follow the trail down the rabbit hole and see how deep it goes.

ISRAELI "GOLIATH" THREATENS ARAB "DAVID"

ONE OF the most spectacular virtual-reality mass illusions in the world today—reinforced constantly by the news media—is the perception that, in the never-ending Arab-Israeli conflict, Israel is the evil aggressor "Goliath" threatening the righteous but powerless Arab "David."

How is this possible? Israel, a sliver of a country the size of New Jersey, is surrounded by twenty-two Arab nations with vastly more population, land, wealth, armies, and oil. Israel has been attacked by its Arab neighbors five times in all-out wars of intended annihilation—the first war coming one day after Israel's founding in 1948! To this day, Israel is obligated to continually defend itself in a perpetual state of war declared by hostile neighbor nations *openly sworn to destroy it* as well as constant terrorist attacks on innocent civilians by jihadist suicide bombers.

To regard the tiny Jewish state as the aggressor in the Arab-Israeli conflict, then, is delusional. It's like putting a seven-year-old in the ring with a heavyweight boxer and seeing the adult boxer as the underdog and the child as the bully.

Here's how this illusion is accomplished. Arab leaders, many of whom have from the start vowed to eliminate the Jewish state from the Middle East, have conspired to attain by guile and deceit what their militaries could not accomplish through repeated wars of aggression. They have cultivated a campaign to establish a "Palestinian state"—directly on top of a vanquished Israel.

The Palestinian cause is a modern-day myth, broadcast and reinforced endlessly by the news media. The Palestinian state is the Trojan horse of the Arab world, designed to get inside Israel by way of deception and promises of peace. The Palestinian leadership doesn't want peace with Israel; it wants Israel.

Like the Palestinian leadership, the other leaders of the Arab world care nothing for the Arab people who call themselves Palestinians—they care only for the destruction of Israel, which they hope the Palestinian cause will ultimately bring. As President Jimmy Carter confessed at a 1979 press conference, "I have never met an Arab leader that in private professed a desire for an independent Palestinian state. Publicly, they all espouse an independent Palestinian state."

Let's pull on just one thread in the fabric of the Palestinian cause and see what happens. Remember the "martyrdom" of twelve-year-old Mohammed al-Dura? It's a classic example of the media matrix. The world was horrified as news broadcasts played the sensational video footage over and over again of the Palestinian boy being shot on September 30, 2000, apparently by Israeli forces, and then dying pitifully in his father's arms.

Heart-wrenching photos of the father and son in death's grip became immortalized in posters that were plastered up and down the streets of the West Bank and Gaza, inspiring many a youthful suicide bomber to join Mohammed in martyr's paradise. He became the poster boy and rallying cry of the bloody intifada that claimed hundreds of lives.

Although the Israeli military initially assumed responsibility for the incident, it soon became apparent that the Israelis could not have shot the boy, due to a large barrier between the Israeli military outpost across the remote junction in Gaza and the position of the boy and his father. In 2003 an independent journalistic investigation concluded that the al-Dura affair was actually a piece of Palestinian street theater, similar to the dramatic Palestinian funeral processions that were observed after the Israeli incursion into the Jenin refugee camp. During that public spectacle, a martyred "corpse" twice fell off the stretcher, only to hop back up and retake his place in the procession. (The Palestinians had claimed three thousand deaths in Jenin—the actual toll turned out to be fifty-two.)

It turns out many Palestinians were playing to the camera on the day Mohammed al-Dura was "martyred." Israeli commentator Amnon Lord's account of the larger scene at Netzarim Junction when the boy was supposedly shot to death describes "incongruous battle scenes complete with wounded combatants and screeching ambulances played out in front of an audience of laughing onlookers, while makeshift movie directors do retakes of botched scenes."

Palestinian journalist Sami El Soudi echoes Lord's observation, revealing that "almost all Palestinian directors take part more or less voluntarily in these war commissions, under the official pretext that we should use all possible means, including trickery and fabulation, to fight against the tanks and airplanes the enemy has and we don't. . . . Our official press reported 300 wounded and dead at Netzarim junction the day when Mohammed was supposedly killed. Most of the cameramen there were Palestinians. . . . They willingly took part in the masquerade, filming fictional scenes, believing they were doing it out of patriotism. When a scene was well done the onlookers laughed and applauded."

"It is incredible," says French journalist Gérard Huber, "how many people were calmly filming the battle of Netzarim on September 30th,

2000. Not only professionals—some of them standing no more than ten meters away from the al-Dura incident—but amateurs as well. The rushes [video clips] are full of surprising incongruities: Children smile as ambulances go by. A 'wounded' Palestinian collapses and two seconds later an ambulance pulls up to take him to the hospital. It looks as if the driver had been cued in, knew in advance where the Palestinian was going to fall, or was waiting in the upper right hand corner just out of the photographic field ready to zoom in on signal."

Street theater. The Mohammed al-Dura story—which rather than documenting Israeli brutality toward Palestinians shows instead the Arab propaganda machine being enabled, magnified, and laundered by the "mainstream press"—is but one story. There are hundreds and hundreds of similar shabby episodes—from the "Jenin massacre" to the "murder" of Rachel Corrie—that together create and reinforce this preposterous virtual-reality illusion of Israel as the aggressor. The truth is, the Palestinian cause is itself a giant piece of street theater, just as the separate scenes—Mohammed al-Dura's "martyrdom," children being told they'll go to heaven if they commit mass murder, leaders like the late Yasser Arafat pretending to seek peace with Israel (in English) while simultaneously urging violent jihad (in Arabic)—are the little charades that comprise the whole.

It takes an incredible amount of effort and energy on the part of the news media to maintain such an obviously outrageous suspension of reality. But what would happen if the press reported accurately, objectively, and courageously on the Middle East conflict? Media reports would reflect, truthfully, that Israel is a Western democracy surrounded by dozens of backward, repressive, terror-supporting Arab police states dedicated to Israel's annihilation. They'd show that the Nobel Peace Prize–winning Arafat was the father of modern terrorism. They'd show that the so-called Palestinian problem was cynically created for the precise purpose of eliminating the Jewish state by deception. The media would reveal that the Palestinian leadership is not now, nor has it ever been, interested in a *separate* Palestinian state next to Israel, but rather, in taking over *all* of Israel.

"Well, what about the West Bank?" you say. "Doesn't that belong rightfully to the Palestinians?"

When did it belong to the Palestinians? Before 1967, when Israel seized it in an unprovoked war of intended annihilation launched by neighboring Arab nations, the West Bank was part of Jordan. So whence comes this idea that it belonged to the Palestinians? It's a myth, a lie—a matrix program—created in the Arab Middle East and presented endlessly by the Western press as though it were reality.

"Pedophile Priests" and Boy Scouts

We've seen in the preceding examples just how flagrant the media's distortion of reality can get. Now consider how subtle it can get.

Let's focus for a few moments on one of the most sensational news stories of recent years, the Catholic Church's clergy sex scandal, usually identified by the ubiquitous news tag "Pedophile Priests." It's a great headline—short, punchy, and with that nice double-P alliteration. The only problem is, it's not true.

It turns out, the vast majority of the offending priests' misdeeds do *not* involve "pedophilia"—sexual contact between an adult and a prepubescent youth. Rather, they amount to sexual seductions of teenage boys by predatory homosexual men who have abused their position of authority and trust. Stephen Rubino, a lawyer who has represented more than three hundred alleged victims of priest abuse, estimates that 85 percent of the victims have been teenage boys, according to *National Review*'s Rod Dreher.[4]

If you recall, the American press was white-hot in exposing the Catholic hierarchy's inexcusable toleration of known sex offenders, transferring them to other posts and generally looking the other way rather than reporting their crimes to the police, ejecting them out of the clergy and into jail. Yet a horrendous hypocrisy accompanied the media's coverage of "pedophile priests."

You see, there's been another major ongoing news story involving homosexuality—namely, the controversy over the "discriminatory" policies of the Boy Scouts of America.

For several years now, many Americans, organizations, and corporations have withdrawn their financial and moral support from the Boy Scouts and condemned the organization as prejudiced and bigoted. At least fifty United Way chapters have ceased to fund the Boy Scouts, some local governments and school districts have declared it to be discriminatory, and the American Civil Liberties Union attacks it endlessly.

And what did the century-old Boy Scouts of America—one of the most beloved and beneficial organizations in history, having helped lead *tens of millions* of boys into responsible adulthood—do to deserve this vilification?

Just this: unlike the Catholic Church in America, the scouting organization doesn't knowingly allow homosexual men to hold official positions of trust and authority over young males.

Indeed, historically the Boy Scouts of America has had its own problem with sexual offenses committed by adult leaders against Scouts—so serious that prevention has become a major preoccupation, with constant leader screening and training, the "two-deep leadership" requirement, and programs for Scouts to identify warning signs of inappropriate advances by adults.

The scouting folks understand the undeniable reality that adults interested in sexual contact with young people gravitate toward careers and volunteer positions allowing proximity to their prey—positions such as coaches, teachers, scoutmasters, and priests.

The scouts simply refuse to allow what the Catholic Church has allowed—letting known homosexuals occupy positions of authority and trust, positions too easily and too often used to prey on vulnerable young people.

So the big question: Why does the mainstream press condemn the Catholic Church for allowing predatory homosexuals to destroy the lives of boys while simultaneously condemning the Boy Scouts of America for trying to avoid precisely the same thing in their organization?

What? You don't see the media condemning the Boy Scouts? (Remember, I said "subtle.") The press provides widespread and sympathetic journalistic voice to the absurd arguments and campaigns of those reviling the Scouts, cutting off their funding, and portraying them as a hateful, "discriminatory" organization. Without this media cheerleading, the shrill condemnations of radical homosexuals and ACLU lawyers would be seen for what they are—shameful attempts to destroy one of the most positive institutions America has ever known.

Today's mainstream news organizations—which, as we have seen, include a considerable number of agenda-driven homosexuals who cynically regard the press as just a powerful activist tool—are quick to reflect the gay rights movement's condemnation of the Boy Scouts' organization and the Catholic Church, both of which officially oppose homosexuality.

The only problem for pro–gay rights journalists is, How do you get around the fact that it's none other than *smooth-talking predatory homosexuals* who are the cause of the problems within both the Catholic Church and the Boy Scouts of America?

No problem. Just call the homosexual priests "pedophiles," which they are not. That takes the spotlight off homosexuality. And simultaneously pretend there is no connection between the issue of allowing homosexuals to become adult Scout leaders and the very real problem of homosexual Scout leaders molesting Scouts. That is the schizophrenic manner in which the media have played both stories, and thus with great subtlety they have advanced the gay rights agenda by protecting it from some very bad publicity.

"Okay," you might be saying. "So you're picking out a few horror stories where the media got it wrong. What's the point?"

These are not horror stories. They're normal. They are the very fabric of the daily news coverage churned out by today's journalism organizations.

Throughout this book, from "gay rights" to "multiculturalism" to "sexual liberation," we've seen at every turn the central role the news media have played in selling radical agendas to Americans:

Gay rights. Abortion rights. Gun control. Hate crimes. Separation of church and state. Behind these and other facile news labels are what amount to virtual-reality constructs, sophisticated marketing products composed of lies and truth seamlessly sewn together. Poke at them a little and they burst—spilling out marketing slogans, half-truths, emotionalized reasoning, distortions and bald-faced lies. Whatever the focus, today's so-called mainstream news coverage is rooted in powerfully propagandistic impulses and results in a web of matrix-like delusions— which most of us think of as the real world.

WHAT'S BEHIND THE MEDIA MATRIX?

IN TRUTH, propagandists within the news media, just like all of the other marketers of evil discussed in this book (in other words, the "authority" class the average person looks to for experts and role models), are themselves pawns in a great cosmic game of deception. In a very real sense they're also caught up in and subject to a matrix program—but one that's been running, not only during this generation, but in one way or another for as long as man has been around. And this real-world matrix is every bit as powerful, consuming, and seemingly inescapable as that in the science-fiction thriller.

Of course, I'm talking about *evil*, the real matrix of deception in this world, the dark spiritual dimension that "waits upon" the human race to tempt and ensnare as many of us as possible. Evil approaches each of us mainly through other people, who typically don't realize the role they're playing in leading us astray. One need only think of a fourteen-year-old boy seducing a thirteen-year-old girl to get this concept; he doesn't realize the harm he's doing to both of them. Indeed, most of us, from the time we're born, are pressured, at one time or another, by parents, family, friends, teachers, employers, and the larger culture to become something other than what the Good Lord intended us to become. With the promise of reward and/or the threat of punishment—through intimidation, false love, cruelty, seduction, and endless other ways people appeal to the various hidden weaknesses in all of us—our lives are shaped and molded by outside influences.

In a sense, I'm describing the very machinery of life within the matrix that all of us—even the most decent and noble—get caught up in to one degree or another. But this life also causes us to suffer, and it is that very suffering that prompts us to desire to be free of the matrix of evil. Although some people descend into loving the matrix, others are not at all happy living there and, like Neo, yearn to be free. If that sounds far-fetched, consider twentieth-century history. We've all seen how many people living under Communist or Nazi propaganda succumbed to the lies of totalitarianism. Some even reveled in it, rising to become leaders. And yet other people resisted the lie—even unto death. We should never underestimate the power of appeals to the dark impulses of human nature.

Consider a current example of this kind of extreme matrix programming. In some parts of the Islamic world, children are bred and nurtured for what they are taught is their "highest purpose"—attaching explosives to their God-given bodies and vaporizing themselves while they take with them as many innocent people as possible. All in the insane belief they are thereby earning their way into heaven.

The thoughts, feelings, and beliefs of such youngsters are not their own thoughts, feelings, and beliefs. Rather, they have been cruelly injected into them, by means of the same sorts of brainwashing techniques that have been used by cult leaders like Charles Manson and Jim Jones. Powerful emotions of hatred, false love, pride and envy, lying philosophies about who God is and how to please Him, all tend to appeal to the victim's lower nature—the brainwasher's best ally in this conversion process. Indeed, what Christianity calls "pride" and psychology calls "ego" is full of weaknesses that can easily be exploited.

The jihadist child's desire for glory and his mortal fear of shaming his family—remember, the sick subculture he lives in literally revolves around honor and shame, not right and wrong—can be played like a musical instrument by a skillful manipulator desiring to implant hatred and call it forth to action. Whether you call it conditioning, programming, or mind control, you must admit that, whatever it is, it must be very strong to induce young people to overcome their own natural desire to live, to have a family, to be happy.

Don't think for a minute that this dynamic of being programmed by others occurs only in far-off lands. It goes on right here in the good old USA, in your state, in your town—perhaps in your home. Of course, for most of us, particularly in America, the pressures are usually less obvious than they are for those living under horrendous "isms" like Communism and radical Islamism. But the principles are exactly the same.

Pick a behavior—say, body piercing. Do you really think millions of people independently arrived at the idea that it's a great thing to bore holes in multiple parts of their bodies (and I'm not talking about earrings) and embed metal objects there? Obviously, people do this because they see others doing it, yet somehow they still believe it's their own idea! No one likes to think he or she has a weak mind and is acting out the suggestions of other people.

But here's the key point about being influenced and shaped by peer pressure: If you're unwilling to recognize there's something wrong with your programming, with the way you think and act and feel, that means you're firmly in its grip. But if you are more self-aware—if you're introspective and sincere enough to recognize there's something wrong with the way you are living—then you can break out of the peer-pressure matrix. God rewards honest people, those who are willing to give up the lie, no matter how painful that is or how damaging to our pride.

But since we all seem to have this part of our nature that is somehow more inclined to believe flattering con men than prophets telling us painful truths, it's essential that our nation's culture revolve around reality. That's what true civilization is. A culture that affirms good as good and evil as evil acts as a mirror of sorts, helping each of us keep a firm grip on public and private morality.

A well-known Bible verse says, "Woe unto them that call evil good, and good evil; that put darkness for light, and light for darkness; that put bitter for sweet, and sweet for bitter!" (Isaiah 5:20). Indeed, this book is about how evil is packaged and perfumed to look good—and good made to appear evil.

Unfortunately, today's establishment press, the primary filter through which we receive most of our information about the world, does not revolve around reality. As a matter of fact, over the past few decades no institution has been more culpable for making evil appear good and good appear evil than the media.

"The Evil of the Age"

Hiding behind the pretense of journalistic impartiality, de facto activists masquerading as objective, dispassionate reporters use the same seductions, the same expert packaging of corruption, the same propaganda techniques that professional marketers use. In America, what was once a free press—the hallmark of a free country—has largely become just another public relations establishment, intent on advancing ideologies and agendas that are hostile to traditional American values. (For the ultimate case in point, in the next chapter we'll take an in-depth look at the most shocking and dishonest public relations crusade of all—namely, the campaign to legalize abortion.)

Make no mistake, it is because of the news media that abortion destroys more than a million lives in America every year. Most members of the establishment press want abortion to be legal, and that is why it is legal.

But what would happen if today's news media were to report accurately, objectively, and courageously on abortion—as the *New York Times* did way back in the 1870s when it headlined its groundbreaking investigative series on abortion in New York, "The Evil of the Age"?

What if reporters and editors cut through the high-flying rhetoric of civil rights and constitutional freedom and women's health and brought the issue down to little, perfectly formed human babies—three thousand of them every day, the same number of people as perished on 9-11—being painfully ripped apart, suctioned, chemically burned, sliced up, or decapitated?

What if the press diligently reported on the proven and devastating physical and psychological effects abortion has on women or on the many studies that show abortion leads to an increased risk of breast cancer? What if the press actually broadcast pictures or video of abortions?

What if the press reported—not just once, equivocally and in subdued tones, as it is prone to do with facts it doesn't like but feels obligated to report—but aggressively and relentlessly, with saturation coverage, as today's *New York Times* did with dozens upon dozens of front-page stories on the Abu Grahib prison scandal?

Can there be any doubt as to the result? Americans would see the truth once again, and the realization of the horror of abortion would, as it did for centuries before this generation, seep into and eventually permeate the public consciousness. Abortion would not only become illegal once again, but would widely be recognized as grossly immoral, barbaric and criminal.

Are you ready? It's time to unplug the abortion matrix program . . .

9

BLOOD CONFESSIONS

*How Lying Marketers Sold America on
Unrestricted Abortion*

WOMEN MUST HAVE CONTROL over their own bodies."

"Safe and legal abortion is every woman's right."

"Who decides? *You* decide!"

"Abortion is a personal decision between a woman and her doctor."

"Who will make this most personal decision of a woman's life? Will women decide, or will the politicians and bureaucrats in Washington?"

"Freedom of choice—a basic American right."

In one of the most successful marketing campaigns in modern political history, the "abortion rights" movement—with all of its emotionally compelling catchphrases and powerful political slogans—has succeeded in turning what once was a crime into a fiercely defended constitutional right.

During the tumultuous 1960s, after centuries of legal prohibition and moral condemnation of abortion, a handful of dedicated activists launched an unprecedented marketing campaign. Their aim was twofold: first, to capture the news media and thus public opinion, and then to change the nation's abortion laws.

Their success was rapid and total—resulting in abortion being legalized in all fifty states for virtually any reason and throughout all nine months of pregnancy. Since the Supreme Court's controversial *Roe v. Wade* decision in 1973, American doctors have performed well over forty million abortions.

Although polls consistently show Americans *disapprove* of unfettered abortion-on-demand by a three-to-one margin, the movement's well-crafted, almost magical slogans—appealing to Americans' deeply rooted inclination toward tolerance, privacy, and individual rights—have provided the abortion camp a powerful rhetorical arsenal with which to fight off efforts to reverse *Roe,* which struck down all state laws outlawing abortion.

In marketing wars, the party that frames the terms of the debate almost always wins. And the early abortion marketers brilliantly succeeded in doing exactly that—diverting attention from the core issues of exactly what abortion does to both the unborn child and the mother, and focusing the debate instead on a newly created issue: choice. No longer was the morality of killing the unborn at issue, but rather "who decides."

The original abortion-rights slogans from the early '70s—they remain virtual articles of faith and rallying cries of the "pro-choice" movement to this day—were "Freedom of choice" and "Women must have control over their own bodies."

"I remember laughing when we made those slogans up," recalls Bernard Nathanson, M.D., cofounder of the pro-abortion vanguard group NARAL, reminiscing about the early days of the abortion rights movement in the late '60s and early '70s. "We were looking for some sexy, catchy slogans to capture public opinion. They were very cynical slogans then, just as all of these slogans today are very, very cynical."

Besides having served as chairman of the executive committee of NARAL—originally the National Association for the Repeal of Abortion Laws and later renamed the National Abortion and Reproductive Rights Action League—as well as its medical committee, Nathanson was one of the principal architects and strategists of the abortion movement in the United States. He tells an astonishing story.[1]

Changing the Law on Abortion

"In 1968 I met Lawrence Lader," says Nathanson. "Lader had just finished a book called *Abortion,* and in it had made the audacious demand that abortion should be legalized throughout the country. I had just finished a residency in obstetrics and gynecology and was impressed with the number of women who were coming into our clinics, wards and hospitals suffering from illegal, infected, botched abortions.

"Lader and I were perfect for each other. We sat down and plotted out the organization now known as NARAL. With Betty Friedan, we set up this organization and began working on the strategy.

"We persuaded the media that the cause of permissive abortion was a liberal, enlightened, sophisticated one," recalls the movement's cofounder. "Knowing that if a true poll were taken, we would be soundly defeated, we simply fabricated the results of fictional polls. We announced to the media that we had taken polls and that 60 percent of Americans were in favor of permissive abortion. This is the tactic of the self-fulfilling lie. Few people care to be in the minority. We aroused enough sympathy to sell our program of permissive abortion by fabricating the number of illegal abortions done annually in the U.S. The actual figure was approaching 100,000, but the figure we gave to the media repeatedly was 1 million.

"Repeating the big lie often enough convinces the public. The number of women dying from illegal abortions was around 200–250 annually. The figure we constantly fed to the media was 10,000. These false figures took root in the consciousness of Americans, convincing many that we needed to crack the abortion law.

"Another myth we fed to the public through the media was that legalizing abortion would only mean that the abortions taking place illegally would then be done legally. In fact, of course, abortion is now being used as a primary method of birth control in the U.S. and the annual number of abortions has increased by 1,500 percent since legalization."[2]

NARAL's brilliantly deceitful marketing campaign, bolstered by fraudulent research, was uncannily successful. In New York the law outlawing abortion had been on the books for 140 years. "In two years of work, we at NARAL struck that law down," says Nathanson. "We lobbied the legislature, we captured the media, we spent money on public relations. . . . Our first year's budget was $7,500. Of that, $5,000 was allotted to a public relations firm to persuade the media of the correctness of our position. That was in 1969." New York immediately became the abortion capital for the eastern half of the United States.

"We were inundated with applicants for abortion," says Nathanson. "To that end, I set up a clinic, the Center for Reproductive and Sexual

Health (CRASH), which operated in the east side of Manhattan. It had 10 operating rooms, 35 doctors, 85 nurses. It operated seven days a week, from 8 a.m. to midnight. We did 120 abortions every day in that clinic. At the end of the two years that I was the director, we had done 60,000 abortions. I myself, with my own hands, have done 5,000 abortions. I have supervised another 10,000 that residents have done under my direction. So I have 75,000 abortions in my life. Those are pretty good credentials to speak on the subject of abortion."[3]

"A Window into the Womb"

After two years, Nathanson resigned from CRASH and became chief of the obstetrical service at St. Luke's Hospital in New York City, a major teaching center for Columbia University Medical School. At that time, in 1973, a raft of new technologies and apparatuses had just become available, all designed to afford physicians a "window into the womb."

Nathanson recalls the dazzling array of cutting-edge technologies back then:

Real-time ultrasound: an instrument which beams high frequency sound into the mother's abdomen. The echoes that come back are collected by a computer and assembled into a moving picture;

Electronic fetal heart monitoring: We clamp an apparatus on the mother's abdomen, and then continuously record the fetal heart rate, instant by instant;

Fetoscopy: an optical instrument put directly into the womb. We could watch that baby, actually eyeball it.

Cordocentesis: taking a needle, sticking it into the pregnant mother's uterus and, under ultrasound, locating the umbilical arteries and actually putting a needle into the cord, taking the baby's blood, diagnosing its illnesses, and treating it by giving it medicine.

"Anyway," says Nathanson, "as a result of all of this technology—looking at this baby, examining it, investigating it, watching its metabolic functions, watching it urinate, swallow, move and sleep, watching it dream, which you could see by its rapid eye movements via ultrasound, treating it, operating on it—I finally came to the conviction that this was my patient. This was a person! I was a physician, pledged to save my patients' lives, not to destroy them. So I changed my mind on the subject of abortion.

"There was nothing religious about it," he hastens to add. "This was purely a change of mind as a result of this fantastic technology, and the new insights and perceptions I had into the nature of the unborn child."

Nathanson expressed some doubts about abortion in an editorial in the *New England Journal of Medicine.* "I was immediately summoned to a kangaroo court and was discharged from the pro-abortion movement, something I do not lose sleep over."

In 1985, intrigued by the question of what really happens during an abortion in the first three months of a pregnancy, Nathanson decided to put an ultrasound machine on the abdomen of a woman undergoing an abortion and to videotape what happens.

"We got a film that was astonishing, shocking, frightening," he says.

"It was made into a film called *The Silent Scream.* It was shattering, and the pro-abortion people panicked. Because at this point, we had moved the abortion debate away from moralizing, sermonizing, sloganeering and pamphleteering into a high-tech argument. For the first time, the pro-life movement now had all of the technology and all of the smarts, and the pro-abortion people were on the defensive."

Nathanson's film provoked a massive campaign of defamation on the part of the pro-abortion movement, including charges that he had doctored the film. He hadn't. "I was accused of everything from pederasty to nepotism. But the American public saw the film."

In 1987 Nathanson released another, even stronger film called *Eclipse of Reason,* introduced by Charlton Heston. "*The Silent Scream* dealt with a child who was aborted at twelve weeks," said Nathanson. "But there are four hundred abortions every day in this country that are done after the third month of pregnancy. Contrary to popular misconception, *Roe v. Wade* makes abortion permissible up to and including the ninth month of pregnancy. I wanted to dramatize what happens in one of these late abortions, after the third month.

"They took a fetuscope, which is a long optical instrument with a lens at one end and a strong light at the other. They inserted the fetuscope into the womb of a woman at 19½ weeks, and a camera was clamped on the eyepiece and then the abortionist went to work.

"This procedure was known as a D&E (dilation and evacuation). It involves dilating the cervix, rupturing the bag of waters, taking a large crushing instrument and introducing it way high up into the uterus, grabbing a piece of the baby, pulling it off the baby, and just repeating this procedure until the baby has been pulled apart, piece by piece.

"Then the pieces are assembled on a table, put together like a jigsaw puzzle, so the abortionist can be sure that the entire baby has been removed. We photographed all this through the fetuscope. This is a shattering film."[4]

Thus did Bernard Nathanson, a cofounder and top strategist of the pro-abortion movement, come to be staunchly committed to the cause of ending legalized abortion in America. Nathanson is by no means the only abortionist to switch sides in the abortion war. Indeed, in recent years hundreds of abortion providers have left their profession. On its Web site, NARAL bemoans "the dwindling number of doctors willing or trained to perform abortions."

If we really want to understand how abortion has been so successfully marketed, there's no better source than those who have worked in the abortion industry. They, like no one else, really know firsthand what it's like to sell and perform abortions for a living.

Deceptive Counseling

CAROL EVERETT of Dallas, Texas, got involved in the abortion industry in 1973, the year of *Roe v. Wade*, after having an abortion herself. She set up referral clinics in Texas, Louisiana, and Oklahoma, then worked in two clinics in which eight hundred abortions were performed monthly, and eventually ran five abortion clinics. She describes how women coming to her clinics were counseled:

Those kids, when they find out that they are pregnant, may not want an abortion; they may want information. But when they call that number, which is paid for by abortion money, what kind of information do you think they're going to get? Remember, they sell abortions—they don't sell keeping the baby, or giving the baby up for adoption, or delivering that baby. They only sell abortions.

The counselor asks, "How far along are you? What's the first day of your last normal period?"

They've got their wheel there and they figure it out. The counselor is paid to be this girl's friend and authority figure. She is supposed to seduce her into a friendship of sorts—to sell her the abortion.[5]

Surprisingly, professional public relations firms are commonly brought in to train clinic personnel to sell women on the abortion option. Nita Whitten worked as chief secretary at another Dallas abortion clinic, that of Dr. Curtis Boyd. Whitten concurs with Everett about the often-obsessive profit motive of abortion clinics.

"I was trained by a professional marketing director in how to sell abortions over the telephone," she said. "He took every one of our receptionists, nurses and anyone else who would deal with people over the phone through an extensive training period. The object was, when the girl called, to hook the sale so she wouldn't get an abortion somewhere else, or adopt out her baby, or change her mind."

With disarming candor, Whitten adds, "We were doing it for the money."[6]

Kathy Sparks, who worked in a Granite City, Illinois, abortion clinic, describes the manipulative counseling practices used at her clinic:

One particular worker was very good. She could sit down with these girls during counseling and cry with them at the drop of a pin. She would immediately draw them out, asking them all kinds of good questions, to find out what their pressure point was—what was driving them to want the abortion.

Whatever that pressure point was, she would magnify it. If the girl was afraid her parents would kill her, and didn't know how to tell them, the counselor would proceed by saying, "Well, that's why abortion is here, we want to help you; this is the answer to your problems." If it was money, she would tell the girl how much baby items cost: "You know it costs $3,000 to have a baby now," or "You know, baby shoes are $28. Sleepers are $15. But you know, that's what's so wonderful about abortion. We can take care of this problem and you don't have to worry about it until you are financially prepared to have a child."[7]

The salesmanship at her clinic was so effective, says Sparks, ninety-nine out of every one hundred women would decide to have an abortion. But abortion clinics, and particularly Planned Parenthood, the world's largest abortion provider, insist publicly that they offer all alternatives—keeping the baby, adoption, abortion—without coercion or preference.

"The women were never given any type of alternatives to abortions," says Debra Henry, who worked as an assistant and counselor for six months at an ob-gyn office in Levonia, Michigan. "They were never told about adoption agencies, that there were people out there willing to help them, to give them homes to live in, to provide them with care, and even financial support."[8]

Carol Everett relates what happened after the initial counseling of her clinic's clients:

After the basic questions, the girls were told briefly about what was to happen to them after the procedure. All they were told about the procedure itself was that they would experience slight cramping, similar to menstrual cramps. They were not told about the development of the baby, or about the pain that the baby would be experiencing, or about the physical or emotional effects the abortion would have on them.

The two questions they always ask are: No. 1, "Does it hurt?" And the answer would always be, "Oh, no. Your uterus is a muscle. It's a cramp to open it, a cramp to close it—just a slight cramping sensation." And the girl thinks, "That's no problem. I can stand that. I've been through it before." Then the client asks question No. 2: "Is it a baby?" "No," would come the answer, "it's a product of conception," or "it's a blood clot," or "it's a piece of tissue." They don't even call it a fetus, because that almost humanizes it too much, but it's never a baby."

There are two standard reactions in the recovery room, says Everett:

The first is: "I've killed my baby." It amazed me that this was the first time the patients called it a baby, and the first time they called it murder. But the second reaction is: "I am hungry. You kept me in here for four hours and you told me I'd only be here for two. Let me out of here." That woman is doing what I did when I had my abortion. She's running from her abortion, not dealing with it.[9]

WHY DOCTORS DO ABORTIONS

MANY DOCTORS who perform abortions cite the same contributory factors to their getting started—the media, women's rights groups, and their medical training itself. In addition, doing abortions makes for a very lucrative practice.

Joseph Randall, M.D., of Atlanta, Georgia, frankly admits that he was attracted to the large income potential that abortions offered. Over the ten years that he did abortions, Randall estimates that he performed thirty-two thousand.

"The media were very active early on," recalls Randall. "They were probably one of the major influences on us, telling us that abortion was not only legal, but that it was to serve women. It was to give women a choice, more or less give them a freedom to grow and to take their rightful place in society where they had been kind of pushed down prior to that. We also believed the lie that there were tens of thousands of women being maimed and killed from illegal abortions prior to legalization of abortion law."

Remember, as Nathanson admits, the number of women dying from illegal abortions was only a tiny fraction of what the marketers claimed.

"As part of our medical training," added Randall, "abortions became a necessary procedure, according to the chief of my department. This was in 1971, before the law had changed in the country, but it had changed in New York a few years before. We needed to serve women, we needed to know all the procedures that we had to do for women, and we had to know how to do them well. Otherwise, we weren't considered effectively trained. Our chief said that if we didn't do the abortions, we might as well get out of obstetrics and gynecology because we just wouldn't be complete physicians."[10]

"Why do doctors do abortions?" asks Anthony Levantino, M.D., an ob-gyn who provided abortions for his patients in his Albany, New York, office for eight years. "Why did I do abortions? If you are pro-choice, or, as a lot of people like to say, 'morally neutral' on the subject, and you happen to be a gynecologist, then it's up to you to take the instruments in hand and actively perform abortions. It's part of your training. I've heard it many times from other obstetricians: 'Well, I'm not really pro-abortion, I'm pro-woman.'

"The women's groups in this country have done a very good job of selling that bill of goods to the population, that somehow destroying a life is being pro-women. I can tell you a lot of obstetricians believe it. I used to.

"Along the way," says Levantino, "you find out that you can make a lot of money doing abortions. I worked 9 to 5. I was never bothered at night. I never had to go out on weekends. And I made more money than my obstetrician brethren. And I didn't have to face the liability. That's a big factor, a huge perk. I almost never, ever had to worry about her lawyer bothering me.

"In my practice, we were averaging between $250 and $500 per abortion—and it was cash. It's the one time as a doctor you can say, 'Either pay me up front or I'm not going to take care of you.' Abortion is totally elective. Either you have the money or you don't. And they get it."[11]

Cash payment is common in the abortion industry, says Everett.

"I've seen doctors walk out after three hours' work and split $4,500 dollars between them on a Saturday morning—more if you go longer into the day," she said. "Of the four clinics I've worked in, none of them ever showed that they collected the doctors' money; they collect it separately, and do not show it on any of the records in those clinics. That way, the doctors are independent contractors and the clinic doesn't have to be concerned with their malpractice insurance, and doesn't have to report their income to the IRS."

"Every single transaction that we did," adds Whitten, "was cash money. We wouldn't take a check, or even a credit card. If you didn't have the money, forget it. It wasn't unusual at all for me to take $10,000 to $15,000 a day to the bank—in cash."

Beverly McMillan, M.D., founded the first abortion clinic in Mississippi and did a large volume of business. She makes the provocative observation that not only do many abortion clinics require payment in cash, but they also do not report that income to the government.

"A lot of these folks do not declare all their income," she says flatly. "When you're dealing in cash, unless you're honest, you can just not have a record for that patient, not make an entry on your ledger. I know some people who were paid under the counter. They would get half of their salary in cash, and they never had to pay taxes on that. Why the IRS doesn't go after these guys, I don't understand."[12]

THE HEART OF THE MATTER

ULTRASOUND, THE great awakener of Bernard Nathanson, is routinely employed today to check on the progress of developing babies. In an ironic and shadowy parallel, ultrasound is also used to aid in abortions.

Joseph Randall observed: "The nurses have to look at the ultrasound picture to gauge how far along the baby is for an abortion, because the larger the pregnancy, the more you get paid. It was very important for us to do that. But the turnover definitely got greater when we started using ultrasound. We lost two nurses—they couldn't take looking at it. Some of the other staff left also."

What about the women having the abortions? Do they see the ultrasound?

"They are never allowed to look at the ultrasound because we knew that if they so much as heard the heartbeat, they wouldn't want to have the abortion," said Randall.

A peculiar problem in the abortion clinic is fetal disposal.

"We basically put them down the garbage disposal if they were small enough," said Nita Whitten. "We hardly ever sent anything to the laboratory for pathology unless there was something weird going on and the doctor wanted to make sure he wouldn't get sued."

Kathy Sparks recalled a different disposal method: "Oftentimes, second trimester abortions were performed and these babies we would not put in the little jar with the label to send off to the pathology lab. We would put them down a flush toilet—that's where we would put these babies."

"THERE ARE NO WORDS TO DESCRIBE IT"

EVERY YEAR in the United States more than a million abortions are performed—including tens of thousands of late-term abortions (after the twelfth week). Some of these late abortions are carried out by means of amniotic infusion (the injection of a foreign substance into the amniotic sac) of saline, prostaglandin, urea, or another agent designed to kill the unborn baby.

"Saline abortions have to be done in the hospital because of complications that can arise," says ob-gyn staffer Debra Henry. "Not that they can't arise during other times, but more so now. The saline, a salt solution, is injected into the woman's sac and the baby swallows it. The baby starts dying a slow, violent death. The mother feels everything, and many times it is at this point when she realizes that she really has a live baby inside of her, because the baby starts fighting violently for his or her life. He's just fighting inside because he's burning."

"One night a lady delivered, and I was called in to see her because she was uncontrollable," said David Brewer, M.D., of Glen Ellyn, Illinois. As a military physician in Fort Rucher, Alabama, Brewer performed abortions for ten years. "I went in the room, and she was going to pieces; she was having a nervous breakdown, screaming and thrashing. The nurses were upset because they couldn't get any work done, and all the other patients were upset because this lady was screaming. I walked in, and here was her little saline abortion baby kicking. It had been born alive, and was kicking and moving for a little while before it finally died of those terrible burns, because the salt solution gets into the lungs and burns the lungs, too."

"I'll tell you one thing about D&E," lamented Anthony Levantino. "You never have to worry about a baby's being born alive. I won't describe D&E other than to say that, as a doctor, you are sitting there tearing, and I mean tearing—you need a lot of strength to do it—arms and legs off of babies and putting them in a stack on top of a table."

Commenting on late-term D&E abortions, Carol Everett recalled: "My job was to tell the doctor where the parts were, the head being of special significance because it is the most difficult to remove. The head must be deflated, usually by using the suction machine to remove the brain, then crushing the head with large forceps."

The question of how doctors could tear apart a virtually full-grown baby is painful, perplexing, mystifying.

"Psychologically," noted Everett, "the doctors always sized the baby at 'twenty-four weeks.' However, we did an abortion on one baby I feel was almost full-term. The baby's muscle structure was so strong that it would not come apart. The baby died when the doctor pulled the head off the body."

Kathy Sparks described a second-trimester abortion: "The baby's bones were far too developed to rip them up with this curette, and so he would have to try to pull the baby out with forceps, in about three or four major pieces. Then he scraped and suctioned and scraped and suctioned, and then this little baby boy was lying on the tray. His little face was perfectly formed, little eyes closed and little ears—everything was perfect about this little boy."

"There are no words to describe how bad it really is," added Carol Everett. "I've seen sonograms of the baby pulling away from the instruments as they are introduced into the vagina. And I've seen D&E's through thirty-two weeks done without the mother's being put to sleep. And yes, they hurt and they are very painful to the baby, and yes, they are very, very painful to the woman. I've seen six people hold a woman on the table while they did her abortion."

"MY HEART GOT CALLOUSED"

PHYSICIANS ARE manipulated into going against their consciences and performing abortions, says David Brewer, all in the name of helping women. He described witnessing a suction abortion for the first time during his medical training.

> I can remember . . . the resident doctor sitting down, putting the tube in, and removing the contents. I saw the bloody material coming down the plastic tube, and it went into a big jar. My job afterwards was to go and undo the jar, and to see what was inside.
>
> I didn't have any views on abortion; I was in a training program, and this was a brand new experience. I was going to get to see a new procedure and learn. I opened the jar and took the little piece of stockingette stocking and opened that little bag. The resident doctor said, "Now put it on that blue towel and check it out. We want to make sure that we got it all." I thought, "That'll be exciting—hands-on experience looking at tissue." I opened the sock up and put it on the towel, and there were parts of a *person* in there.

I had taken anatomy, I was a medical student. I *knew* what I was looking at. There was a little scapula and an arm, I saw some ribs and a chest, and a little tiny head. I saw a piece of a leg, and a tiny hand and an arm and, you know, it was like somebody put a hot poker into me. I had a conscience, and it *hurt*. Well, I checked it out and there were two arms and two legs and one head and so forth, and I turned and said, "I guess you got it all." That was a very hard experience for me to go through emotionally.

Here I was with no real convictions, caught in the middle. And so I did what a lot of us do throughout our life. We don't do anything. I didn't talk with anybody about it, I didn't talk with my folks about it, I didn't *think* about it. I did nothing. And do you know what happened? I got to see another abortion. That one hurt too. But again I didn't do anything, and so I kept seeing abortions. Do you know what? It hurt a little bit less every time I saw one.

Then I got to sit down and do an abortion. Well, the first one that I did was kind of hard. It hurt me again like a hot poker. But after a while, it got to where it didn't hurt. My heart got calloused. I was like a lot of people are today—afraid to stand up. I was afraid to speak up. Or some of us, maybe we aren't afraid, but we just don't have our own convictions settled yet.

One particular abortion changed Brewer's life.

I remember an experience as a resident on a hysterotomy (a late-term abortion delivered by Caesarean section). I remember seeing the baby move underneath the sack of membranes as the caesarean incision was made, before the doctor broke the water.

The thought came to me, "My God, that's a *person*." Then he broke the water. And when he broke the water, it was like I had a pain in my heart, just like when I saw the first suction abortion. And then he delivered the baby, and I couldn't touch it. I wasn't much of an assistant. I just stood there, and the reality of what was going on finally began to seep into my calloused brain and heart.

They took that little baby that was making little sounds and moving and kicking, and set it on the table in a cold, stainless steel bowl. And every time I would look over while we were repairing the incision in the uterus and finishing the Caesarean, I would see that little person kicking and moving in that bowl. And it kicked and moved less and less, of course, as time went on. I can remember going over and looking at that baby when we were done with the surgery and the baby was still alive. You could see the chest was moving and the heart beating, and the baby would try to take a little breath like that, and it really hurt inside, and it began to educate me as to what abortion really was.

"Everything Changes"

Anthony Levantino, the "pro-woman" ob-gyn from Troy, New York, relates the revealing and very personal story of what happened that caused him to stop performing abortions.

There was this tremendous conflict going on within me. Here I am, doing my D&Cs (an early term suction abortion), five and six a week, and I'm doing salines on a nightly basis whenever I was on call. The resident on call got the job of doing the salines, and there would usually be two or three of those. They were horrible, because you would see one intact, whole baby being born, and sometimes they were alive. And that was very, very, very frightening. It was a very stomach-turning kind of existence.

My wife and I were looking desperately for a baby to adopt, even while I was throwing them in the garbage at the rate of nine and ten a week. The thought occurred to me even then, "I wish one of these people would just let me have their child." But it doesn't work that way.

We were lucky; it just took four months before we adopted a healthy little girl, and we called her Heather.

We can talk about why doctors do abortions, and I think that the reasons tend to be more or less universal. But why doctors change their minds, I think, is very personal, very different from one doctor to the next. My reasons for quitting were very personal:

Life was good until June 23, 1984. On that date I was on call, but I was at home at the time. We had some friends over and our children were playing in the back yard. At 7:25 that evening, we heard the screech of brakes out in front of the house. We ran outside, and Heather was lying in the road. We did everything we could, but she died.

Let me tell you something. When you lose a child—your child—life is very different. Everything changes. And all of a sudden the idea of a person's life becomes very real. It's not an embryology course anymore; it's not just a couple of hundred dollars. It's the real thing. It's your child you buried.

The old discomforts came back in spades. I couldn't even think about a D&E abortion anymore, no way. Then you start to realize, this is somebody's child. I lost my child—someone who was very precious to us. And now I'm taking somebody's child, and I'm tearing them right out of their womb. I'm killing somebody's child. That's what it took to get me to change. My own sense of self-esteem went down the tubes. I began to feel like a paid assassin. That's exactly what I was. You watch the movies, when somebody goes up to a hit man and pays them to kill someone; that's exactly what I was doing. It got to a point that it just wasn't worth it to me anymore. The money wasn't worth it. "Poor women," my butt. I don't care. This was coming out of my hide, costing me too much personally. For all the money in the world, it wouldn't have made any difference. So I quit.

PUTTING THE GENIE BACK IN THE BOTTLE

IN THE strangest of ironies, Bernard Nathanson, perhaps the closest thing to being "the man who started it all" for the pro-choice movement—the Edward Teller of abortion—now spends his days trying to put the abortion genie back in the bottle. Like Norma McCorvey—who as the barefoot-and-pregnant "Jane Roe" was the pro-abortion plaintiff in the Supreme Court's momentous and fateful *Roe v. Wade* decision—Nathanson also is today dedicated to putting an end to what both now see as a national tragedy akin to the Nazi Holocaust.

"Let me share with you my own personal perception of the abortion tragedy," Nathanson told one California audience:

I'm going to set it against my Jewish heritage and the Holocaust in Europe. The abortion holocaust is beyond the ordinary discourse of morality and rational condemnation. It is not enough to pronounce it absolutely evil. Absolute evil used to characterize this abortion tragedy (forty-three million and counting) is an inept formulation. The abortion tragedy is a new event, severed from connections with traditional presuppositions of history, psychology, politics and morality. It extends beyond the deliberations of reason, beyond the discernments of moral judgment, beyond meaning itself. It trivializes itself to call itself merely a holocaust or a tragedy. It is, in the words of Arthur Cohen, perhaps the world's leading scholar on the European Holocaust, a *mysterium tremendum,* an utter mystery to the rational mind—a mystery that carries with it not only the aspect of vastness, but the resonance of terror, something so unutterably diabolic as to be literally unknowable to us.

This is an evil torn free of its moorings in reason and causality, an ordinary secular corruption raised to unimaginable powers of magnification and limitless extremity. Nelly Sachs, a poetess who wrote poems on the Holocaust in Europe and who won the Nobel Prize in 1966, wrote a poem called "Chorus of the Unborn." Permit me to give you a few lines. She said:

> We, the unborn, the yearning has begun to plague us
> as shores of blood broaden to receive us.
> Like dew, we sink into love but still
> the shadows of time lie like questions over our secret.[13]

When we honestly face the sheer barbarism and brutality of abortion—some of which amounts to infant torture and murder—we're left with a dilemma. Most people who consider themselves pro-choice are, by all appearances, reasonable and caring human beings. And yet they condone, and some even champion, the right to perpetrate the very acts of deception, betrayal, mutilation, torture, and killing described in these pages. How can this be?

In searching for an explanation, Bernard Nathanson compares America's abortion holocaust with what occurred in Europe during World War II. While some would object to the comparison, there are at least a couple of parallels that are both stunning and inescapable—and very instructive when it comes to marketing evil.

During the Nazi era, it's a fact that many apparently reasonable and caring Germans somehow came to regard Jews as less than human. Somehow their perception had been so tampered with that, although their physical eyes would see a human being, in their minds they saw the Jew as something less than human and therefore disposable.

For that matter, even in our own nation during the early nineteenth century, the Supreme Court in its infamous *Dred Scott* decision denied the full personhood of Americans of African origin and ruled that they could never become U.S. citizens. Writing for the court majority, Chief Justice Roger B. Taney said blacks have "no rights which the white man was bound to respect; and that the negro might justly and lawfully be reduced to slavery for his benefit. He was bought and sold and treated as an ordinary article of merchandise and traffic, whenever profit could be made by it."

But what about the Declaration of Independence, with its bedrock affirmation that "all men are created equal"? How did the Supreme Court get around that? According to Chief Justice Taney: "It is too clear for dispute, that the enslaved African race were not intended to be included, and formed no part of the people who framed and adopted this declaration."[14] As it has so many times throughout history, this same dehumanizing phenomenon—complete with an illegitimate blessing by the U.S. Supreme Court—has occurred once again, this time with unborn children as the victims.

Whereas once upon a time pregnant mothers were respectfully, lovingly referred to as being "with child," today we coldly refer to the unborn, not as a child, but as a fetus. Indeed, the word *fetus* has taken on qualities and characteristics convenient to the pro-abortion viewpoint—implying something less than human, with little intrinsic worth, and therefore disposable. If an abortionist or pro-choicer looks at a fetus, his eyes will see a perfectly formed human child—for that is what a fetus actually is—but his mind will see something else, an ugly, nonhuman, disposable lump of tissue.

Interestingly, if there were no word for fetus, such a switch of realities would be more difficult. The word itself becomes a convenient carrier of the ugly, nonhuman characteristics, and is thus a key tool for denying the humanity of the unborn human child.

We're dealing with very deep denial here. More than two decades ago, as a news reporter, I confronted a Planned Parenthood attorney with a photograph of a five-gallon white plastic bucket filled with dead, late-term human babies—the results of one day's abortions at a Canadian hospital. His response was to deny that what he saw were really human babies, and suggested that perhaps they were actually dead monkeys. Mind you, this man made his living defending the world's largest abortion provider—but when he saw real abortions, he denied what was right in front of his own eyes.

Babies? fetuses? monkeys? This sleight-of-hand substitution of a false reality for the real one may make more sense when you consider that a skilled hypnotist can cause his subject to see a doll as a real baby and, more chillingly, to see a real baby as only a doll. But we're not talking about hypnosis here—or are we?

When a stage hypnotist can so quickly and dramatically alter his subject's perceptions—making an educated adult forget his own name, believe he's a yodeling champion, or strut around on stage clucking like a rooster—isn't it reasonable to think that whatever mysterious dynamics allow this sort of mental manipulation on stage would also crop up, perhaps in more disguised ways, in real life? If so, how does a population get itself into such a trance, such a grotesque and deadly delusion, all the while believing it has embraced something enlightened and liberating?

In the case of Nazi Germany, the answer is obvious. There was one national hypnotist in chief, a leader-manipulator who understood the wounded pride of a people crushed by their total loss after World War I and humiliated by the subsequent Treaty of Versailles. Understanding their latent anti-Semitism, their angers, and their intense need for a scapegoat to excuse their defeat and help them reclaim their national pride, Adolf Hitler played the German people like a virtuoso violinist plays a Stradivarius—not only with emotional speeches, but with a massive, relentless propaganda campaign backed by intimidating rallies and terrorizing street bullies. Bypassing reason, he appealed directly and intensely to raw emotion, and he radically altered their perception of reality.

In America, the process is much more subtle but no less pervasive. First, over the last few decades our nation embraced the notion that total sexual freedom, without restriction of any kind, is a right, an entitlement. We've been seduced into blaming moralists as oppressors, and thus separating sexuality from its God-ordained purpose—the sanctified union between husband and wife within the protective confines of marriage, from which issues the most precious of all things: our children. We have abandoned reason and self-restraint in favor of the self-indulgent fulfillment of our personal desires and lusts. And logically, if sex without consequences is the top priority—which it has become—then abortion simply *has* to be an option, no matter what.

Second, a huge factor in making abortion acceptable, indeed a "fundamental American right," has been the change in American law.

Whether in Nazi Germany or in *Roe v. Wade* America, legalizing something is immensely powerful in persuading people of the moral acceptability of immoral acts. In fact, for a great many people, legal *equals* moral.

In America today, the unborn baby is the obvious victim of the abortion holocaust. But there are other victims. Vulnerable young women are deceived by manipulative counselors and unscrupulous "health professionals" into believing their unborn babies are not human, only to find out too late, in the recovery room or shortly thereafter, that they ended the lives of their own children. What crueler trick could one play on a mother?

In truth, millions of people who think of themselves as pro-choice are victims of sophisticated marketing campaigns designed to appeal to their deepest feelings about freedom and equality while simultaneously hooking them through powerful appeals to their selfishness. Understand that marketing evil is different from marketing blue jeans. In the commercial world, you profile people in your target market and map out strategies for selling to them. You're appealing to them, yes, but you're not *changing* them, just understanding their mental-emotional-cultural makeup and reaching in and pushing buttons to elicit the desired response.

In marketing evil, however, a much more profound process is at work. You're in the business of changing, seducing, corrupting people. And the way back is not so easy, because we all exist in a state of pride, which means we don't like to see we've done something wrong. So once we've been tempted to cross the line—in this case, to have an abortion—our very consciousness and loyalties often change.

In the same way, many of the physicians who perform abortions have also been victims of sorts, pressured to do so by an amoral and cowardly medical establishment. Each in his own way has fallen prey to the appealing rhetoric of the abortion marketer who justifies their destructive acts and anesthetizes their consciences with intimidating slogans.

As Dr. David Brewer explained, medical students act against their conscience by learning to perform abortions, because their residency chief insists they must perform abortions if they ever want to become doctors. The residency chief is an authority, and authorities exert a powerful, persuasive influence on suggestible people. (Indeed, people's vulnerability to an authority's suggestion is a core principle of hypnosis.) And what makes the subject here suggestible? The fact that the med student's career is at stake provides a strong inducement for him to give up his principles to fulfill the requirements for success in his chosen field.

When people are the victims of con men, they often are loath to recognize that they have been deceived, simply because they don't want to think they have exercised bad judgment or done anything wrong. In this example, once a medical student starts performing abortions, before long he can no longer see that it is wrong. Moreover, the decreasing conflict he feels each time he performs an abortion is evidence of a movement away from conscience as his involvement progresses. This mirrors the pattern in all corruption—the first lie, the first act of embezzlement, the first rape, the first murder is always the hardest.

The Bible describes this seduction process whereby we ignore our conscience so we can obtain some perceived advantage, but this results instead in spiritual blindness: "Hearing ye shall hear, and shall not understand; and seeing ye shall see, and not perceive: For the heart of this people is waxed gross, and their ears are dull of hearing, and their eyes have they closed; lest they should see with their eyes, and hear with their ears, and understand with their heart, and should be converted, and I should heal them" (Acts 28:26–27).

WAKING UP

FROM ITS inception in the 1960s, America's legal and cultural embrace of abortion has been based on lies, deception, greed, and monumental selfishness. Bernard Nathanson courageously exposed the cynical marketing campaign he led—the fabricated statistics, the slogans, the issue positioning by public relations professionals, and the cowardly cooperation of a servile news media. The other repentant abortion providers profiled here, courtesy of the Pro-Life Action League's "Meet the Abortion Providers" program, further illustrate the emotional manipulation and deceit—not to mention the betrayal, suffering, and death—that have characterized the abortion movement from the start.

But these are only a few stories. There's not enough room to go into the utter fraud of Planned Parenthood, the world's largest abortion provider, founded by the racist eugenicist Margaret Sanger, who preached the inferiority of nonwhite races and had close ties to Hitler's director of genetic sterilization, Ernst Rudin.

Likewise, there's not enough room to go into detail about Norma McCorvey—the original "Jane Roe" on behalf of whom the *Roe v. Wade* case was fought and won. Guess what? McCorvey now admits *Roe v. Wade* was a fraud, and that she was used by abortion rights attorneys in their quest to legalize the procedure. In fact, in 2003 McCorvey filed suit in federal court to have *Roe v. Wade* overturned. Among her 5,437 pages of evidence were affidavits from more than 1,000 women who testified that having an abortion had devastating emotional, physical, and psychological effects on them. Today McCorvey is passionately and publicly committed to undoing the damage she did in her earlier years and ending legalized abortion in America.

Ah, but this is not easily done. McCorvey has encountered the same bizarre denial that Nathanson has on his journey to personal redemption. After years of promoting abortion and helping to make it acceptable in the minds of the media and the public, Nathanson could not undo his earlier manipulations. Once he sold his followers on the abortion idea, he could not unsell them—even by explaining the mechanics of behind-the-scenes manipulation or by producing films showing frighteningly clear video footage of the horrors of abortion.

In truth, it's one thing to make a person do something wrong by deceiving him into thinking that it was right, but it is quite another thing to get him to face the fact that it was wrong and that he has been deceived. The human ego doesn't like to see that it is wrong, and it especially doesn't like to admit it was manipulated by another.

Whether this seduction comes by way of an instructor in medical school, by peer pressure from friends or parents to have an abortion, or by Planned Parenthood (an authority figure for scared teenagers), the seduced no longer sees reality as he or she once saw it, but instead, as the seducer/authority sees it. Of course, there is a temporary comfort in this for the victim. He or she has been set free to pursue whatever course is most convenient or advantageous or pleasurable—thanks to abortion.

However, due to the unnaturalness of the conditioning process, the pain of suffering and tragedy can often jolt people back into a state of consciousness and awakening. Dr. Anthony Levantino mysteriously woke up from his trance to the horror of his abortion practice when his own daughter died. Dr. Beverly McMillan woke up while standing at the sink at the back of her clinic, examining the ripped-apart body of a little aborted baby. Although she had done this examination hundreds of times before, this time, for some mysterious reason, her consciousness was awakened as she realized for the first time that this was a human baby. Sometimes self-deception, like a rubber band, can be stretched only so far before it breaks or snaps back to normal.

When the Nazi Holocaust finally came to an end, Allied soldiers led the horrified German population—the law-abiding, government-believing, reasonable and caring people of the day—through the concentration camps. Newsreels of this guided tour show women crying convulsively, stunned men with heads bowed low in shock and dismay. Filing past piles of emaciated corpses, the stench of death everywhere, an unspeakable horror permeated their souls. All at once they realized that the nagging doubt in the back of their minds—the secret fear that the rumors of genocide might actually be true, but which they had disbelieved, thinking such negative thoughts to be from the demon of disloyalty—had actually been the desperate cry of inner truth. The soft, velvety denial they had lived in vanished instantly, and in its place, the agony of guilt and betrayal.

Don't look down on these people. At least they faced their sins of omission and tacit complicity, having believed their leaders and ignored the urgings of their own conscience. They were forced to acknowledge the horror they had previously denied.

What about us? Will we one day tour through the wreckage of our own culture of death and weep? What will we then think of the marketers' slogans?

"WOMEN MUST have control over their own bodies."

"Safe and legal abortion is every woman's right."

"Who decides? *You* decide!"

"Abortion is a personal decision between a woman and her doctor."

"Who will make this most personal decision of a woman's life? Will women decide, or will the politicians and bureaucrats in Washington?"

"Freedom of choice—a basic American right."

Despite all the clever marketing, this has been a story of great horror and injustice. But it is also one of hope. After all, if people who have performed thousands of abortions can find the courage and love to face the painful reality of what they have done in the past, and now embrace life rather than death, maybe there's hope that the rest of America can join in their confession and share their healing.

LAST, BEST HOPE

The Fall and Rise of American Christianity

DESPITE DECADES OF RELENTLESS attacks on its moral and spiritual foundations, America is still overwhelmingly a Christian nation. Or is it? The numbers certainly give that impression. Four out of five Americans describe themselves as Christians—54.7 percent self-identifying as Protestant, 22 percent as Roman Catholic, and another 2.7 percent as "other Christian," according to a 2004 survey by the Pew Forum on Religion and Public Life. That's almost 80 percent, an overwhelming majority of citizens—and voters.[1]

Our leadership gives that impression. Virtually all of America's presidents have called themselves Christians, from George Washington right on into our own time. Jimmy Carter talked openly and frequently of being a born-again Baptist, while Ronald Reagan, a Presbyterian, was more private, yet had a deep faith. George H. W. Bush, a churchgoing Episcopalian, was succeeded by Bill Clinton, a Baptist who liked to be seen carrying around a large Bible under his arm. And Methodist George W. Bush has spoken of his faith and its centrality to his life more than any other president in our lifetime.

Our church attendance gives that impression. In contrast with Europeans, Americans are still a churchgoing people. On any given weekend, 45 percent of us attend worship services.[2] Tens of millions have bought Rick Warren's *The Purpose-Driven Life,* making it one of the best-selling books in publishing history. And Christians made the much-maligned Mel Gibson film *The Passion of the Christ* one of the top-grossing movies of all time. America appears to be bursting its seams with vibrant Christianity.

There's just one problem.

While a vast majority of the nation's citizens consider themselves Christians, America's popular culture, its laws, its public education system, its news media, and other major institutions have become progressively *un*-Christian—even *anti*-Christian, as we have documented in these pages. The reason for this, of course, is that Christians, like everyone else, have been seduced by the marketers of evil.

For example, they've been taken in by no-fault divorce—the failure rate for marriages among Christians is virtually the same as among non-Christians. Similarly, Christians have fallen prey in mass numbers to abortion, sexual liberation, gay rights, multicultural madness, and all the rest of the marketing seductions of our age.

This is very troubling to church leaders who are increasingly aware they are losing a spiritual tug-of-war with the powerful and corrupting secular culture. Many in their congregations are being converted before their eyes, becoming strangers to the church that once was their spiritual home.

Indeed, it's a dangerous situation for America. The churches are, and always have been, the seat of this nation's moral strength. Revolutionary War citizen-soldiers were commonly recruited from the pulpit, slavery was excoriated from the pulpit, our war dead have been memorialized from the pulpit, and our citizens have ever been exhorted and challenged and comforted from the pulpit. It is from the pulpit that every social evil to plague this nation has been confronted and rebuked while a higher, better road to glory has been promoted.

Even today, despite what amounts to an all-out war on the nation's founding values waged from without and within, the churches remain the last, best hope Americans have for bringing about a rebirth of Western Judeo-Christian culture. But for this very reason, it shouldn't surprise us to discover, as we soon shall, that America's churches themselves have been the number-one target of the marketers of evil.

Unfortunately, once the churches—the fortresses of America's goodness and strength—are overcome, there is no longer a substantial defense against the forces of corruption. And there is no longer a powerful counterforce to fight for a spiritually wholesome culture in which future generations may grow up safely and soundly. Thus it is imperative that we look honestly, dispassionately, and courageously at America's churches, at those who lead them, and at those who attend them. In other words, it is time to focus our spotlight of inquiry on ourselves.

To heal our troubled churches, we must exercise a physician's objective powers of observation. Once we identify the symptoms, we'll be able to diagnose the disease. Likewise, once we've explored honestly and completely the underlying causes and nature of the malady, the cure will be self-evident.

First, the symptoms.

"Like Everyone Else"

A RECENT study by respected Christian pollster George Barna showed that born-again Christian adults in the United States think and act virtually the same as nonbelievers. Questioning respondents about everything from parenting priorities to education and from moral absolutes to the importance of their religious beliefs, Barna said there was almost no difference between those professing to be born-again Christians and non-Christians.

"For years we have reported research findings showing that born-again adults think and behave very much like everyone else," he said. "It often seems that their faith makes very little difference in their life. This new study helps explain why that is: Believers do not train their children to think or act any differently. When our kids are exposed to the same influences, without much supervision, and are generally not guided to interpret their circumstances and opportunities in light of biblical principles, it's no wonder that they grow up to be just as involved in gambling, adultery, divorce, cohabitation, excessive drinking and other unbiblical behaviors as everyone else."[3]

Not only do far too many Christians apparently think and act just like unbelievers these days, but the number and variety of different and contradictory Christian world views and practices—all presumably based on the same Bible—have grown astronomically.

In recent decades, it seems, myriad new types of churches have evolved to accommodate every conceivable temperament and world view, regardless of whether that world view is biblical. Thus, for example, there are now the new "Metropolitan" churches created especially for homosexuals.

No matter what kind of person you are, a form of Christianity has evolved just for you. There's a politically liberal Christianity and a politically conservative Christianity. There's an acutely activist Christianity and an utterly apolitical Christianity, a Christianity that holds up a high standard of ethical behavior and service, and a Christianity for which both personal ethics and good works are irrelevant. There's a raucous, intensely emotional Christianity drenched in high-voltage music, and there's a quiet, contemplative Christianity. There's a loving Christianity and a hateful, racist Christianity, a Christianity that honors Jews as God's chosen people and a Christianity that maligns Jews as Satan's children.

The variations are endless and sometimes bizarre. There are churches that believe in handling venomous snakes and drinking poison as a test and proof of their faith. Mostly in the Southeast, these churches stake their identity on Jesus' words recorded in the Gospel according to Mark: "And these signs shall follow them that believe; In my name shall they cast out devils; they shall speak with new tongues; they shall take up serpents; and if they drink any deadly thing, it shall not hurt them; they shall lay hands on the sick, and they shall recover" (Mark 16:17–18).

Of course, common sense tells us—however we interpret Jesus's actual meaning—that He didn't intend for the faithful to tempt God by drinking strychnine and strutting around on stage with rattlers and cottonmouths, practices that every year result in one or more deaths being reported from these churches.

To bring this heavenly issue of biblical interpretation down to earth a bit, consider the difficulty people have in agreeing on the meaning of a much shorter, more recent, and more concrete document—the Constitution of the United States. Unlike the Bible, which is mystical, written by many different authors in different languages over the course of many centuries, the Constitution was written with simplicity and clarity of expression in mind by a single group of people only two centuries ago (except for the later amendments). Moreover, it was written in English, so translation is not an issue. To top it off, there's an abundance of contemporaneous writings, most important *The Federalist Papers,* explaining clearly what the Founding Fathers meant. And yet, depending on their agenda and political views, politicians, bureaucrats, attorneys, judges, and others come up with fantastically divergent and contradictory interpretations of the simple document that is meant to be America's common rule book.

In the same way it appears that millions of Christians interpret the Bible—their religion's constitution, if you will—to be compatible with their world view and attitudes, rather than to convey the original meaning and intent of the Holy Scriptures. If it can be interpreted in so many ways, imagine how confused things get when we start radically changing the Bible itself, as is happening with increased frequency.

In one recent example, the Archbishop of Canterbury, Rowan Williams, head of the seventy-million-member Anglican Church, enthusiastically endorsed a brand-new version of the Bible that flatly contradicts traditional core Christian beliefs on sex and morality. Titled *Good as New,* the new Bible was rewritten by former Baptist minister John Henson for the "One" organization, to produce what the group calls a "new, fresh and adventurous" version of the Christian Scriptures.

Although Williams described it as a book of "extraordinary power," he admitted many would be startled by its content. "Instead of condemning fornicators, adulterers and 'abusers of themselves with mankind,'" wrote Ruth Gledhill, the London *Times* religious affairs correspondent, "the new version of his first letter to Corinth has St. Paul advising Christians not to go without sex for too long in case they get 'frustrated.' . . . The new version, which Dr. Williams says he hopes will spread 'in epidemic profusion through religious and irreligious alike,' turns St. Paul's strictures against fornication on their head."

The One organization that produced the new Bible version is dedicated to "establish[ing] peace, justice, dignity and rights for all." Echoing all the familiar leftist code words, the group claims it is also dedicated to "sustainable use of the earth's resources," challenging "oppression, injustice, exclusion and discrimination" as well as accepting "one another, valuing their diversity and experience."

Here, quoted from the London *Times,* are a few sample passages from this "adventurous" new Bible:

MATTHEW 23:25

KJV: "Woe unto you, scribes and Pharisees, hypocrites!"

New: "Take a running jump, Holy Joes, humbugs!"

MATTHEW 26:69–70

KJV: "Now Peter sat without in the palace: and a damsel came unto him, saying, 'Thou also wast with Jesus of Galilee.' But he denied before them all, saying, I know not what thou sayest."

New: "Meanwhile Rocky was still sitting in the courtyard. A woman came up to him and said: 'Haven't I seen you with Jesus, the hero from Galilee?' Rocky shook his head and said: 'I don't know what the hell you're talking about!'"

1 CORINTHIANS 7:1–2

KJV: "Now concerning the things whereof ye wrote unto me: [It is] good for a man not to touch a woman. Nevertheless, [to avoid] fornication, let every man have his own wife, and let every woman have her own husband."

New: "Some of you think the best way to cope with sex is for men and women to keep right away from each other. That is more likely to lead to sexual offences. My advice is for everyone to have a regular partner."

1 CORINTHIANS 7:8–9

KJV: "I say therefore to the unmarried and widows, It is good for them if they abide even as I. But if they cannot contain, let them marry: for it is better to marry than to burn."

New: "If you know you have strong needs, get yourself a partner. Better than being frustrated."[4]

Such disconcerting "symptoms" as we've been describing here—surveys showing born-again believers think and act the same as nonbelievers, endless and contradictory versions of the same gospel, wacky Bible translations that smile on fornication and homosexuality—become suddenly understandable when we identify the underlying disease. And disease is an apt metaphor, since the church has been under relentless invasion by foreign elements attempting to sicken and cripple the body of Christ. Let's examine some of the major invaders.

"THE RELIGIOUS LEFT"

MANY CHURCHGOING Christians scratch their heads and wonder why America's mainline denominations so frequently seem to support leftist organizations. It's because many of these mainline churches, at least at the leadership level, have virtually *become* leftist organizations! Front and center is the notoriously radical umbrella group, the National Council of Churches, which represents three dozen denominations, including the United Church of Christ, the United Methodist Church, the Presbyterian Church (USA), the Episcopal Church, and the Evangelical Lutheran Church in America.

How can an organization supposedly championing the interests of tens of millions of Bible-believing Christians be so passionately, obviously—indeed, almost comically—supportive of hardcore leftist causes? Writer Jacob Laskin explains in "The Church of the Latter-Day Leftists":

> Founded in 1950, the New York City–based NCC has, for more than half a century, remained faithful to the legacy of its forerunner, the Communist front-group known as the Federal Council of Churches. At one time an unabashed apostle of the Communist cause, the NCC has today recast itself as a leading representative of the so-called religious Left. Adhering to what it has described as "liberation theology"—that is, Marxist ideology disguised as Christianity—the NCC lays claim to a membership of 36 Protestant, Anglican and Orthodox Christian denominations, and some 50 million members in over 140,000 congregations.
>
> Since the collapse of the Soviet Union, the NCC has soft-pedaled its radical message, dressing up its demands for global collectivization and its rejection of democratic capitalism in the garb of religious teachings. Yet the organization's history suggests that it was—and remains—a devout backer of a gallery of socialist governments.[5]

Recounting the NCC's support for Communist regimes and uprisings all over the world, Laskin shows, for example, how the group—in conjunction with its Geneva-based parent organization, the World Council of Churches—financially supported Soviet-sponsored invasions of Africa in the 1970s, "aiding the terrorist rampages of Communist guerrillas in Zimbabwe, Namibia, Mozambique, and Angola." To this day, he adds, the NCC "remains an unwavering ally of the Cuban government."

Noting that some of the more conservative Protestant elements, including Southern Baptists and evangelicals, have criticized the NCC for "elevating political activism above its spiritual calling," Laskin says the group has turned elsewhere in search of funding for its leftist activism.

"Compensating somewhat for sagging private donations, the NCC has received funding from a handful of left-wing foundations in recent years," he writes. "In 2000 the NCC took in $100,000 from the Ford Foundation, $149,400 from the Annie E. Casey Foundation in 2000–2001, $150,000 from the Beldon Fund in 2001, $500,000 from the Lilly Endowment in 2002, $50,000 from the Rasmussen Foundation in 2003, and $75,000 from the Rockefeller Brothers Fund that same year."[6]

Although the National Council of Churches justifies its controversial political activities as support for human rights, it consistently condemns Israel—the one nation whose very right to exist is threatened more often and more severely than any other. In a world filled with totalitarian regimes inflicting unimaginably brutal human rights abuses, the NCC seems most offended by the Mideast's tiny Jewish democracy, surrounded by hostile Arab neighbors sworn to annihilate it. A study by the Institute of Religion and Democracy, Laskin notes, found that "of the seven human rights criticisms [the NCC] issued from 2000–2003, Israel received four, the United States two, and Sudan one."[7]

In the same way, some of America's largest mainline Protestant denominations—just like the National Council of Churches and the World Council of Churches—have taken to attacking Israel as though it were a singularly evil blight on the modern world. In July 2004 the Presbyterian Church (USA), which claims three million members, voted by an overwhelming 461-to-62 majority of its general assembly to side with Palestinian Arabs and against Israel, choosing to divest from the Jewish state as it has done only once before—with apartheid-era South Africa.[8] Shortly thereafter, some leaders of the Anglican Church, which in America includes the Episcopal Church, announced they were considering joining the Presbyterian Church (USA) in the divestment campaign against the Jewish state.[9]

But the Anglican Church's most controversial position recently has been its open embrace, on both sides of the Atlantic, of homosexual clergy. In America, the consecration by the Episcopal Church (USA) of openly homosexual Gene Robinson as New Hampshire bishop in 2003, as well as its decision to bless same-sex unions, has threatened to split the church in two. And in Britain that same year, after becoming the Anglican Church's new leader, Rowan Williams immediately made waves by supporting homosexual priest Dr. Jeffrey John as the bishop of Reading. Although John ultimately withdrew in the face of widespread and intense opposition, Williams has continued with his open support of homosexuals ever since.[10]

If the Protestant world—already divided between the liberal mainline denominations and the conservative evangelicals and others—is facing new and stunning denominational splits over homosexuality, the Roman Catholic Church has been downright devastated by the issue.

HOMOSEXUAL INFILTRATION

JUST AS a grown man can be defeated by a nearly invisible virus, even great institutions can be severely impacted by malevolent invasions that go all but unnoticed for years. The Roman Catholic Church has striven mightily against the tides of immorality in an increasingly secular world and held with admirable strength to traditional, biblical, life-affirming principles. But it has also—at least in the United States—been profoundly affected not only by the leftist liberation theology but also by a major infiltration of its seminaries by homosexuals. In fact, widespread cases of predatory homosexual priests have created a full-blown crisis for the church.

"The real problem the Catholic Church faces," explains Father Donald B. Cozzens, author of *The Changing Face of the Priesthood,* is the "disproportionate number of gay men that populate our seminaries."[11]

Former California Congressman Bob Dornan states it more bluntly when he says, "The Catholic Church in this country has been penetrated by an aggressive homosexual network."[12] And *National Review* senior writer Rod Dreher puts it even more bluntly: "This is chiefly a scandal about unchaste or criminal homosexuals in the Catholic priesthood. . . . For Catholics, to start asking questions about homosexuality in the priesthood is to risk finding out more than many Church members prefer to know. For journalists, to confront the issue is to risk touching the electrified third rail of American popular culture: the dark side of homosexuality."[13]

One journalist who's not afraid to touch the issue is Paul Likoudis, longtime editor of the *Wanderer,* one of America's oldest Catholic newspapers. Likoudis's love and reverence for the Roman Catholic Church does not prevent him from fully exposing the deadly virus that has infected it. In his book, *Amchurch Comes Out: The U.S. Bishops, Pedophile Scandals and the Homosexual Agenda,* Likoudis explains how "homosexuals, pedophiles and other perverse persons in the priesthood rose to prominence in the Church," especially in the United States and Canada—the "Amchurch." Revealing that these subversive elements "began carefully plotting and promoting a sexual liberation agenda that would take Catholics by surprise, an agenda that first manifested itself in the new catechetical texts rushed into print during the Second Vatican Council," Likoudis lays out an agenda that would be unthinkable, except for the fact that it has all come true:

> The immediate attacks were on Church teaching regarding masturbation, fornication, adultery and contraception and divorce; but by the middle of the 1980s, it became clear this was only the first stage, to be followed by the aggressive promotion of homosexuality, bisexuality and "transgenderism."[14]

"The evidence," says Likoudis, "is now irrefutable that an influential and very powerful coterie within the Catholic Church—well-embedded and well-protected by the Roman Catholic hierarchy and their peers in the police, the courts, legislatures and the media—is successfully advancing a sexual liberation agenda that will not end until every social stigma attached to any sexual activity, no matter how bizarre, has been erased."

Ever since the first major case of a sexually predatory priest, that of Gilbert Gauthe in 1984, says Likoudis, "close to a thousand similar cases" have occurred, "involving tens, if not hundreds of thousands of victims, costing the Church an estimated $1 billion," although that figure may be low. All the while, Likoudis adds, "the leadership in the Catholic Church in the United States has pursued a homosexualizing

agenda in its grammar and high schools, colleges and seminaries, its social service agencies, initiatives in art, architecture and liturgy, catechet-
ics, and pastoral ministries at the diocesan and parish levels."

For Likoudis, the biggest shock has been the response by the
church's authorities to the epidemic of priests' sex crimes:

> When I began working for *The Wanderer* in 1987, I had no idea how the
> Amchurch's sexual liberation agenda would play out, how Church agencies
> were honeycombed with homosexuals and the queen bees choreographing
> each successive move. I naively assumed that the exposure of sexual per-
> verts would prompt episcopal action to root out the abusers and to insti-
> tute strict reforms to remove potential threats, especially in seminaries. But
> in the 15 years since I reported on my first sexual abuse case in the priest-
> hood, sexual scandals have become more egregious, the legal tactics more
> bare-knuckled, the payoffs larger, while Amchurch's leaders only accelerate
> their education agenda to advance the cause of sexual liberation.

Although Likoudis "firmly believes that the Catholic Church was established by Christ and is protected by Him," the truth must be exposed, he explains, that "cliques of 'devils'—to use Dostoyevsky's
term—managed to come to power in the Church, and have used their
power and the Church's resources *to destroy her from the inside,* to wreck
her credibility, to sully her image, to make her appear ridiculous in the
eyes of the world and in the minds of the faithful. In the end," concludes
Likoudis, "they will be on the losing side of history, but the damage they
will have wrought will be enormous."[15]

ABANDONMENT

AS WE have seen, churches that are more structured as top-down
authority-based institutions can readily be subverted from the top. The
ultimate authority church on earth, the Roman Catholic Church, has
been attacked (in North America) by an invasion at the authority level—
that is, in its seminaries. In the same way, the big, traditional, top-down
mainline Protestant denominations under the umbrella of the National
Council of Churches have drifted so far to the left that they demonstrate
little disagreement with the dominant, secular culture.

But what about the bottom-up churches—like those in the evangelical world—where religious doctrine and practice are more decentralized and less dependent on a vertical hierarchy of authority? Obviously, if top-down, authority-based organizations are vulnerable at the top, bottom-up faith-based or relationship-based churches are susceptible at the bottom. In other words, churchgoers and pastors alike are in danger of being influenced and corrupted by the powerful currents of the surrounding culture.

Let's take a close look at the millions of American evangelicals, and those the media derisively like to label fundamentalist Christians, who still hold strongly to traditional values. First, let's give credit where it's due. Many evangelicals, just like many believers from other regions of Christendom, not only take their religion seriously, "walking their talk" and putting biblical principles first in their lives, but they also believe they have a duty to stand up for God's principles in the larger world. Some are active in homeschooling while others are politically engaged, along with many Catholics, in trying to fight evils like abortion and euthanasia. Indeed, it is evangelical Christians who comprise the most active and passionate component of the Republican Party and who are most responsible for getting out the vote at election time.

Courageous attorneys—both Protestant and Catholic—give up lucrative private practices to defend Americans' religious liberties and fight daunting legal battles against abortion and same-sex marriage. In other words, there are Christians today who are true successors to America's founding generation, putting everything on the line to keep America both great and good. But then there are also large numbers of Bible-believing, traditional-values-affirming Christians who are, for want of a better term, just waiting for the end to come. This is not a criticism of Christians who have an interest in end-times prophecy— that's a shared interest in *all* believers as it's a major theme of the New Testament. Rather, we're talking about Christians who have become "invisible"—that is, of no account when it comes to standing up to the evil all around them.

In his book *Abandonment Theology*, author John W. Chalfant describes how the "Abandonment Clergy," as he calls certain types of pastors, have responded to the increasingly audacious attacks on Christian America during the past half-century:

Incredibly, this was the ultimate hour for the Abandonment Clergy to see the light of truth. They faced blatant godlessness at every turn. They could have abandoned their own ways and made a comeback to the faith of the Founding Fathers. But what did they do?

They observed the horrible, deteriorating conditions in America, determined that she was headed into rubble just like pagan Rome and that we must be living in the prophesied "last days" and "end times." Therefore, with the end and the "rapture of the church" so apparently near, why fight?

"After all," these clergymen said, "We're in this world, not of it, so to heck with it," and "Compared to eternity we're here only for an instant." They told us that all that really counts is that we "lead as many people as possible to salvation and let our corrupted country continue on its death course."

Faulty religious teaching, Chalfant contends, is the only way to explain why so many well-meaning Christians have been paralyzed into inaction:

The Abandonment Clergy and their followers have been teaching, preaching and saturating the media and their church members with the doctrine of surrender and political non-involvement. They are not teaching us to surrender to Christ through obedience to the commandments of God. Rather, they tell us that America is finished, that the collapse of our heritage and our freedoms has been predetermined within a definable near-future time frame and is therefore beyond our control.

Chalfant takes direct aim at those too focused on their own imminent "rapture":

The legitimate study of eschatology (the future in prophecy) has been converted into a doctrine of futility and surrender by the clergy who, in defiance of Christ's injunction (see Mark 13:32–33), insist upon assigning near-future dates to the "last days," the "rapture of the church" and the "second coming" of Christ. . . . At the very least the clergy should understand that their "last days" teachings are nothing more than personal speculations.[16]

With their beloved country being de-Christianized at 100 miles per hour, what is this powerful seduction that has succeeded in neutralizing so many Christians from mounting any effective defense?

"Invisible" Christians

FRANCIS A. SCHAEFFER is widely regarded as one of the most influential evangelical thinkers of the twentieth century, having written twenty-three books translated into twenty-five languages, including *The God Who Is There, Escape from Reason,* and *How Should We Then Live?* Shortly before he died in 1984, Schaeffer published a book with the spine-straightening title *The Great Evangelical Disaster.* In it, he reflected, just as we are in these pages, on the culture wars raging in America and why Christians were so seemingly absent from the struggle.

"Most of the evangelical world has not been active in the battle," Schaeffer lamented, "or even been able to see that we are in a battle. And when it comes to the issues of the day the evangelical world most often has said nothing; or worse has said nothing different from what the world would say.

"Here," he said, "is the great evangelical disaster—the failure of the evangelical world to stand for truth as truth. There is only one word for this—namely *accommodation:* the evangelical church has accommodated to the world spirit of the age."

The dangers of this accommodation were Schaeffer's final warning to Christendom:

> This accommodation has been costly, first in destroying the power of the Scriptures to confront the spirit of our age; second, in allowing the further slide of our culture. Thus we must say with tears that it is the evangelical accommodation to the world spirit around us, to the wisdom of this age, which removes the evangelical church from standing against the further breakdown of our culture. It is my firm belief that when we stand before Jesus Christ, we will find that it has been the weakness and accommodation of the evangelical group on the issues of the day that has been largely responsible for the loss of the Christian ethos which has taken place in the area of culture in our country over the last forty to sixty years.

To Schaeffer, who for decades nurtured, exhorted, and lectured Christian audiences worldwide, this accommodation was no light matter of secondary importance to the believer's Christian walk. It was a sign of grossest hypocrisy, he said.

> And let us understand that to accommodate to the world spirit about us in our age is nothing less than the most gross form of worldliness in the proper definition of that word. And with this proper definition of worldliness, we must say with tears that, with exceptions, the evangelical church is worldly and not faithful to the living Christ.[17]

These were, and are, stunning words from one of our era's most revered evangelical leaders. But other respected Christian authors have sounded the same alarm over what Schaeffer called accommodation. Theology professor David F. Wells of Gordon-Conwell Theological Seminary asks in his book *No Place for Truth:* "Why is it that with more than a third of the nation's adults in 1990 claiming a born-again experience and many more beyond that claiming allegiance to Christian values, the society moves on oblivious to its religious citizens, reshaping laws and policies as if they were not there?"

Chillingly, Wells explains, "The answer, in a sense, is that they are not there. They are the people of the inner life whose relation to the external world is largely a matter of cognitive disjuncture. Whatever follies the Marxists committed—and their follies and wickedness have been manifold—they always had the wisdom to know that if they yielded their world view, they yielded their reason for existence. Evangelicals are not quite so wise."[18]

Schaeffer and many other Christian leaders have long bemoaned this disastrous Christian accommodation, and indeed much of it emanates from very commonplace human weaknesses like doubtfulness, fear of rejection, need for acceptance and approval, and desire for advantage. However, because evangelical Christians are especially focused on the Great Commission—the supreme task Christ gave His disciples to spread the gospel—another reason for this "becoming just like the rest of society" syndrome has evolved, and it is this: to get the attention of the unsaved, you have to go where they are, even look like them and act like them, in hopes of winning their trust, and hopefully their conversion.

After all, Jesus hung out with prostitutes and other sinners—and even worse, with tax collectors!

On one hand, we have to honor the wisdom of such classic evangelical thinking. The missionary not only has to put himself in the midst of the unsaved, he also has to make himself as credible and nonthreatening as possible. "We've got to go where these kids are if we're going to retrieve them," goes the evangelical logic. For this reason, for example, youth pastors at some point started to dispense with their formal attire and instead appeared before teenagers without coat and tie, so as not to appear a stuffed shirt. That's a reasonable accommodation. But what happens when the youth leader's strategy of going tie-less turns into his dressing like a rap singer, talking jive, and wearing earrings? That's what's happened in Christian pop culture today.

Far too much of today's evangelical world has been swept up in the powerful magnetic field of the secular popular culture. Thinking they're doing God's work behind the enemy lines of the atheistic popular culture, they've gradually and inadvertently taken on many more characteristics and attitudes of the enemy than they realize.

That's why, when I drive in my car and turn on the radio, it sometimes takes several minutes before I can figure out whether I'm listening to a regular, secular rock song or a Christian rock song. They often sound uncannily the same—the Christian song being a virtual clone of the secular. In turn, the powerful popular culture ridicules evangelicals for their lame imitation of the real thing. Here's one recent example.

Walter Kirn, literary editor for *GQ* magazine, wrote a biting critique of contemporary evangelical Christian culture, bearing the familiar title, "What Would Jesus Do?" "But more important," says the magazine's mocking introduction to Kirn's odyssey, "what were Jesus' fitness secrets? If you were one of the growing millions of Americans living in the multimillion-dollar Christian alternaculture—in which everything in mainstream culture gets cloned and then leached of 'sinful' content—you'd know. Walter Kirn spends seven strange days walking in the shoes of the faithful."

Yes, it's cynical. Yes, *GQ* is not a Christian magazine—far from it. It's a worldly, upscale, and sophisticated fashion magazine for young professional males, similar to *Esquire*. And yes, Kirn doesn't sound like he's a believer, but rather, a skeptical, secular journalist. However, there is enough truth in what he writes to paint a disturbing portrait of what has happened to evangelical Christian culture in America:

> Today I will leave behind the fallen world of secular American pop culture and enter the self-contained parallel universe of American Christian pop culture, within which I've vowed to dwell, exclusively for seven days and nights, watching PAX instead of NBC and letting Pat Robertson be my Tom Brokaw.
>
> The old Ark, the biblical Ark, constructed to save the chosen from the Great Flood, had two of every creature in existence. The new Ark, the cultural Ark, built to save the chosen from the Great Media Flood, also has two of everything, I'm learning. You say you're a Pearl Jam fan? Check out Third Day. They sound just like them—same soaring guttural vocals, same driven musicianship, same crappy clothes, just a slightly different message: Repent! You say you like Grisham- and Clancy-style potboilers? Grab a copy of Ted Dekker's "Heaven's Wager"—same stick-figure characterizations, same preschool prose, just a slightly different moral: Repent! Your kids enjoy Batman, you say? Try Bibleman. Same mask, same cape, just a slightly different . . .
>
> That's the convincing logic of the Ark: If a person is going to waste his life cranking the stereo, clicking the remote, reading paperback pulp and chasing diet fads, he may as well save his soul while he's at it. Holy living no longer requires self-denial. On the Ark, every mass diversion has been cloned, from Internet news sites to MTV to action movies, and it's possible to live inside the spirit, without unplugging oneself from the modern life, twenty-four hours a day.

Describing his trip to a Christian store in Bozeman, Montana, where he bought his "Ark supplies," Kirn recalls how "a poster above the music racks matches name-brand acts from secular radio with their closest sanctified equivalents."

For the atheist teen who has suddenly been converted and wants to carry into his new life as many of his old attitudes and tastes as he can safely manage, such a chart would prove helpful, I imagine, much as a cookbook of sugar-free recipes might help a chocoholic with diabetes. For me, though, the chart confirmed a preconception that Christian rock is a cultural oxymoron—a calculated, systematic rip-off, not a genuine surge of inspired energy.[19]

What about television? For Christian fare, says Kirn, "you get shows like the Sky Angel network's 'Ten Most Wanted'—a low-voltage rip-off of those MTV music-video-countdown programs. The twenty-ish host has a fuzzy soul patch, a grungy plaid shirt and a shock of spiky hair that like most Christian versions of 'downtown' style, is years out of date and ever so slightly too clean. Plus, his earrings look suspiciously like clip-ons."

Kirn describes how the show's host deftly glides from the popular culture into the alternate dimension of Christian evangelism to deliver the message, and then back into the comfortable world of pop culture:

An ad comes on for a pro-life pregnancy hot line, and then it's back to the shabby veejay, who drops his rebel pose, earnestly asks his young viewers to come to Christ ("call 877–949-HELP") and then slips back into jive talk for the sign-off: "Thanks for hangin' wit' me. I'll see you guys later." Such lame mimicry is the curse of most youth ministries.[20]

Whether you like the mocking tone or not, Kirn's conclusion is thought-provoking:

What makes the stuff . . . so thin, so weak and cumulatively so demoraliz-ing (even to me, a sympathetic journalist who'd secretly love to play the brash contrarian and rate the "Left Behind" books above Tom Clancy) has nothing to do with faith. The problem is lack of faith. Ark culture is a bad Xerox of the mainstream, not a truly distinctive or separate achieve-ment. Without the courage to lead, it numbly follows, picking up the major media's scraps and gluing them back together with a cross on top.[21]

How far can this Christian mimicry of a thoroughly unchristian popular culture go? Under sway of the vain belief that we're somehow gaining the trust of the unsaved in hopes of leading them to Christ, are there any lower limits beyond which we won't go? Unfortunately, in some cases today's evangelical accommodation has led to some very strange and scary things.

GROSS-OUT GAMES

PICTURE THIS: a youth pastor at a New Year's Eve party at his church, in an effort to capture the imagination of the young people present, chews up a disgusting mixture of dog food, sardines, meat, sauerkraut, cottage cheese, salsa and eggnog. Then he spits it all out into a glass and invites the youths present to drink it.[22] This actually happened at an Indiana church. In fact, when some of the youngsters who drank the mixture became sick, four sets of parents sued the church.

As Gene Edward Veith explained in *World* magazine, "The youth pastor said that the 'gross-out' game, called the Human Vegematic, was just for fun and that the church forced no one to participate. The lawsuit accused the adults in charge of pressuring 13- and 14-year-olds into activities that caused them physical and mental harm."

Why am I taking up space describing such a bizarre case of terrible judgment on the part of a youth pastor? Obviously, outrageous activities like this must be rare in youth ministries, right? Wrong. "Such 'gross-out' games have become a fad in youth ministry," says Veith. "Since adolescents are amused by bodily functions, crude behavior, and tastelessness—following the church-growth principle of giving people what they like as a way to entice them into the kingdom—many evangelical youth leaders think this is a way to reach young people."

The games—many of them contributed by youth ministry leaders—are listed on "The Source for Youth Ministry," a well-known and widely used online resource center for Christian youth leaders. Some of the games, writes Veith, are "designed to appeal to adolescents' hormones":

> These include kissing games like "Kiss the Wench." "Leg Line Up" has girls feel boy's legs to identify who is who. Some of them have odd homosexual subtexts, like "Pull Apart," in which guys cling to each other, while girls try to pull them apart. Another has girls putting makeup on guys, leading to a drag beauty show. Then there is the embarrassingly Freudian "Baby Bottle Burp," in which girls put a diaper (a towel) on a boy, then feed him a bottle of soda, and cradle him until he burps!
>
> These are presented as just ordinary games, good ways to break the ice at youth group. But there is another category of "Sick and Twisted Games." Many of these involve eating and drinking gross things, like at

the Indiana church. ("Toothbrush Buffet" has youth group leaders brushing their teeth and spitting into a cup. Each then passes it along to the next in line, who uses what is in the cup to brush his teeth. The last one drinks down everyone's spit.) Others are scatological, and are too repellent to describe.[23]

Obviously, these activities are degrading and in some cases unhealthful. But they do appeal to many youths, so if keeping them coming back for more is the church's primary object, and if that could in turn lead to their conversion or membership in the church, then such "harmless icebreakers" are seen by some youth leaders as a good thing.

In reality, such activities are both corrupting and unchristian, and they teach some very questionable lessons to impressionable young people, as Veith notes:

- Lose your inhibitions. Young people usually have inhibitions against doing anything too embarrassing or shameful. These exercises are designed to free people from such hang-ups.

- Give in to peer pressure. Defenders of these kinds of activities maintain that they help create group unity. The way they work, though, is to overcome a teenager's inhibitions with the greater desire to go along with the group.

- Christianity is stupid. Status-conscious teenagers know that those who are so desperate to be liked that they will do anything to curry favor are impossible to respect. Young people may come to off-the-wall youth group meetings, but when they grow up, they will likely associate the church with other immature, juvenile phases of their lives, and Christianity will be something they will grow out of.[24]

Veith is right, but it's actually much worse than that. Degrading someone is a classic preparatory step to brainwashing him. I'm not saying church youth leaders are intentionally trying to brainwash anyone. But the fact is, someone who has been tempted to cross ethical boundaries—in response to peer pressure, or out of fear of ridicule or other adverse consequences—is wide open to being reprogrammed by a strong personality. This dynamic is made all the more powerful by the presence of a group pulling in the same direction as the leader.

Yes, you're hearing me right. I'm saying drinking the leader's "Human Vegematic" spit or violating our own God-given inhibitions by engaging in shameful or titillating games at church is not just tasteless and moronic. It can also make us vulnerable to a counterfeit religious experience. When we're angry, emotional, upset, or just excited, we're simply more susceptible to outside suggestion than when we're calm and composed. But when, in addition, we have actually violated the subtle laws of God—"going against our conscience," we call it—out of weakness, insecurity, and a need for approval, any religious experience or even religious feeling that may follow surely has nothing to do with being touched by God. But it has everything to do with being emotionally reprogrammed, which can lead to lots of religious words and feelings, but no actual connection to God. Scary but true. And that's why this sort of mind game is much more dangerous and "gross" than we may realize.

We could go down many more dark alleys and explore countless other instances of strange practices, strange beliefs, and, frankly, strange people in our churches. But it's not necessary. We all know there's a big problem. The question now, after observing the various symptoms and identifying some of the key invaders and disease factors infecting the church body is, What is the cure?

THE BOTTOM LINE

AMERICA IS full of people who have accepted the idea that Jesus Christ died for their sins and that this belief guarantees them a place in heaven. Some are very sincere. They are truly mortified at their former sins, genuinely contrite before God and those they have offended, and they grieve over their continuing compulsions. They have awakened from their former life of gross sin and now want nothing more than to do the will of their Creator—whatever that may be, wherever it may lead them, whatever they may suffer. They take seriously the commandments and principles given by their Savior and make their life revolve around emulating Him to the best of their ability. They are, quite literally, followers of Christ—in other words, Christians.

They are a wholesome and upgrading influence wherever they go and whatever they do. They are "salt and light," to use the popular expression. It is because of them that America hasn't fallen completely into the socialistic, post-Christian, secular decadence and deadness that already grips Europe. They are the reason there is still hope for America.

Others are not so sincere. There are countless Christians who believe they have a ticket to heaven, and nothing else really matters very much to them. They live lives of shallowness and selfishness, of petty emotions and jealousies, of gossip and escape, of ego and pride, and sometimes of gross corruption and treachery. The worst of them are prideful, selfish, and brazen. Living it up under the smug delusion that they're "saved," they drive other people crazy (and away from real Christianity) with their hypocrisy. Such people, whether in family or business relationships, whether as church leaders or leaders of nations, sow confusion, rebellion, and suffering everywhere they go.

Others are more decent but powerfully in the grip of sin and confusion. They go to church and sing hymns and sometimes read the Bible. They may even "try to be a good Christian," but they're basically clueless. Their marriage is on the rocks, and their children are wearing tongue studs. They believe in society's atheistic experts, and they're even addicted to Internet porn. They are easily taken in by the marketers of evil.

This is not a judgment of these people. Many are moving in the direction of being more Christian, but many, unfortunately, are moving in the direction of being less Christian. In fact, some so-called Christians, I'm sorry to say, are actually worse off after being "saved" than before. (I put *saved* in quotes because of course I'm not referring here to the real thing.) At least before they were "saved," they had a natural respect for, or fear of, ultimate justice—an inborn sense that somehow we all reap what we sow. After being "saved," that's gone for the insincere "Christian." For him or her, belief in Jesus amounts to a "get out of hell free" card, a sort of spiritual diplomatic immunity. It's like the profligate teenage son of an important Arab diplomat who knows he won't be prosecuted under U.S. law while living here, so he drives recklessly, molests women, and generally lives it up with impunity. And because the natural and *necessary* fear of consequences has been unwisely removed from his life, he falls that much more easily to the temptations of his lower nature.

For millions of us, Christianity has been dumbed down into a bumper-sticker religion. Simply by mouthing, one time, a single phrase—"I accept Jesus Christ as my savior"—we somehow believe we're guaranteed eternal life in heaven no matter how insincere or selfish or shallow our motives for doing so, no matter how corrupt and unrepentant a life we live after our "conversion."

But is this the kind of salvation Jesus referred to when He said, "But he that shall endure unto the end, the same shall be saved" (Matthew 24:13)? *Endure to the end? What's with that? I thought this salvation thing was all settled by that altar call back in '95.*

Is this what He meant when He said, "If ye keep my commandments, ye shall abide in my love; even as I have kept my Father's commandments, and abide in his love" (John 15:10)? Many Christians don't bother to pay any attention at all to God's commandments. *Hey, what difference does it really make? I'm already saved!*

Is this what Paul referred to when he said, "I die daily" (1 Corinthians 15:31)? The apostle's poignant and intensely meaningful reference to the duty of man to give up the life of pride in all its forms, to die to the "carnal mind"—considered central to Christians of past eras—is all but absent from many of today's churches. *"Die daily"? Man, I don't even know what you're talking about.*

Christianity—the deepest, most meaningful and awe-inspiring religion ever, the magnificent driving force behind Western civilization, and the transcendent hope of mankind's future—has been dumbed down by such as these into a caricature, a comic-book religion. Turn on your radio or TV and listen to how the time-honored altar call, responsible for introducing countless souls to the Christian life, has been turned into a shallow, irreverent recruitment effort: "Hey, friend! Do you want to go to hell—*forever?* Do you want to miss out on eternal life? Then why not say yes to Jesus right now, just to make sure? It'll only take a minute. You'll like it—it's a natural high."

Such cynical calls to conversion are little more than an insurance pitch, as if to say: "Hey, buy a little extra insurance, then you can go on with your selfish life and be guaranteed a place in heaven no matter what." Just repeat the salvation "formula"—like an Eastern mantra—and you're saved. Period.

For this type of "Christian," there's no need to stand up to evil, because they're "saved by grace, not works" (despite repeated biblical admonitions that "faith without works is dead"). No need to obey God's commands, because they're already saved, so why bother? No need to try to help make it a better world, no need to help widows and orphans, because they're going to be "raptured" soon, and those who remain behind can sort out the mess.

Is it any wonder that the church—and America—are in such trouble? What's missing in all of this, of course, is a genuine love of truth.

"This people draweth nigh unto me with their mouth, and honoureth me with their lips; but their heart is far from me," said Jesus (Matthew 15:8).

There are all kinds of truth. Two plus two equals four. The sky is blue. But the kind of truth we're talking about here is a special kind—and I'm not even talking about theological doctrine. Rather, the truth that sets the sincere child of God apart from the insincere imitation revolves around our humility and willingness to patiently face our own imperfections and failings. If we stand close to God, He illuminates what's wrong with us so we can repent and change. It's no coincidence that Jesus's first recorded word of ministry was, "Repent."

We all like to assume that we embrace truth. But in reality, truth can be painful to bear. It puts us on edge. It makes us squirm. Why? Because we're "born in sin" and have a certain part of us called pride that is at war with reality. Thus many of us bristle when confronted with the truth about our defects and shortcomings. (In fact, a lot of us spend virtually our entire lives escaping from truth—usually without ever realizing that's what we're doing.)

So what do I mean by "love of truth"?

For one thing, if you have a love of truth, you're never really satisfied with anything else. Counterfeit religious experiences and exciting escapes don't satisfy you. You're always hungry for real experiences, for a genuine relationship with God, for true repentance and change, even if you don't know how to get there. You want to know the truth about everything—*especially* about yourself. If you're wrong about something, you *want* to know it. If you've been living a lie, you're willing to see it—no matter what the cost.

Is it good enough to say, "Well, I follow the Bible"?

That depends. As we have seen, depending on our personal honesty, or lack thereof, we can justify virtually *anything* with the Bible. Every deluded belief, every perverted lust, every selfish ambition—whether it's to become rich, advance communism, live a self-serving and self-satisfied life, prove you're righteous by drinking poison, celebrate homosexuality, or hate the Jews—has generated a form of "Christianity" to justify that particular form of prideful deception, all sugarcoated with selected and even retranslated Bible verses.

What we need is that missing ingredient—the spirit of humility and honesty that invites self-understanding and repentance, which will faithfully guide our true understanding of the Scriptures. Ask yourself, Is stealing wrong because the Bible says it's wrong, or does the Bible say stealing is wrong because it *is* wrong? Which came first? What about murder? Was murder wrong before God gave Moses the Ten Commandments? When Cain slew Abel, there was no Bible and no Ten Commandments. Yet God held Cain accountable and set a curse upon him. But why should Cain have known killing his brother was wrong if there was no law?

The truth, of course, as the Bible makes clear in Romans 1, is that God's living law, the inborn ability to discern right from wrong, was written in Cain's heart, as it is in every human being who has ever lived. The word *conscience* literally means "with knowing." We all know. We all know, deep down, right from wrong. We're self-contained truth machines if only we'd pay attention. It's only our pride, our willfulness to have our own way, to be the god of our own lives, to rationalize our compulsions and sins—and the inevitable denial of truth that follows—that disconnects us from it.

When my daughter, Sarah, was three years old, I used the occasion of her misbehaving with her younger brother to introduce her to the Golden Rule. I remember my amazement when I realized that she clearly understood what I was saying. The "do unto others as you would have them do unto you" message went right home, immediately and full force, into her heart. I remember thinking to myself, "Oh my gosh, a three-year-old can understand Jesus's message!" The fact that she could recognize the truth and rightness of the Golden Rule when she heard it for the first time in her life means she had the essence of its message already inside of her. Otherwise, how could she *recognize* it and respond to it when I spoke those few words to her?

We're talking about real faith—our invisible life-support connection with our Creator. Did you ever do the wrong thing and then, looking back to the moments just before you made the mistake, recall that you had experienced an intuitive flash, a little bit of a wordless warning, like an aversion or feeling not to do it? Like most of us, you ignored it and did the wrong thing anyway. But that "still, small voice"—a voiceless voice, really—tried to steer you away from a wrong action. That's from God. Typically, people learn to honor and respect such intuitive leadings first in hindsight, as they realize they ignored God's loving nudge, and later in foresight, as they discover by experience which impulses to obey and which to resist in life.

Inside every truly sincere person there is an inner witness, a wordless knowing, a quiet confirmation of all truth. When you reverently inquire into the meaning, not only of the Holy Scriptures, but of everything in life, and—very important—when you have the courage to believe and hold onto the little glimpses of insight God gives you in response to your sincere searching, you are living by faith.

Our quiet inner belief that stealing and murder are wrong just because we can plainly see they're wrong, this instant embrace of the Golden Rule just because we can see for ourselves that it's right, this deep and wordless understanding of both life and Scripture that graces us from beyond the borders of our education and experience—which we regard too lightly as common sense—is in reality God's communication with us through faith.

Let's look at one final example of love of truth in action in our daily lives. Say you suffer from envious thoughts. To covet is to break one of the Ten Commandments. So how do we deal with these troublesome feelings? Certainly not by wallowing in them and indulging them. But also not by repressing them or attempting to manufacture "good" thoughts and feelings in their place or by escaping from them. The Christian answer might be to pray, but what form of prayer? As pastors often say, prayer isn't always talking to God. It's often better just to listen. So, in this case, if you notice envious thoughts, just observe them—honestly, sincerely, without escaping or trying to change them or making excuses for them or justifying them or getting upset over them. Just see what God shows you about yourself, with poise and dignity, and quietly, wordlessly, cry inwardly to Him for help. He will. This is true transparency, which is resignation of your will to His. It's how we're supposed to be.

By the same token, to the truth-seeking soul, the story of Christ—not as told by a "plastic Christian," but as told by someone who's *real,* whether pastor or layman or mom or dad—has an internal reverberation of truth in the listener's soul. It has the quality of a wonderful old story you heard long ago, in your childhood, but had forgotten. At the core of this life-changing faith—this truest of all ways of living—is the individual believer's love and appreciation and acceptance and embrace of Christ's perfect sacrifice, the ultimate demonstration of our heavenly Father's love for His wayward children.

But in far too many pulpits across America, and broadcasting over the nation's airways, Christianity is presented in such a shallow way that it doesn't require a love of truth—which is tantamount to a love of Him. This dumbed-down version of Christianity doesn't require honest introspection or courage or self-denial or patience. The only ingredient it needs is a guilty person who's sick of feeling guilty, wants relief, wants to feel better about himself, and desires an insurance policy to keep him out of hell. But even the most insincere person wants to feel better about himself, wants relief from guilt, and fears death and what may lie beyond.

The compartmentalization and trivialization of Christianity into a mantra of belief—but separated from works, from obedience to God's laws, and even more fundamentally, separated from basic honesty, integrity, love of truth, and true repentance—has ushered in a generation of shallow, ineffectual, and invisible Christians. Fortunately, in America there are also many deeply principled and committed believers who have stood firm and held back the tide of atheism from fully sweeping over the land. These Americans love the truth, but they are, sadly, in the minority, which is why the marketers of evil have been winning the war for America's soul.

Yet it is precisely this affinity for truth—the kind that is sometimes painful and always humbling because it exposes us to our own pride and folly—that is the cure, the antidote for the toxic marketing campaigns that have poisoned American culture, including many of her churches.

In this book, we've surveyed the marketers of evil—who they are, what they've sold us, why they did it, and what the disastrous results of their efforts were. But every transaction has both a seller and a buyer. Every con job requires not only a con man but also a hapless victim that somehow didn't see the obvious.

Americans didn't see the obvious. We didn't see the obvious because the marketers of evil fed us the beguiling lies that a hidden, selfish part of us wanted to embrace—just as the proverbial serpent in the Garden of Eden, according to the biblical account, seduced Adam and Eve by telling them lies they secretly wanted to believe.

It's time to give up the life of pride—the impatient, vain, self-serving, pleasure-seeking, egotistical, and utterly faithless part of us that has made all of us such absurdly easy targets for con men throughout the ages. The fox in Pinocchio is alive and well and is still selling us on the joys of Pleasure Island.

It's often said the Christian church in America needs revival. But this doesn't necessarily mean ever-bigger tents with tens of thousands of us swaying back and forth, singing songs, giving speeches, and getting pumped up—and then going home and watching television. America's real revival and genuine rebirth will be much less dramatic in the beginning. We might never even realize exactly how it came about. But it can happen, and we must pray that it will.

How will it come to pass? It'll happen, dear friends, when we all simply go to our rooms, close the door, take a deep breath, and take a good, long, hard, honest look at ourselves. And then, quietly and humbly and fervently, we ask the living God for help, for insight, for direction—for salvation.

When that happens, the spell will be broken, the sun will shine again, and every marketer of evil will have to go out and get an honest job.

ACKNOWLEDGMENTS

NOTES

INDEX

ACKNOWLEDGMENTS

I WANT TO EXPRESS my sincere appreciation to the people who made this book possible, including Ronald E. Pitkin, president of Cumberland House, and Stacie Bauerle, assistant publisher for WND Books (an imprint of Cumberland), for believing so strongly in *The Marketing of Evil.* My gratitude also to Ed Curtis for his experienced hand in editing the book and for expertly helping me over the various prepublication hurdles.

Likewise, a special thank-you goes to my longtime designer Linda Daly for conceiving and executing the perfect cover design.

I also want to thank my colleagues at WorldNetDaily. I'm particularly indebted to Bob Just, WND columnist and veteran talk-radio host, for his steadfast encouragement, friendship, wise counsel, and invaluable and tireless editing help. Bob, you made the book better.

Most important, I want to thank WorldNetDaily CEO Joseph Farah for giving me the opportunity to write this book. Joseph is both a true journalism pioneer and an entrepreneur, having founded not only WND Books but also, along with his wife, Elizabeth, WorldNetDaily.com, one of the world's most popular and respected independent news Web sites, as well as *Whistleblower* magazine. I am honored to be associated with both entities as managing editor and to be part of the larger information revolution we call the "New Media."

It's fitting that I end this book with an acknowledgment of the New Media in all its various forms, from Internet news to the blogs to talk radio to cable news. Of all the trends, both positive and negative, developing in America today, probably the single most hopeful one in terms of counteracting the pervasive "marketing of evil" described in this book is the emergence and growth of a truly free press.

Sadly, until recently, no institution was more complicit in making evil appear good and good appear evil to Americans than the "Old Media." Today, however, the longtime monopoly of network TV news and the rest of the "elite media" is rapidly coming to an end. To my colleagues in the New Media—and you all know who you are—go my thanks and the greatest respect.

Finally, I want to thank my family—my wife, Jean, and our children, Joshua and Sarah—for their endless patience and enthusiastic support while I was writing this book. A project of this sort demands endless hours, including lots of late nights and weekends, and they graciously endured my scarcity during this often-grueling writing marathon. In addition, theirs were the first ears to hear each chapter as I finished it, and their input was more valuable than they know. I am greatly blessed.

NOTES

INTRODUCTION

1. M. Scott Peck, *People of the Lie: The Hope for Healing Human Evil* (New York: Simon & Schuster, 1983), 42.
2. Ibid., 66.

CHAPTER 1: MARKETING BLITZ

1. Robert Bauman, *The Gentleman from Maryland: The Conscience of a Gay Conservative* (New York: Morrow, 1986), 163.
2. Ibid., 180.
3. Ibid., 183, 197.
4. Ibid., 190.
5. Ibid., 202.
6. Alan P. Bell and Martin S. Wineburg, *Homosexuality: A Study of Diversity among Men and Women* (New York: Simon & Schuster, 1978), 308.
7. David Kupelian, "The Battle over AIDS," *New Dimensions,* March 1990, 21.
8. Ibid.
9. David Kupelian, "The New McCarthyism," *New Dimensions,* July 1990, 20.
10. Ibid.
11. Marshall Kirk and Hunter Madsen, *After the Ball: How America Will Conquer Its Fear and Hatred of Gays in the '90s* (New York: Penguin, 1989), 163.
12. Ibid., xxvii.
13. Ibid., xxviii.
14. Paul E. Rondeau, "Selling Homosexuality to America," *Regent University Law Review,* vol. 14 (2002):443, citing Kirk and Madsen, *After the Ball.*
15. Kirk and Madsen, *After the Ball,* 146.
16. Rondeau, "Selling Homosexuality to America," 443.
17. Ibid.
18. *Today,* NBC News Transcripts, October 13, 1998.
19. *Today,* NBC News Transcripts, October 12, 1998.
20. Kirk and Madsen, *After the Ball,* 155.
21. Ibid., 155–56.
22. Ibid., 154.
23. Ibid., 188.
24. Ibid., 189.
25. Rondeau, "Selling Homosexuality to America," 443.
26. Kirk and Madsen, *After the Ball,* 221.

27. William L. Shirer, *The Rise and Fall of the Third Reich* (New York: Simon & Schuster, 1960), 38.

28. Peter LaBarbera, "Gay Journalists Turn Activists," WorldNetDaily.com, September 14, 2000, online at http://www.wnd.com/news/article.asp?ARTICLE_ID=16422.

29. Joseph Farah, "Activist-Journalists out of the Closet," WorldNetDaily.com, September 13, 2000, online at http://www.wnd.com/news/article.asp?ARTICLE_ID =15046.

30. *Seventeen* Magazine (May 2000): 214, cited by Dr. Judith Reisman, "Crafting Bi/Homosexual Youth," *Regent University Law Review,* vol. 14, no. 2 (Spring 2002).

31. William C. Holmes, MD, MSCE, and Gail B. Slap, MD, MS, "Sexual Abuse of Boys: Definition, Prevalence, Correlates, Sequelae, and Management," *Journal of the American Medical Association,* December 2, 1998, online at http://jama.ama-assn.org/cgi/content/abstract/280/21/1855.

32. Reader Feedback, *Whistleblower* magazine (August 2002): 43.

33. Kirk and Madsen, *After the Ball,* 184.

CHAPTER 2: BUYING THE BIG LIE

1. David Barton, "Keys to Good Government" (n.p.: WallBuilders, 2000); *Roberts v. Madigan,* 702 F. Supp. 1505 (D. Colo. 1989), 921 F. 2d 1047 (10th Cir. 1990).

2. Barton, "Keys to Good Government"; *Commonwealth v. Chambers,* 599 A. 2d 630 (Sup. Ct. Pa. 1991), 643–44.

3. Barton, "Keys to Good Government"; *Warsaw v. Tehachapi,* U.S. District Court, Eastern District of California, No. CV F-90–404 and CV F-90–404 EDP (1990).

4. Joseph Story, *Commentary on the Constitution of the United States,* as quoted by U.S. Supreme Court Chief Justice William Rehnquist, dissenting opinion in *Wallace v. Jaffree,* 1985, "United States Not Founded on Absolute Church-State Separation," online at http://www.belcherfoundation.org/wallace_v_jaffree_dissent.htm.

5. Rehnquist, dissenting opinion, *Wallace v. Jaffree.*

6. "O'Connor Praises International Law," WorldNetDaily.com, October 27, 2004, online at http://www.wnd.com/news/article.asp?ARTICLE_ID=41143.

7. Ibid.

8. Cynthia L. Cooper, "Daughter of Justice Blackmun Goes Public About Roe," Women's eNews, February 29, 2004, online at http://www.womensenews.org/article.cfm/dyn/aid/1732/context/cover.

9. John T. Elson, "Toward a Hidden God," *Time* magazine, April 8, 1966, 82–87.

10. Ibid., 82–87.

11. Jim Henderson, letter to the editor, *Whistleblower* magazine, December 2003, 43.

12. Rehnquist, dissenting opinion, *Wallace v. Jaffree.*

CHAPTER 3: KILLER CULTURE

1. Patricia Hersch, *A Tribe Apart: A Journey into the Heart of American Adolescence* (New York: Ballantine, 1998), 82–83, 85.

2. "The Merchants of Cool," *Frontline,* PBS, February 27, 2001; see http://www .pbs.org/wgbh/pages/frontline/shows/cool. By the way, I highly recommend you and your teenage children view "The Merchants of Cool," which is available at www.shoppbs.org.

3. Ibid.

4. Ibid.

5. Ibid.

6. Ibid.

7. Ibid.

8. Ibid.

9. Ibid.

10. Ibid.

11. Ibid.

12. Ibid.

13. Ibid.

14. Ibid.

15. Dr. Laura Schlessinger, "Looking for Love," WorldNetDaily.com, July 1, 2002, online at http://www.wnd.com/news/article.asp?ARTICLE_ID=28138.

16. Gregory A. Freeman, "Bug Chasers: The Men Who Long to Be HIV+," *Rolling Stone,* February 26, 2003.

17. Steven Levenkron, *Cutting: Understanding and Overcoming Self-Mutilation* (New York: Norton, 1998), 44–45.

18. Bob Just, "Killer Culture: A Call to the Churches," WorldNetDaily.com, January 26, 2004, online at http://www.wnd.com/news/article.asp?ARTICLE_ID=36769.

CHAPTER 4: MULTICULTURAL MADNESS

1. Emma Lazarus, "The New Colossus" (1883), from *The Poems of Emma Lazarus,* 2 vols. (New York: Houghton Mifflin, 1889).

2. Robert H. Bork, *Slouching Towards Gomorrah: Modern Liberalism and American Decline* (New York: Regan Books, 1996), 304.

3. Ibid., discussing Richard Bernstein's *Dictatorship of Virtue: Multiculturalism and the Battle for America's Future* (New York: Knopf, 1994).

4. "Judge: Witches Can Pray at County Meeting," WorldNetDaily.com, November 15, 2003, online at http://www.wnd.com/news/article.asp?ARTICLE_ID=35628.

5. Duncan Gardham, "Devil Warship: Navy Tells the NCO in Black Robes He Can Perform His Satanic Rituals at Sea," *Daily Mail* (London), October 25, 2004.

6. *Vogue* magazine, cited by Howard Calhoun, "Should Ohio Ban Hunting of Mourning Doves? A Specious Animal-Rights Agenda," *Cleveland Plain Dealer,* September 4, 1998.

7. Carol Iannone, "Homeland Security," *New York Press,* October 16, 2001.

8. Daniel Pipes, "The Snipers: Crazy or Jihadis?" *New York Post,* October 30, 2002.

9. Robyn Dixon, Jack Leonard, and Rich Connell, "Those Who Knew LAX Killer Say Personal Agenda Died with Him," *Los Angeles Times,* July 14, 2002.

10. Don Phillips, "Doomed Jet's Final Second; Co-Pilot Calm in 1999 Crash, Agency Says," *Washington Post,* August 12, 2000.

11. Larry Witham, "Reporters Asked to Handle 'Islamic' Jargon with Care," *Washington Times,* September 24, 2001.

12. "To Put It Another Way," *Washington Post,* October 7, 2001.

CHAPTER 5: FAMILY MELTDOWN

1. Tom Hoopes, "Breaking Vows: When Faithful Catholics Divorce," *Crisis* magazine, July 8, 2004, online at http://www.crisismagazine.com/julaug2004/hoopes.htm.

2. Judith S. Wallerstein, Julia M. Lewis, and Sandra Blakeslee, "The Unexpected Legacy of Divorce: A 25 Year Landmark Study," *Hyperion* (2000): xxiii.

3. Stephen Baskerville, "Divorce as Revolution," *Salisbury Review,* vol. 21, no. 4 (Summer 2003), online at http://www.fatherhoodcoalition.org/cpf/newreadings/2003/Divorce_as_Revolution_SBsum03.htm.

4. Ibid.

5. Cathy Young, "The Faults of Ending No-Fault Divorce," *Detroit News,* March 19, 1996.

6. Baskerville, "Divorce as Revolution."

7. Dennis E. Powell, "Divorce-on-Demand: Forget About Gay Marriage: What About the State of Regular Marriage?" National Review Online, October 27, 2003, online at http://www.nationalreview.com/magazine/20031027/digital/102703.asp#powell.

8. Julie Foster, "Pro-Marriage Book Harvard Dumped Does Well," quoting *Wall Street Journal* columnist Stanley Kurtz, WorldNetDaily.com, January 28, 2001.

9. Catharine MacKinnon, *Feminism Unmodified: Discourses on Life and Law* (Cambridge, MA: Harvard University Press, 1987), 59, as quoted in Patrick F. Fagan, Robert E. Rector, and Lauren R. Noyes, "Why Congress Should Ignore Radical Feminist Opposition to Marriage," Heritage Foundation, June 16, 2003.

10. Linda J. Waite and Maggie Gallagher, *The Case for Marriage: Why Married People Are Happier, Healthier, and Better Off Financially* (New York: Doubleday, 2000), 1.

11. Robin Morgan, *Sisterhood Is Powerful* (New York: Random House, 1970), 537, as quoted in Fagan, Rector, and Noyes, "Why Congress Should Ignore Radical Feminist Opposition to Marriage."

12. Germaine Greer, *The Female Eunuch* (New York: McGraw-Hill, 1971), 317, 320, as quoted in Fagan, Rector, and Noyes, "Why Congress Should Ignore Radical Feminist Opposition to Marriage."

13. Andrea Dworkin, "Feminism: An Agenda (1983)," in *Letters from a War Zone* (Brooklyn, NY: Lawrence Hill Books, 1993), 146, as quoted in Fagan, Rector, and Noyes, "Why Congress Should Ignore Radical Feminist Opposition to Marriage."

14. Jill Johnston, *Lesbian Nation: The Feminist Solution* (New York: Simon and Schuster, 1973).

15. Claudia Card, "Against Marriage and Motherhood," *Hypatia,* vol. 11, no. 3 (Summer 1996): 8, online at www.indiana.edu/~iupress/journals/hypatia/hyp11–3

.html, as quoted in Fagan, Rector, and Noyes, "Why Congress Should Ignore Radical Feminist Opposition to Marriage."

16. Wallerstein, Lewis, and Blakeslee, "Unexpected Legacy of Divorce," xxi–xxii.

17. Ibid., xxii.

18. Peter Schweizer, *Reagan's War: The Epic Story of His Forty-Year Struggle and Final Triumph over Communism* (New York: Doubleday, 2002), 15.

19. Michael Reagan and Jim Denney, *Twice Adopted* (Nashville: Broadman & Holman, 2004), 44.

20. Glenn T. Stanton, "What No-Fault Divorce Can Teach Us About Same-Sex Marriage," *Citizen Link,* June 17, 2004, online at http://www.family.org/cforum/fosi/marriage/ssuap/a0032550.cfm.

21. Schweizer, *Reagan's War*, 8.

22. Mikhail Heller, *Cogs in the Wheel* (New York: Knopf, 1988), 168–79, cited in Charles E. Corry, "Evolution of Society," online at http://www.ejfi.org/Civilization/Civilization-2.htm.

23. Jerry Bock and Sheldon Harnick, "Miracle of Miracles," from *Fiddler on the Roof,* MGM/UA, 1971.

CHAPTER 6: OBSESSED WITH SEX

1. Kelly Hollowell, "America's Sexual Holocaust," WorldNetDaily.com, April 3, 2004.

2. "American Porn," *Frontline,* PBS/WGBH, February 7, 2002.

3. Bruce Rind et al., "A Meta-Analytic Examination of Assumed Properties of Child Sexual Abuse Using College Samples," *American Psychological Association's Psychological Bulletin,* 124, no. 1 (July 1998): 22–53.

4. Jordan Riefe and Megan Lehmann, "Nicole Defends New Movie's Tub Scene with Boy, 10," *New York Post,* October 19, 2004.

5. Scott McLemee, "The Man Who Took Sex out of the Closet," Salon.com, November 5, 1997.

6. Judith Reisman, "Sex, Lies and Kinsey," *Whistleblower* magazine (July 2002).

7. Ibid.

8. Ibid.

9. McLemee, "Man Who Took Sex out of the Closet."

10. Ibid.

11. Reisman, "Sex, Lies and Kinsey."

12. Caleb Crain, "Doctor Strangelove," *New York Times,* October 3, 2004.

13. Reisman, "Sex, Lies and Kinsey."

14. Ibid.

15. "Where Did the Childhood Sexual Data Come From?" Kinsey Institute Web site, http://www.indiana.edu/~kinsey.

16. Crain, "Doctor Strangelove."

17. Reisman, "Sex, Lies and Kinsey."

18. E. Michael Jones, *Libido Dominandi: Sexual Liberation and Political Control* (South Bend, IN: St. Augustine's Press, 2000), 571–72.

19. James H. Jones, "Dr. Yes," *New Yorker,* September 1, 1997, 100–101, cited by Linda Jeffrey, "Restoring Legal Protections for Women and Children: A Historical Analysis of the States Criminal Codes," *State Factor* (April 2004).

20. Dennis Prager, "Judaism, Homosexuality and Civilization," *Ultimate Issues,* 6 no. 2 (April–June 1990): 2–3.

21. Ibid., 3.

22. Anton Szandor LaVey, The Satanic Bible (1976), Lucifer 3:14.

23. Ibid., number 7 of the 9 Satanic Statements.

24. Ibid., Lucifer 3:37–38.

25. G. K. Chesterton, *G.K.'s Weekly,* January 29, 1928.

CHAPTER 7: SABOTAGING OUR SCHOOLS

1. Gerald Beals, "Thomas Edison Quotes," online at http://www.thomasedison.com/edquote.htm.

2. James Dobson, "Bringing Up Boys," speech delivered at the National Religious Broadcasters Convention, Nashville, Tennessee, March 2002.

3. Diana Lynne, "Islam Studies Spark Hate Mail, Lawsuits," WorldNetDaily.com, January 16, 2002.

4. "Is Declaration of Independence Unconstitutional?" WorldNetDaily.com, November 23, 2004.

5. Julie Foster, "Zero-Tolerance Policies Victimize 'Good' Kids," WorldNetDaily.com, June 7, 2000.

6. Julie Foster, "Boy Hero Appeals Suspension," WorldNetDaily.com, May 20, 2001.

7. "Boys Suspended for Tiny G.I. Joe Guns," WorldNetDaily.com, January 29, 2004.

8. Foster, "Zero-Tolerance."

9. Ibid.

10. "Student Expelled 1 Year for Advil," WorldNetDaily.com, December 5, 2003.

11. Foster, "Zero-Tolerance."

12. Peter G. Mode, *Sourcebook and Bibliographical Guide for American Church History,* Menasha, WI: Banta, 1921), 74–75, cited on www.bible-history.com.

13. John Taylor Gatto, *The Underground History of American Education* (New York: Odysseus Group, 2001), xxviii.

14. Ibid.

15. Ibid., 37.

16. Wilhelm Wundt, cited by Paolo Lionni, *The Leipzig Connection: The Systematic Destruction of American Education* (Sheridan, OR: Delphian Press, 1989).

17. Samuel L. Blumenfeld, "Dumbed Down: The Deliberate Destruction of America's Education System," *Whistleblower* (October 2001): 10.

18. Ibid., 16–17.

19. Gatto, *Underground History of American Education,* 45.

20. William Bradford, *Of Plymouth Plantation: Bradford's History of the Plymouth Settlement 1608-1650.*

CHAPTER 8: THE MEDIA MATRIX

1. Media quotes courtesy of Media Research Center, Alexandria, Virginia, online at http://www.mediaresearch.org.
2. Andy Wachowski and Larry Wachowski, *The Matrix,* Warner Studios, 1999.
3. David Limbaugh, "Why Are the Media AWOL?" WorldNetDaily.com, August 17, 2004, online at http://www.wnd.com/news/article.asp?ARTICLE_ID=40000.
4. Rod Dreher, "The Gay Question: Amid the Catholic Church's Current Scandals, an Unignorable Issue," *National Review,* April 22, 2002.

CHAPTER 9: BLOOD CONFESSIONS

1. David Kupelian and Mark Masters, "Pro-Choice 1990: Skeletons in the Closet," *New Dimensions* magazine (October 1990): 25.
2. David Kupelian, "Abortionist Whistleblowers Tell All," *Whistleblower* (January 2003): 9.
3. Kupelian and Masters, "Pro-Choice 1990," 26.
4. Ibid., 26–27.
5. *Meet the Abortion Providers* (Chicago: Pro-Life Action League, 1989).
6. Ibid.
7. Ibid.
8. Ibid.
9. Ibid.
10. Ibid.
11. Ibid.
12. Ibid.
13. Ibid.
14. Paul Finkelman, *Dred Scott v. Stanford* (Boston: Bedford Books, 1997) as referenced on the PBS Web site at http://www.pbs.org/wgbh/aia/part4/4h2933.html.

CHAPTER 10: LAST, BEST HOPE

1. Pew Forum on Religion and Public Life, "The American Religious Landscape and Politics, 2004," online at http://pewforum.org/docs/index.php?DocID=55.
2. The Barna Group, "Church Attendance," 2005, online at http://www.barna.org/FlexPage.aspx?Page=Topic&TopicID=10.
3. The Barna Group, as cited in "Christians Parent No Different than 'World,'" WorldNetDaily.com, March 3, 2005, online at http://www.wnd.com/news/article.asp?ARTICLE_ID=43128.
4. "New Bible Translation Promotes Fornication," WorldNetDaily.com, June 24, 2004, online at http://www.wnd.com/news/article.asp?ARTICLE_ID=39114.
5. Jacob Laskin, "The Church of the Latter-Day Leftists," FrontPageMagazine.com, January 13, 2005, online at http://frontpagemag.com/Articles/ReadArticle.asp?ID=16625.
6. Ibid.
7. Ibid.

8. "Presbyterians to Divest from Israel," WorldNetDaily.com, July 17, 2004, online at http://www.wnd.com/news/article.asp?ARTICLE_ID=39504.

9. "Episcopal Church Next to Shun Israel?" WorldNetDaily.com, September 24, 2004, online at http://www.wnd.com/news/article.asp?ARTICLE_ID=40603.

10. "Anglican Church Head: Don't Criticize 'Gays,'" WorldNetDaily.com, December 1, 2004, online at http://www.wnd.com/news/article.asp?ARTICLE_ID=41707.

11. Donald B. Cozzens, *The Changing Face of the Priesthood,* cited by Stephen Batesin, "Priesthood 'Becoming Mainly Gay,'" *Manchester Guardian Weekly,* August 16, 2000.

12. Judith Reisman, "Child Atrocities in the Church," WorldNetDaily.com, January 10, 2003, online at http://www.worldnetdaily.com/news/article.asp?ARTICLE_ID =30419.

13. Rod Dreher, "The Gay Question: Amid the Catholic Church's Current Scandals, An Unignorable Issue," National Review Online, April 22, 2002, online at http://www.nationalreview.com/flashback/flashback-dreher042202.asp.

14. Paul Likoudis, *Amchurch Comes Out: The U.S. Bishops, Pedophile Scandals and the Homosexual Agenda* (Petersburg, IL : Roman Catholic Faithful, 2002), xv, available from www.rcf.org.

15. Ibid., xxv–xxvi.

16. John W. Chalfant, *Abandonment Theology: The Clergy and the Decline of American Christianity* (Winter Park, FL: American—A Call to Greatness, 1996), 8–9.

17. Francis A. Schaeffer, *The Great Evangelical Disaster* (Westchester, IL: Crossway Books, 1984), 36–38.

18. David F. Wells, *No Place for Truth: Or Whatever Happened to Evangelical Theology?* (Grand Rapids: Eerdmans, 1993), 136.

19. Walter Kirn, "What Would Jesus Do?" *GQ* magazine (September 2002): 476.

20. Ibid., 495.

21. Ibid., 497.

22. Gene Edward Veith, "Stupid Church Tricks," *World* magazine, August 22, 2002, online at http://www.worldmag.com/displayarticle.cfm?id=6259.

23. Ibid.

24. Ibid.

INDEX